OUT OF OUR MINDS

OUT OF OUR MINDS

Learning to be creative

FULLY REVISED AND UPDATED EDITION

SIR KEN ROBINSON

"Ken Robinson writes brilliantly about the different ways in which creativity is undervalued and ignored ..."

John Cleese

CAPSTONE

First edition published 2001
Revised and updated edition published 2011

Registered office
Capstone Publishing Ltd. (A Wiley Company), The Atrium, Southern Gate, Chichester, West Sussex, PO19 8SQ, United Kingdom

For details of our global editorial offices, for customer services and for information about how to apply for permission to reuse the copyright material in this book please see our website at www.wiley.com.

Library of Congress Cataloguing-in-Publication Data
is available

ISBN 9781907312472 (cloth), ISBN 9780857081032 (emobi),
ISBN 9780857081049 (epub), ISBN 9780857081490 (ebook)

A catalogue record for this book is available from the British Library.

Set in 11/14 pt Plantin by Sparks – www.sparkspublishing.com

Printed in the Unites States by Courier Westford, Inc., Westford, MA

For Terry, who makes everything possible.

IN PRAISE OF *OUT OF OUR MINDS* (1ST EDITION)

"Out of Our Minds *explains why being creative in today's world is a vital necessity. This is a book not to be missed. Read and rejoice.*"
Ken Blanchard, Co-author, *The One Minute Manager* and *The Secret*

"*If ever there was a time when creativity was necessary for the survival and growth of any organization, it is now. This book, more than any other I know, provides important insights on how leaders can evoke and sustain those creative juices.*"
Warren Bennis, Distinguished Professor of Business, University of Southern California; Thomas S. Murphy Distinguished Research Fellow, Harvard Business School, best-selling author, *Geeks and Geezers*

"*This really is a remarkable book. It does for human resources what Rachel Carson's* Silent Spring *did for the environment. It makes you wonder why we insist on sustaining an education that is narrow, partial, entirely inappropriate for the 21st century and deeply destructive of human potential when human beings have so much latent creative ability to offer. A brilliant analysis.*"
Wally Olins, Founder, Wolff-Olins

"*The best analysis I've seen of the disjunction between the kinds of intelligence that we have traditionally honored in schools and the kinds of creativity that we need today in our organizations and our society. I learned a lot.*"
Howard Gardner, A. Hobbs Professor in Cognition and Education, Harvard Graduate School of Education; best-selling author, *Frames of Mind*

"*Books about creativity are not always creative. Ken Robinson's is a welcome exception: a set of wide ranging, provocative and useful reflections for anyone concerned with bringing new ideas to fruition in business, academia, or the arts.*"
Mihaly Csikszentmihalyi, C.S. and D.J. Davidson, Professor of Psychology, Claremont Graduate University; Director, Quality of Life Research Center; best-selling author, *FLOW*

CONTENTS

ABOUT THE AUTHOR

S IR KEN ROBINSON, PHD is an internationally recognized leader in the development of creativity, innovation and human resources. He has worked with governments in Europe, Asia and the USA, with international agencies, Fortune 500 companies, and some of the world's leading cultural organizations. In 1998, he led a national commission on creativity, education and the economy for the UK Government. "All Our Futures: Creativity, Culture and Education" (*The Robinson Report*) was published to wide acclaim in 1999. He was the central figure in developing a strategy for creative and economic development as part of the Peace Process in Northern Ireland, working with the ministers for training, education enterprise and culture. He was one of four international advisors to the Singapore Government for its strategy to become the creative hub of South East Asia.

For twelve years, he was Professor of Education at the University of Warwick in the UK and is now Professor Emeritus. He has received honorary degrees from the Open University, the Central School of Speech and Drama, Birmingham City University, Rhode Island School of Design, Ringling College of Art and Design and the Liverpool Institute for Performing Arts. He has been honored with the Athena Award of the Rhode Island School of Design for services to the arts and education; the Peabody Medal for contributions to the arts and culture in the United States, and the Benjamin Franklin Medal of the Royal Society of Arts for outstanding contributions to cultural relations between the United Kingdom and the United States. In 2005 he was named as one of *Time/Fortune*/CNN's Principal Voices. In 2003, he received a knighthood from Queen Elizabeth II for his services to the arts. He speaks to audiences throughout the world on the creative challenges facing business and education in the new global economies. His renowned talks at the annual TED conference (2006 and 2010) continue to be viewed by many millions of people around the world.

Sir Ken was born in Liverpool, England as one of seven children. He is married to Therese (Lady) Robinson. They have two children, James and Kate, and live in Los Angeles, California.

Also by Sir Ken Robinson: *The Element: How Finding Your Passion Changes Everything* (Penguin/Viking 2009) is a *New York Times* Best Seller, which has been translated into 20 languages.

PREFACE

"We will not succeed in navigating the complex environment of the future by peering relentlessly into a rear view mirror. To do so, we would be out of our minds."

CREATIVITY IS THE GREATEST GIFT of human intelligence. The more complex the world becomes, the more creative we need to be to meet its challenges. Yet many people wonder if they have any creative abilities at all. *Out of Our Minds* is about why creativity matters so much, why people think they are not creative, how we arrived at this point, and what we can do about it. The first edition of this book was published in 2001. What you have in your hands now is a completely new and revised edition. So, why a new edition, and how new is it, really?

I wrote the original edition of *Out of Our Minds* during 2000. The first reason for a new edition is that so much has happened since then, both in *the* world and in *my* world. On almost every front, the pace of change has become ever more frantic and the issues at the heart of this book have become more pressing. Consider the rate of change in technology. Ten years ago, the Internet was still a novelty for most people. There were no smart phones, iPods; no Facebook, Twitter, YouTube or most of the social media sites that are now transforming culture and economics around the world. Many other things have happened too – from the global impact of the events of 9/11 to the compounding effect of the Great Recession – that simply could not have been anticipated ten years ago: in politics, the economy, in culture and in the environment. The sheer unpredictability of human affairs lies right at the heart of my argument for cultivating our powers of creativity: in business, in education and in everyday life.

The second reason for this new edition is that I now have more to say about many of the core ideas in the book and about what we should do to put them into practice. During the past ten years I have presented and debated these ideas with people at all levels in every sort of field; including CEOs of multinational corporations and not-for-profit organizations, politicians, artists, scientists, students, parents and educators. These experiences have deepened my conviction about the importance and the urgency of the arguments put forward in *Out of Our Minds*; and the need to represent them to an even wider audience.

The third reason is, not only has the world moved on in the last ten years, I have too. Literally. When I wrote the first edition, my family and I were living in Stratford on Avon, a small market town in England and birthplace of William Shakespeare. I wrote the new edition in Los Angeles, where we live now. The architect Frank Lloyd Wright once said that if you were to turn the world on its side and shake it, everything loose would land in Los Angeles. Just after the first edition of *Out of Our Minds* was published, my family and I shook loose and did just that. You can imagine what a seamless transition that turned out to be. Since then, I have traveled all over the United States meeting many extraordinary people and seeing fascinating initiatives. All of these experiences have informed this new edition, which has a much stronger emphasis on developments in the Americas and Asia as well as in Europe. The fact is that these really are global issues.

In 2006, I spoke at the world-renowned TED conference (Technology, Entertainment, Design) in Monterey, California and touched on some of the core themes of this book. That talk has since been downloaded over 5 million times in over 100 countries.[1] Mind you, our son James and daughter Kate, showed me a 30 second video on YouTube of two kittens that seem to be talking to each other and that has been downloaded 30 million times. So I am keeping this in perspective. I do know though, that unlike the cats' video, my TED talk has been shown at large and small conferences, meetings and training events, all around the world. As a result, it has been seen by an estimated 100 million people to date. That is one indication of the level of interest in these issues. I gave a second TED talk in 2010 and that too is drawing a powerful response.[2]

During 2008, I wrote *The Element: How Finding Your Passion Changes Everything*, published in the USA in January 2009[3] and in many editions around the world since then. That book looks at the nature of personal talent and creativity and the conditions in which it flourishes. In many ways, *Out of Our Minds* is a natural companion to *The Element*. It looks in much more depth at why the need to develop our natural talents – especially creativity – is so pressing, and at how and why organizations in general and education in particular tend to stifle them in the first place. Consequently, I was delighted when Capstone suggested I work on a new edition of *Out of Our Minds* to mark the tenth anniversary of its first publication. I have to admit that initially I had in mind a less sweeping revision. I pictured spending a long weekend with a casual bottle of claret and a spell check program, sprucing up the original text. In the event I have virtually rewritten the entire book: to include new material, to make the arguments sharper and the overall tone more accessible. So if you did read the first edition, you should not be deterred from buying (or borrowing) and reading this new one. It is very different in many ways and I think you will find enough that is new to repay a second look. If you are picking this book up for the first time, whether you work in business, education, the not-for-profit sector, or if you are concerned about your own creative potential, I trust you will find a great deal here to interest and engage you.

My aims in this book are to help individuals to understand the depth of their creative abilities and why they might have doubted them; to encourage organizations to believe in their powers of innovation and to create the conditions where they will flourish; and to promote a creative revolution in education.

I said in the original introduction that I had called the book *Out of Our Minds* for three reasons. I still have three reasons and here they are. First, human intelligence is profoundly and uniquely creative. We live in a world that's shaped by the ideas, beliefs and values of human imagination and culture. The human world is created out of our minds as much as from the natural environment. Thinking and feeling are not simply about seeing the world as it is, but having ideas about it, and interpreting experience to give it meaning. Different communities live differently according to the ideas they have and the meanings they experience. In a literal sense, we create the worlds we live in. We can also re-create them. The great revolutions in human history have often been brought about by new ideas: by new ways of seeing that have shattered old certainties. This is the essential process of cultural change.

Second, realizing our creative potential is partly a question of finding our medium, of being *in our element*. Education should help us to achieve this, but too often it does not and too many people are instead displaced from their own true talents. They are out of their element and out of their minds in that sense. Finally, there is a kind of mania driving the present direction of educational policy. In place of a reasoned debate about the strategies that are needed to face these extraordinary changes, there is a tired mantra about raising traditional academic standards. These standards were designed for other times and for other purposes – as I will explain. We will not succeed in navigating the complex environment of the future by peering relentlessly into a rear-view mirror. To stay on this course we should be out of our minds in a more literal sense.

Ken Robinson
Los Angeles, February 2011

OUT OF OUR MINDS

"When people say to me that they are not creative, I assume that they haven't yet learnt what is involved."

How creative are you? How creative are the people you work with? How about your friends? Next time you are at a social event, ask them. You may be surprised by what they say. I have worked with people and organizations all over the world. Everywhere I go, I find the same paradox. Most children think they're highly creative; most adults think they're not. This is a bigger issue than it may seem.

CREATING THE FUTURE

We are living in a world that is changing faster than ever and facing challenges that are unprecedented. How the complexities of the future will play out in practice is all but unknowable. Cultural change is never linear and rarely predictable. If it were, the legions of media pundits and cultural forecasters would be redundant. It was probably with these dynamics in mind that the economist J.K. Galbraith said, "The primary purpose of economic forecasting is to make astrology look respectable."

As the world spins faster and faster, organizations everywhere say they need people who can think creatively, communicate and work in teams: people who are flexible and quick to adapt. Too often they say they can't find them. Why not? My aim in this book is to answer three questions for anyone with a serious interest in creativity and innovation, or in simply understanding their own creative potential.

- **Why is it essential to promote creativity?** Business leaders, politicians and educators emphasize the vital importance of promoting creativity and innovation. Why does this matter so much?

- **What is the problem?** Why do people need help to be creative? Young children are buzzing with ideas. What happens as we grow up to make us think we are not creative?

- **What is involved?** What is creativity? Is everyone creative or just a select few? Can creativity be developed and, if so, how?

Everyone occasionally has new ideas, but how can creativity be encouraged as a regular and reliable part of everyday life? If you are running a company or an organization or a school, how do you make creativity systematic and routine? How do you lead a culture of innovation?

RETHINKING CREATIVITY

To answer these questions it is important to be clear about what creativity is and how it works in practice. There are three related ideas, which I will elaborate as we go on. They are *imagination*, which is the process of bringing to mind things that are not present to our senses; *creativity*, which is the process of developing original ideas that have value, and *innovation*, which is the process of putting new ideas into practice. There are various misconceptions about creativity in particular.

Special people?

It is often thought that only special people are creative: that creativity is a rare talent. This idea is reinforced by histories of creative icons like Martha Graham (1894–1991), Pablo Picasso (1881–1973), Albert Einstein (1879–1955) and Thomas Edison (1847–1931). Companies often divide the workforce into two groups: the 'creatives' and the 'suits'. You can normally tell who the creatives are because they don't wear suits. They wear jeans and they come in late because they have been struggling with an idea. I don't mean to suggest that the creatives are not creative. They can be highly creative, but so can anybody if the conditions are right, including the suits. Everyone has huge creative capacities. The challenge is to develop them. A culture of creativity has to involve everybody, not just a select few.

"My starting point is that everyone has huge creative capacities as a natural result of being a human being. The challenge is to develop them. A culture of creativity has to involve everybody, not just a select few."

Special activities?

It is often thought that creativity is about special activities, like the arts, or advertising, or design, or marketing. All of these can be creative; but so can anything, including science, mathematics, teaching, working with people, medicine, running a sports team or a restaurant. Schools sometimes have 'creative arts' departments. I am an uncompromising advocate of better provision for the arts in schools. I will explain why later. But creativity is not confined to the arts. There are many reasons for teaching the arts in schools, including their role in fostering creativity; and there are others that are just as compelling. At the same time, other disciplines, including science and mathematics can be just as creative as music and dance. Creativity is possible whenever we're using our intelligence.

In business too, different companies are creative in different areas. Apple, for example, is famously good at creating new products. Others, like Wal-Mart, haven't created any products at all; their area of innovation is in systems, such as supply chain management and pricing. The coffee chain, Starbucks, is creative in providing services. Starbucks didn't invent coffee; it created a particular type of culture around coffee. Actually, it did invent the $5 cup of coffee, which was a bit of a breakthrough, I thought. An innovation in any part of an organization can transform its fortunes.

My starting point is that everyone has huge creative capacities as a natural result of being a human being. The challenge is to develop them. A culture of creativity has to involve everybody not just a select few.

Learning to be creative

It's often thought that creative people are either born creative or not, just as they may have blue or brown eyes, and there is not much they can do about it. The fact is, there is a lot you can do to help people become more creative. If someone tells you they cannot read or write, you don't assume that they are not capable of reading and writing, but that they haven't been taught how. It is the same with creativity. When people say to me that they are not creative, I assume they just haven't yet learnt what is involved.

Letting go?

Creativity is sometimes associated with free expression, which is partly why some people worry about creativity in education.

Critics think of children running wild and knocking down the furniture rather than getting on with serious work. Being creative does usually involve playing with ideas and having fun; enjoyment and imagination. But creativity is also about working in a highly focused way on ideas and projects, crafting them into their best forms and making critical judgments along the way about which work best and why. In every discipline, creativity also draws on skill, knowledge and control. It's not only about letting go, it's about holding on.

Why are these issues important anyway?

THREE THEMES

Running throughout this book there are three fundamental themes:

- The first is that we are living in times of revolution.

- The second is that if we are to survive and flourish we have to think differently about our own abilities and make the best use of them.

- The third is that in order to do so we have to run our organizations and especially our education systems in radically different ways.

I go into each of these issues in more detail in the chapters ahead, but let me quickly summarize my argument.

Facing the revolution

No matter where you are or what you do, if you are alive and on earth you are caught up in a global revolution. I mean this literally not metaphorically. There are forces at work now for which there are no precedents. I know this is a bold claim but it is justified. Human affairs have always been turbulent. What is distinctive now is the rate and scale of change. The two great driving forces are technological innovation and population growth. Together they are transforming how we live and work; they are putting a vast strain on the Earth's natural resources and changing the nature of politics and culture.

New technologies are revolutionizing the nature of work everywhere. In the old industrial economies they are massively reducing the numbers of people in industries and professions that were once labor-intensive. New forms of work rely increasingly on high levels of specialist knowledge, and on creativity and innovation. The new technologies in particular require wholly different capacities from those required by the industrial economy. Manufacturing is shifting to the emergent economies, especially in Asia and South America, and so too are many of the new forms of work that depend on high levels of skill in design and information technologies. Given the speed of change, governments and businesses throughout the world recognize that education and training are the keys to the future, and they emphasize the vital need to develop powers of creativity and innovation. First, it is essential to generate ideas for new products and services, and to maintain a competitive edge. Second, it is essential that education and training enable people to be flexible and adaptable, so that businesses can respond to changing markets. Third, everyone will need to adjust to a world where, for most people, secure lifelong employment in a single job is a thing of the past.

These technological changes, combined with population and climate changes, are affecting everyone on earth and the outcomes are essentially unpredictable. What is certain is that in the next 50 to 100 years, our children will need to confront challenges that are unique in human history. In the first section of the book, I outline what these forces are and some of the challenges they present.[1]

Reframing our potential

In December 1862, Abraham Lincoln gave his second annual address to Congress. He was writing one month before he signed the Emancipation Proclamation, and in his message he urged the Congress to see the situation they faced with fresh eyes. He said this: "The dogmas of the quiet past are inadequate to the stormy present. The occasion is piled high with difficulty. As our case is new, so we must think anew and act anew. We must disenthrall ourselves and then we shall save our country." [2]

I love the word: 'disenthrall'. What he meant was that we all live our lives guided by ideas to which we are devoted but which may no longer be true or relevant. We are hypnotized or enthralled by them. To move forward we have to shake free of them.

Given the challenges we face now, the most profound shift has to be in how we think about our own abilities, and those of our children. In my experience, many, perhaps most people have no idea of their real capabilities and talents. Too many think they have no special talents at all. My premise is that we are all born with immense natural talents but that too few people discover what they are and even fewer develop them properly. Ironically one of the main reasons for this massive waste of talent is the very process that is meant to develop it: education.

Education is not always a good word to use socially. If I am at a party and I tell someone I work in education I can sometimes see the blood drain from their face. "Why me?" they're thinking, "Trapped with an educator on my one night out all week." But, if I ask them about their education, or about their children's schooling, they pin me to the wall. They want to talk about their own experiences. Everyone has very strong opinions. Education is one of those topics that runs very deep with people – like religion, politics and money. And so it should. Education is vital to the success of our working lives, to our children's futures and to long-term global development. More than this, it stamps us with an impression of ourselves that is hard to remove.

Some of the most successful people in the world did not do well at school. No matter how successful they have become, they often carry a secret worry that they are not as clever as they are making out. They include teachers, university professors, vice-chancellors, business people, musicians, writers, artists, architects and many others. Many succeeded only *after* they had recovered from their education. Of course, many people loved their time in education and have done well by it. What of those who didn't?

Current approaches to education and training are hobbled by assumptions about intelligence and creativity that have squandered the talents and stifled the creative confidence of untold numbers of people. This waste stems partly from an obsession with certain types of academic ability and from a preoccupation with standardized testing. The waste of talent is not deliberate. Most educators have a deep commitment to helping students do their best. Politicians too, make impassioned speeches about making the most of every student's abilities. The waste of talent may not be deliberate but it is systemic. It is systemic, because public education is a system, and it is based on deep-seated assumptions that are no longer true.

Before the middle of the nineteenth century, relatively few people had any kind of formal education. Being educated was mainly the privilege of the few who could afford it. Mass systems of public education were developed primarily to meet the needs of the Industrial Revolution and, in many ways, they mirror the principles of industrial production. They emphasize linearity, conformity and standardization. One of the reasons they are not working now is that real life is organic, adaptable and diverse.

Some weeks before our son started at university in Los Angeles, we went along for an orientation day. At one point, the students were taken away for a separate briefing on program options and the parents were taken to the finance department for a form of grief counseling. We then had a presentation from one of the professors about our roles as parents during our children's student days. Essentially he advised us to step out of their way and spare them too much of our career advice. He gave the example of his own son who had been a student at the University some years before. He had originally wanted to study the classics. The professor and his wife were not thrilled at the job prospects that a classics degree would open up for him. So they were relieved when at the end of the freshman year he said he had decided to take a major in something that would be more useful. They asked their son what he had in mind and he said philosophy. His father pointed out that none of the big philosophy firms were hiring at the time. His son took some philosophy courses anyway and then eventually majored in art history.

After college he found a job in an international auction house. He traveled, made a good living and loved the work and the life. He got the job because of his knowledge of ancient cultures, his intellectual training in philosophy and his love of art history. Neither he nor his parents could have predicted that path when he started his college studies. The principle is the same for everyone. Life is not linear. When you follow your own true north you create new opportunities, meet different people, have different experiences and create a different life.

The hierarchy of disciplines in schools is based partly on assumptions about supply and demand in the market place. The new economies demand a deeper conception of talent and the organic nature of our lives demands it too. What we become in future is deeply influenced by our experiences here and now. Education is not a linear process of preparation for the future: it is about cultivating the talents and sensibilities through which we can live our best lives in the present and create the best futures for us all.

Acting differently

Given the changes that are now engulfing us, most countries have recognized the need to reform their education systems. This is good but it is not good enough. The challenge now is to transform them. In the second section of the book, I look at the roots of current approaches to education and why they have marginalized the talents of so many people. I suggest a different way of thinking about the real potential of imagination and creativity in our lives. But as Lincoln said, it's not enough to think differently. We also have to act differently.

The recession of 2008 wiped out the credit and asset bubbles that had been fueling over-consumption and over-production around the world. As the recession blew like a hurricane through the old industrialized economies it left a trail of failed businesses, oceans of debt and deep pools of structural unemployment.

Among the worst affected are young people. As I write this, global levels of unemployment among young people, aged from 15 to 24, are the highest on record.[3] In August 2010, the International Labor Organization (ILO) published its report on *Global Employment Trends for Youth 2010*. The report concludes that there are approximately 620 million economically active young people worldwide. At the end of 2009, 81 million of them were unemployed; the highest number ever, and almost 8 million more than in 2007. The youth unemployment rate increased from 11.9 percent in 2007 to 13.0 percent in 2009. The ILO argues that these trends will have "significant consequences for young people as upcoming cohorts of new entrants join the ranks of the already unemployed" and warns of the "risk of a crisis legacy of a 'lost generation' comprised of young people who have dropped out of the labor market, having lost all hope of being able to work for a decent living."

For millions of young people, the future seems bleak and despairing. They have no work and see no prospect of it. Youth unemployment rates have been more sensitive to the economic crisis than adult rates of unemployment and, historically, the recovery of the job market for young men and women tends to lag behind that of adults. For people of all ages, the economic recovery, when it comes, will not be easy; and even when it does arrive, it will not be business as usual. As Thomas Friedman, author of the *World is Flat*, puts it, "Those who are waiting for this recession to end so someone can again hand them work could have a long wait." Rebuilding the communities that have been left bereft by the recession will depend on imagination, creativity and innovation. As the ILO report argues, creating jobs for the millions of young women and men entering the labor market every year is a critical component in the path towards wealthier economies. It is not only the quantity but also the quality of jobs that matters.

Friedman continues, "Those who have the ability to imagine new services and new opportunities and new ways to recruit work ... are the new Untouchables. Those with the imagination to invent smarter ways to do old jobs, energy-saving ways to provide new services, new ways to attract old customers or new ways to combine existing technologies will thrive." The solution is better education and training. Here too, the future cannot be business as usual. "We not only need a higher percentage of our kids graduating from high school and college – more education – but we need more of them with the right education. Our schools have a doubly hard task, not just improving reading, writing and arithmetic but entrepreneurship, innovation and creativity. We're not going back to the good old days without fixing our schools as well as our banks."[4]

All organizations are competing in a world in which the ability to innovate and adapt to change is not a luxury: it is a necessity. In 2010, IBM published *Capitalizing on Complexity*; the fourth edition of its biennial global CEO study series led by the IBM Institute for Business Value.[5] Introducing the report, Samuel J. Palmisano, Chairman, President and Chief Executive Officer of IBM said, "We occupy a world that is connected on multiple dimensions and at a deeper level – a global system of systems." It is this unprecedented level of interconnection and interdependency that underpins the most important findings in the IBM report.

The study found that at the top of the agendas of global business and public sector leaders, there are three widely shared perspectives. First, they believe that a rapid escalation of complexity is the biggest challenge confronting them. They expect it to continue – indeed to accelerate – in the coming years. Second, they are equally clear that their enterprises today are not equipped to cope effectively with this complexity in the global environment.

Third, they agree overwhelmingly that the single most important leadership competency for organizations to deal with this growing complexity is creativity.

The consequences of a lack of creativity can be severe. Organizations that stand still are likely to be swept aside, and corporate history is littered with the wreckage of companies, and whole industries, that have been resistant to change. They became stuck in old habits and missed the wave of change that carried more innovative companies forward. I once spoke at a gala dinner in London to launch a list of the Fortune Global 500 Companies. The top three companies were American. Ten years earlier, the top three companies had all been Japanese. Now an increasing number of Chinese companies are climbing the ranks. No organization has an assured place at the top of any list. Fortunes rise or fall according to how well they adapt to changing circumstances. One way of describing the decline of the Japanese companies is that they were victims of climate change. The world around them changed faster than they did and they suffered the consequences. The economies of China, South America and India, on the other hand, are adapting fast to the new demand for technological innovation.

Few people would dispute that in the eighteenth and nineteenth centuries, Europe and especially Great Britain dominated the world culturally, politically and economically. Britain was the crucible of the Industrial Revolution and its military forces secured the colonies as surely as the English language invaded their cultures. When Queen Victoria ascended to the throne in 1837, she presided over the largest empire in history: the empire on which the sun never set. If you had gone to her court in 1850 and suggested that this empire would be over within a generation, you would have been laughed out of the building. And yet it was true. By the end of World War I in 1918, the empire was fatally wounded and, by the time I was born in 1950, it was a memory. Culturally, politically and economically, the 20th century was dominated by the United States, as surely as Europe had dominated the nineteenth century. Whether it will dominate the 21st century remains to be seen. As award-winning US scientist Jared Diamond has shown, empires tend to collapse rather than fade away.[6] Think of the Soviet Union and its rapid dissolution in the 1980s and 1990s.

All organizations are organic and perishable. They are created by people and they need to be constantly re-created if they are to survive. When organizations fail, the jobs and communities that depend on them falter too. In a world where lifelong employment in the same job is a thing of the past, creativity is not a luxury. It is essential for personal security and fulfillment.

Leading a culture of innovation has radical implications for how institutions are organized – whether they are schools or corporations – and for styles of leadership. Many organizations put on occasional training days to encourage their staff to think creatively; but like the ritual of rain dancing, they often underestimate the problems they are trying to solve. For these reasons, this is not a conventional book on creativity, offering tips for next week's course. It is about the root causes of the problem rather than the symptoms of it. In the final part of the book, I summarize what's involved in tackling these deeper problems.

"The challenge now is to transform education systems into something better suited to the real needs of the 21st century. At the heart of this transformation there has to be a radically different view of human intelligence and of creativity."

CONNECTING EDUCATION, BUSINESS AND CULTURE

During my own career, I have worked with national education systems, with school districts, with principals, teachers and students from kindergarten to university and beyond, including community colleges and adult education associations. I have directed national research projects, taught in universities and trained teachers. I also work now with every type of business, including Fortune 500 companies, with major banks and insurance houses, design companies, media corporations, information technology organizations, and with retail, manufacturing, engineering and service companies. And I work with major cultural centers in the arts and the sciences; with museums, orchestras, and with dance and theatre companies and community arts organizations. My work has taken me to Europe, North America, South America, the Middle East and Asia.

In my experience, education, business and the cultural sector face many common challenges. Some are compounded by the fact that they have so little contact with each other. This book addresses all three of these fields because I believe that the future lies in closer coordination between them.

The problems that business organizations face are immediate. There are some immediate things they can do to tackle them and I say what they are. But the long-term solution lies upstream in the education system. All over the world, governments are pouring vast resources into education reform. In the process, policy makers typically narrow the curriculum to emphasize a small group of subjects, tie schools up in a culture of standardized testing and limit the discretion of educators to make professional judgments about how and what to teach. These reforms are typically stifling the very skills and qualities that are essential to meet the challenges we face: creativity, cultural understanding, communication, collaboration and problem solving. This is not a party-political issue. Politicians of all persuasions are curiously united in this respect. They argue over the funding and organization of education, over access and selection and about the best ways to improve standards. But it is rare to hear politicians of any party raise questions about the absolute importance of academic standards or of standardized systems of education.

Ironically, they promote these policies in the interests of the economy.[7] I say ironically because when I talk with business leaders, they complain that education isn't producing the thoughtful, creative, self-confident people they urgently need: people who are literate, numerate, who can analyze information and ideas; who can generate new ideas of their own and help to implement them; who can communicate clearly and work well with other people. They want education to provide such people, but too often they also cling to an uncritical belief in traditional academic education.

Many educators want to provide a more balanced and dynamic form of education that makes proper use of their own creative energies. Too often they feel they cannot do any of this because of political pressures of conformity and the disaffection of students who suffer under the same malaise.

Meanwhile, parents lie awake at night worrying about the quality of their children's education. Most parents assume that education will help their children to find work and become economically independent. I know I do. I cannot tell you how much I want my children to be economically independent and as soon as possible. Parents also want education to help young people to identify their unique talents and to lead a life that has meaning and purpose. This is also what young people want for themselves. As we grow up, education is meant to guide us from childhood to maturity. It should be high among the ways in which we realize our creative abilities. More often it is why we lose sight of them.

These issues, covered in *Out of Our Minds*, affect all of us, deeply. The book touches on economic globalization and the revolutionary challenges facing business and work. It looks at some of the extraordinary developments in science and technology that will make the changes we have seen so far seem primitive by comparison. It looks at how we run companies and organizations and the changes that are needed in order to cultivate a spirit of creativity and innovation. And it looks at ideas about intelligence and creativity upon which our current systems of education are based and considers why and how they too have to change, and soon. This range of coverage is important if we're to alter the conversation about creativity and deal not just with the symptoms but with the causes of the problems we now face.

BEYOND IMAGINING

In most respects, we human beings are like most other organisms on earth. Our lives are brief in cosmic terms; we pass through a common cycle of mortality from conception to birth to death; we have many of the same physical needs as other species and we depend on nutrients that the earth supplies.

Over the past few centuries of industrialism, more and more people have moved off the land into cities and seem to believe that we can live apart from the rest of nature. The growing climate crisis is a reminder that we cannot. But in one respect at least, human beings are radically different from the rest of life on earth. We have imaginations. As a result we have unlimited powers of creativity.

By imagination I mean the power to see beyond the present moment and our immediate environment. In imagination we can bring to mind things that are not present to our senses. We can visit the past, and not just a single view of the past. We can review and reinterpret the past. We can enhance our sense of the present by seeing with other people's eyes. And we can anticipate many possible futures. We may not be able to predict the future but we can help to shape it.

"We may not be able to predict the future but we can help to shape it."

Biologically, we are probably evolving at the same rate as other species: in cultural terms, we have always evolved at a uniquely furious rate. So far as we can tell, the cultural lives of dogs and cats are not changing that much. Left to their own devices, they seem to be doing what they have always done and to be pre-occupied with the same sorts of things. There is no need to keep checking in with them to see what's new. In human life, there is always something new, because creativity is part of what it is to be human.

It may be that some of the challenges that we have generated, in the natural environment, in politics and in our conflicting beliefs, will overcome us, and maybe sooner rather than later. If so, it will not be because we have made too much use of our imaginations but too little. Now, more than ever, we need to exercise the unique creative powers that make us human in the first place.

· 2 ·

_____

FACING THE REVOLUTION

"By about 2040, there will be a backup of our brains in a computer somewhere, so that when you die it won't be a major career problem."

Ian Pearson[1]

THE PACE OF CHANGE is quickening every day. New technologies are transforming how we think, work, play and relate to each other. At the same time, the population of the earth is larger and growing faster than at any time in history. Many of the challenges that we face are being generated by the powerful interaction of these forces. The problem is that many of our established ways of doing things, in business, in government and education, are rooted in old ways of thinking. They are facing backwards, not forwards. As a result, many people and organizations are having a hard time coping with these changes and feel left behind or alienated by them. To face these challenges we have to understand their nature; to meet them, we have to recognize that cultivating our natural powers of imagination, creativity and innovation is not an option but an urgent necessity. These challenges are global: they affect everyone. They are also personal: they affect all of us as individuals. As this is my book, let's start with me.

GETTING OUT MORE

I was born in Liverpool, England in 1950. Back then, people didn't really go anywhere. A visit to the nearest town was a day's outing. In some regions, dialects were so distinct that it was possible to tell which *village* or part of town someone came from. My father was born in 1914. He lived his whole life in Liverpool and rarely traveled more than 30 miles from the city. My mother was born in 1919 and it was only later in her life that she traveled out of the country for holidays. I have five brothers and a sister. My brother John has been piecing together our family tree. He has found out that in the mid-to-late 19th century, seven of our eight great grandparents grew up within a couple of miles of each other, in Liverpool; in some cases in adjacent streets. That's how they met. On the whole, people then did marry locally and expected, in the main, to live the sorts of lives their parents had led. They weren't besieged with media images of celebrities and reality stars that made them hesitate about settling for the person they had just met at the shops. They lived local lives and most people always did.

In contrast, I now travel so much for my work that I sometimes cannot remember where I've been or when. I went recently to Oslo, Norway to speak at a conference. I flew overnight from Los Angeles, via New York. The plane was delayed and I arrived in Oslo five hours late, tired but looking forward to the event. As I was getting ready to go on stage, one of the organizers asked me whether I'd been in Oslo before. I told her confidently that I hadn't but that the city seemed fascinating. A few hours later, I remembered that I *had* been in Oslo before. For a week! Admittedly it was about fifteen years earlier, but even so. You don't usually just wander into Norway without noticing. In a week, you do all kinds of things: eat, shower, meet people and talk and think about Norwegian things. I'd been to the National Art Gallery and spent time looking at paintings by Edward Munch, including *The Scream*, which is what I felt like doing when I realized I'd forgotten the entire trip. It may be a sign that I am on the move too much. I think it's also a sign of the times.

I used to live in England in a village called Snitterfield (really), which is three miles from Stratford-upon-Avon; the home of William Shakespeare. Snitterfield is also where William Shakespeare's father, John, was born in 1531. When he was 20 years old he decided to leave Snitterfield to seek his fortune in Stratford – three miles away. It is impossible to grasp the differences between his view of the world and ours almost 500 years later, when business travelers routinely fly across continents to attend meetings for the weekend and then forget where they've been. For most of human history, social change was snail-like in comparison with now. Although there were revolutionary developments in the form of the discovery of new continents, spice routes, and inventions during his lifetime, John Shakespeare's daily life probably differed very little from that of his parents, grandparents or great grandparents.

My father never left England. For work or pleasure, I've now been to most countries in Europe, the Far East and many parts of the United States and of Australia. By their early teens my children had visited more

> "To understand how hard it is to anticipate the future now, we need only think of how difficult it proved to predict the future in the past."

countries than I had by the age of 40. When I was growing up in the 1950s and 60s, I thought of my parent's childhood in the 1920s as the Middle Ages: horses in the street, few cars, steam trains, grand ocean liners, no air travel to speak of, no television, and few telephones. When we got our first black and white television in 1959, my family felt we'd reached the last stage of human evolution. My own children now have a similarly quaint view of my childhood: only two television channels, no color or surround sound, no TiVo, no computer games, cell phones, iPods, fast food, Twitter or Facebook. Their world is inconceivably different and an epoch away from those of my grandparents and great grandparents.

The differences are not only in the nature of change but also in the pace of it. The most profound changes haven't happened in 500 years: most have them have happened in the past 200 years and especially in the last 50 and they're getting faster. According to one estimate:

- in 1950 the average person travelled about 5 miles per day;

- in 2000 the average person travelled about 30 miles per day; and

- in 2020 the average person will travel about 60 miles per day.

Imagine the past 3000 years as the face of a clock with each of the 60 minutes representing a period of 50 years. Until three minutes ago, the history of transport was dominated by the horse, the wheel and the sail. In the late 18th century, James Watt refined the steam engine. This changed everything. It was a major tremor in the social earthquake of the Industrial Revolution. The improved steam engine vastly increased the power available for industrial production. It paved the way for faster methods of transport by road and sea and made possible the development of railways, the arterial system of the early industrial world. The steam engine impelled vast movements of humanity at speeds that were never thought possible. Since then, the curve of change has climbed almost vertically:

- 4 minutes ago   internal combustion engine (François Isaac de Rivaz, 1807)

- 2.5 minutes ago   motor car (Karl Benz, 1885)

- 2 minutes ago   first powered airplane flight (Wright brothers, 1903)

- 1.9 minutes ago   rocket propulsion (Robert Goddard, 1915)

- 1.5 minutes ago   jet engine (Hans von Ohain, and Frank Whittle, 1930)

- 1 minute ago   first man-made object orbits the earth (Sputnik 1, 1957)

- 50 seconds ago   first manned moon landing and moon walk (Apollo 11, 1969)

- 30 seconds ago   reusable space shuttle (Discovery, 1981)

- 2 seconds ago   roadable aircraft (Terrafugia Transition, 2009)

- 1 second ago   unmanned spaceplane (X-37B, 2010)

The revolution in transport is one index of the pace of change, but it's not the fastest one.

GETTING THE MESSAGE

Human beings have had access to writing systems for at least 3000 years. For most of that time these systems hardly changed. People communicated by making marks on surfaces, using pens on paper, chisels on stone or pigment on boards. Written documents existed in single copies are had to be copied by hand. Only a privileged few had access to them and only those few needed to be able to read. Between 1440 and 1450, about eleven minutes ago on our clock, Johannes Gutenberg invented the printing press. Since then the process of change has gathered at a furious pace. Think of the major innovations in communication in the past 200 years, and how the gaps on the clock have shortened:

- 11 minutes ago   printing press (1440–1450)

- 3.4 minutes ago   Morse Code (1838–44)

- 2.7 minutes ago   telephone (1875)

- 2.5 minutes ago   radio (1885)

- 1.6 minutes ago   black and white television (1929)

- 54 seconds ago   fax (1966)

- 41 seconds ago   personal computer (1977)

- 38 seconds ago   analog cell phone (1979)

- 25 seconds ago   World Wide Web (1990)

- 22 seconds ago   SMS messaging (1993)

- 13 seconds ago   broadband (2000)

- 1 second ago   3-D TV (2010)

When I was born in 1950, no one had a home computer. The average computer then was about the size of your living room. This was one reason people didn't buy them: they weren't inclined to live outdoors to accommodate a largely useless device. A second reason was the cost. Computers cost hundreds of thousands of dollars. Only government departments and some companies had computers. In 1950 the transistor was invented. In 1970, the silicon chip was developed. These innovations not only reduced the size of computers, they vastly increased their speed and power. The standard memory capacity has increased exponentially since then, from a few hundred kilobytes to several gigabytes.

If you have an iPhone, it probably has more computing power than was available on earth in 1940. Many children's toys have more computing power than 1960s mainframes. In 1960, Jerome Bruner and George Miller founded the Harvard Center for Cognitive Studies; the first institute dedicated to

cognitive science. The Institute was well funded and pur-
chased the first computer used in America for psychological
experimentation: a PDP4 minicomputer. It cost $65,000 in
1962 and came with 2K of memory, upgradable to 64K.[2] The
average digital wristwatch has appreciably more power and
memory than the 1969 Apollo Moonlander: the space vehicle
from which Neil Armstrong took his small step for man and
his giant leap for mankind.

It is now estimated that something in the order of 10^{17}
microchips are being manufactured every year; a number,
I'm told, that's roughly equivalent to the world population
of ants. I repeat it here in the confident knowledge that it
can't be checked or contradicted. This extraordinary rate of
production mirrors the vast range of applications for which
computers are now used. The pace of expansion in computer
technology over the past 70 years has been breathtaking.
Here's a rough chronology:

- 1937–42   First electronic digital computer, created at Iowa
  State University.

- 1951   First commercially produced computer, The
  Ferranti Mark 1 sells nine between 1951 and
  1957.

- 1965   First phone link set up between two computers.

- 1972   First email program created.

- 1974   The term 'Internet' first used.

- 1975   The Altair personal computer spawns home-
  computing culture.

- 1976   Steve Wozniak builds the Apple I with Steve
  Jobs.

- 1981   IBM enters the home-computing market and
  sells 136,000 in first 18 months.

- 1983   Microsoft Word launched.

- 1984   1000 Internet hosts.

- 1989   100,000 Internet hosts.

- 1990   Microchips are invented in Japan that can store 520,000 characters on a sliver of silicon 15 mm by 5 mm.

- 1992   Internet hosts exceed 1 million.

- 1997   Internet hosts rise from 16 million to 20 million by July.

          www.google.com registered as a domain name.

- 2002   The first social networking site Friendster launches in USA.

- 2003   Skype VOIP telephony is launched in Sweden based on software designed by Estonian developers.

- 2004   The term Web 2.0 is devised to describe an increase in user-generated web content.

- 2006   Twitter is launched.

- 2007   Google surpasses Microsoft as the most valuable and most visited online brand.

- 2010   Global number of Internet users nearly 2 billion. (World population approaching 7 billion.) Asia makes up 40 percent of users. The Middle East, Africa and South America are the fastest growing sectors.

The Internet is the most powerful and pervasive communication system ever devised. It grows daily, like a vast, multiplying organism; millions of connections are being added at an ever-faster rate in patterns that resemble dendritic groupings or ganglia in the brain. Just like the brain, the synapses that fire most often have the most robust response.Inventor and futurist Ray Kurzweil points out that the evolution of biological life and of technology have followed the same pattern. They both take a long time to get going but advances build on one another and progress erupts at an increasingly furious pace: "During the 19th century, the pace of technological progress was equal to that of the ten centuries that came before it. Advancement in the first two decades of the 20th century matched that of the entire nineteenth century. Today significant technological transformations take just a few years; ... Computing technology is experiencing the same exponential growth."

Gordon Moore was a co-founder of Intel in the mid-1960s. He estimated that the density of transistors on integrated circuit boards was doubling every twelve months and that computers were periodically doubling both in capacity and in speed per unit cost. In the mid-1970s Moore revised his estimate to about 24 months. It's anticipated that Moore's Law will have run its course around 2020. By then transistors may be just a few atoms in width. The power of computers will continue to grow exponentially, but in different forms. If the technology of motorcars had developed at the same rate, the average family car would be very different by now. It could travel at six times the speed of sound, be capable of about 1000 miles per gallon and would cost you about one dollar to buy. I imagine you'd get one. You'd just have to be careful with the accelerator.

The rate of technological innovation in the past 50 years has been breathtaking. But the indications are that the revolution may only just be getting underway. In the next 50 years we may see changes that are as unimaginable to us now as the iPad would have been to John Shakespeare. One of the portals into this radical future is nanotechnology.

IT'S ONLY JUST BEGUN

Nanotechnology is the manipulation of very small things indeed. Nanotechnologists are building machines by assembling individual atoms. To measure the vast distances of space, scientists use the light year – the number of miles that light travels in a year, which is equivalent to just under 10 trillion kilometers, or 6 trillion miles. I asked a professor of nanotechnology what they use to measure the unthinkably small distances of nanospace. He said it was the nanometer, which is a billionth of a meter. A *billionth* of a meter. It's almost impossible to grasp how small this distance is. Mathematically it is 10^{-9} meter or 0.000000001 meter. Does that help? I understood the idea but couldn't visualize it. I asked, "What is that roughly?" He thought for a moment and said, "A nanometer is roughly the distance that a man's beard grows in one second." I'd never thought about what beards do in a second but they must do something. It takes them all day to grow about a millimeter and they don't do it suddenly. They don't leap out of your face at eight o'clock in the morning. Beards are languid things and our language reflects this. We do not say "as quick as a beard" or "as fast as a bristle." We now have a way of grasping how slow they are: about a nanometer a second.

A nanometer is very small indeed, but it's not the smallest thing around. If you have a nanometer, you can have half of one. There is indeed a picometer, which is a thousandth of a nanometer. Then there is an attometer, which is a millionth of a nanometer. And there is a femtometer, which is a billionth of a nanometer: a *billionth* of a *billionth* of a meter. So if your beard had a beard …

In 1995, Professor Sir Harry Kroto won the Nobel Prize for Chemistry. With others, he discovered the third form of carbon, a nanotube of graphite called the C60 molecule, also known as the Buckminster Fullerene or Bucky Ball after the

American architect Buckminster Fuller. Fuller made extensive use of geodesic shapes that are similar to the structures of the C60 molecule. The C60 has remarkable qualities. It is a hundred times stronger than steel, a tenth of the weight and it conducts electricity like a metal. This discovery triggered a wave of research in engineering, aerospace, medicine and much else. If it can be produced in industrial quantities, the C60 would make possible the construction of airplanes 20 or 50 times their present size but much lighter and more fuel-efficient. Buildings could be erected that go through the atmosphere: bridges could span the Grand Canyon. Motorcars and trains could be a fraction of their current weight with greater fuel economies through the use of solar power.

Theoretically, nanotechnology makes it possible to create any substance or object from the atomic level upwards. While scientists speculate about the practical possibilities, others wonder about the political and economic consequences. As Charles Ostman, Senior Fellow at the Institute for Global Futures, notes, "Right now power and influence in the world is based on the control of natural and industrial resources. Once nanotechnology makes it possible to synthesize any physical object cheaply and easily, our current economic systems will become obsolete. It would be difficult to envision a more encompassing realm of future development than nanotechnology."[3]

Whether or not these possibilities actually materialize, nanotechnology promises radical innovations in fields as disparate as engineering and medicine. Its applications range from "molecular computing, to shape-changing alloys, to synthetic organic compounds, to custom gene construction, to ultra-miniaturized machinery." In medicine, nanomachines with rotor blades on the scale of human hair are being proposed as scrubbers to swim through veins and arteries cleaning out cholesterol and plaque deposits. In Ostman's view, in other medical applications, "the implications for modifying the cellular chemistry of almost any organ of the human body to cure disease, prolong life, or to provide enhanced sensory and mental abilities, are almost beyond comprehension." Artificially growing skin cultures are already being produced, and research in the development of an organic artificial heart is taking place in several different locations.

Nanotechnology is also leading to the extreme miniaturization of computer systems and will further revolutionize how we use them. In the near future, computers will be small and flexible enough to be worn on the body and be powered by the surface electricity of your skin. The problem then will be what to do with the monitor: you won't want a thin film of microprocessors clinging to your wrist and a large monitor strapped on your chest. One solution is retinal projectors that use low-level lasers mounted on spectacle frames and project the display directly into the eyes. A version of this technology is already in use in advanced aircraft systems. Pilots see the navigation displays on the inside of their visors and can change the direction of the aircraft by moving their eyes. You hope they don't sneeze in hostile airspace.

For more everyday use, computers could be woven into clothing. Shirts could have sensors that monitor heartbeat and other vital signs. Hints of serious ill health could be relayed directly to a doctor. Smart shoes could turn the action of walking into enough energy to power wearable computers.[4] Other innovations will soon replace the conventional keyboard. Already, interfaces are available that are controlled purely by the power of thought. Headsets have been designed to monitor brainwaves, which can then be converted directly into instructions. But this is only the beginning. All these devices work outside their users' bodies. Soon, information technologies may move inside our bodies and even into our brains. Computers may be about to merge with our own minds and consciousness.

USING YOUR BRAIN

For generations, scientists developed their understanding of the brain by dissecting dead brains on laboratory tables. This approach had some obvious limitations. Fortunately, in the last 20 years, the technologies of brain scanning have made it possible to study living brains. Neuroscientists now understand much more about the gross functions of the brain: which parts are used in different activities and in which combinations; in speech for example, in recognizing faces, listening to music, or doing mathematics. Neuroscience is using nanotechnology to explore the processes of thought and perception at the molecular level including the transfer of electrical charges at the neural synapses. These studies are generating wholly new approaches in psychology, in the design of drugs and in the treatment of pain.

Some of the most extraordinary implications of these different fields of research in information systems, material sciences and in neuroscience lie in the crossovers between them. It is now possible to conceive of information technologies modeled on the neural processes of the brain. A new generation of computers may be based not on digital codes and silicon but on organic processes: computers that mimic human thought.

I was talking recently with a senior technologist at one of the world's leading computer companies. At the moment, he said, the most powerful computers on earth have the processing power of the brain of a cricket. I don't know if this is true and nor does he. I don't know any crickets and if I did I'd have no way of telling what, if anything, is going on in their brains. His point is that even the most powerful supercomputers are still just mindless calculators. They perform tasks that humans cannot but they don't have any opinions about what they do. They don't think, in any proper sense of the term. Similarly, airplanes are much better than we are at flying at 35,000 feet but there's no point asking them how they feel about it. They don't. This is all changing.

SUPERCHARGING YOUR BRAIN

In the foreseeable future, the most powerful computers may have the processing power of the brain of a six-month-old human baby. At that point we will cross a threshold: computers will be capable of learning. I asked what that means. I was told that they would be able to rewrite their own operating systems, based on their experiences: "their experiences." In some sense, computers may soon become conscious. By 2020, it may be possible for $1000 to buy a personal computer with the same processing power as an adult human brain.[5] How's that going to feel when you're working with a computer that's as smart as you are: maybe not as attractive as you are, or as much in demand socially, but as smart as you? You give this machine an instruction and it hesitates, and says, "Have you thought this through? I'm not sure that you have." By 2030, personal computers, whatever form they take by then, could have the processing power of not one but of a thousand human brains.

Perhaps most significantly, the interaction of genetics, neuroscience and information systems makes it feasible to think about enhancing our own intelligence by physically merging computers with our brains. Computers, in the form of neural implants, are already being placed into people's brains to counteract Parkinson's disease and tremors from multiple sclerosis. Cochlear implants are available to restore hearing. There have been experiments in which a completely blind patient's optic nerve fibers were connected to a computer-driven dot matrix display and the patient was able to see crude patterns. Retinal implants are being developed to provide at least some visual perception in blind individuals by replacing certain visual processing circuits of the brain.

By 2020, neural implants could improve our general sensory experiences, including our powers of memory and reasoning. So, in future, if you have an important examination coming up you might be able to buy another 60 megabytes of RAM and have it implanted in your brain. Or it may be possible to have language implants. Instead of spending five years learning French you can have it implanted in time for your summer holidays. You could probably pay a few dollars more to have the fashion sense module.

Ray Kurzweil, believes that by "the third decade of the 21st century, we will be in a position to create complete, detailed maps of the 'computationally relevant features of the human brain,' and to recreate these designs in advanced neural computers." There will be a variety of bodies for our machines too, "from virtual bodies in virtual reality to bodies comprising swarms of nanobots..." Humanoid robots that walk and have lifelike facial expressions have been developed in several laboratories. They have great popular appeal, as shown by ASIMO, the robot created by Honda; and Pixar's *Wall-E*. Before the end of this century, "...the law of accelerating returns tells us, earth's technology-creating species – us – will merge with our own technology. And when that happens we might ask: what is the difference between a human brain enhanced a million-fold by neural implants and a non-biological intelligence based on the reverse engineering of the human brain that is subsequently enhanced and expanded?"

As Kurzweil notes, "an evolutionary process accelerates because it builds on its own means for further evolution... The intelligence that we are now creating in computers will soon exceed the intelligence of its creators." Ostman conjectures that there may come a time "when machines exhibit the full range of human intellect, emotions and skills, ranging from musical and other creative attitudes to physical movement."

In that case "the very boundaries of philosophical questions concerning where life ends and something else, yet to be defined, begins are at best soon to become a very fuzzy grey zone of definitions, as will the essence of intelligence as it is currently defined."

"An evolutionary process accelerates because it builds on its own means for further evolution."

This may sound far-fetched, but if someone had told you fifteen years ago that you could sit on the beach with a small wireless telephone and search the Library of Congress, send instant mail, download music and videos, book your holidays, arrange a mortgage and check your cholesterol, you would have thought they were being ridiculous. Now we take it for granted. If you could go back in time and hand your iPhone to your great-grandparents, they'd think you were Captain Kirk from *Star Trek*. The impossible yesterday is routine today. Wait until tomorrow.

IT'S GETTING CROWDED

Technological change is one driver of change. But there's another: the sheer numbers of people on the planet and the shifting patterns of population. Here again we are faced with an exponential curve of change. At the beginning of the Industrial Revolution, in the middle of the 18th century, there were one billion people on earth. In 1930, there were two billion. So it took all of human history until about 1800 for the population to reach the first billion and 130 years to reach the second billion. It took only 30 years to add the third in 1960, fourteen years to add the fourth in 1974 and thirteen years to add the fifth in 1987. By the night of the millennium celebrations in December 1999, the world's population had grown by another billion and reached six billion, the most rapid increase ever. Another billion people will have been added by 2011. The United Nations estimates that on current trends the world population in 2050 will be about 9.2 billion. That is more people than have ever lived on the planet at the same time. The issue is not only the size of the human population but also how it is changing. At the same time as the population is growing it is becoming increasingly urbanized. In 1800, the vast majority of people lived in the countryside: only five percent lived in cities. By 1900, the number had risen to twelve percent. By 2000, almost 50 percent of the six billion people on earth lived in cities. It's estimated that in 2050, over 60 percent of the population – more than five and a half billion people – will be living in cities.

These will not all be the small, manicured, well-regulated cities of the American Dream. Many will be vast, sprawling mega cities (that is, a metropolitan area with a population of over ten million people) with vernacular housing created by the people who live there from the raw materials they have at hand. The numbers are daunting. It's estimated that by 2050 there will be over 500 cities with more than a million people and over 50 mega-cities with populations of more than 50 million. Already, Greater Tokyo has a population of 34.6 million, which is more the entire population of Canada, gathered in one urban metropolis.

At the same time, the human world is shifting on its axis. The most significant growth in population is not in the old industrial economies of Western Europe and North America; it is in the emerging economies of South America, the Middle East and Asia. Currently, 84 million people are being added every year to the populations of the less developed countries, compared with about one and a half million in more developed countries, where populations are projected to remain relatively constant throughout this century.[6] China is the world's most populous nation with a population of 1.3 billion. Its population is increasing by one percent each year, assuming minimal migration. India's population is now approaching 1.2 billion. With a higher annual growth rate of about two percent, India is likely to surpass China as the world's most populous country by the middle of the century.

In some countries, including those of the emerging economies, almost half the population is under 25. In others, especially the older industrialized countries, the population is aging.[7] Many are experiencing extremely slow growth and even natural decrease because death rates have risen above birth rates. By mid 2010, deaths exceeded births in thirteen European countries including Russia, Germany, Latvia and Serbia.[8]

In some countries net immigration provides the only population growth. The United States is the third most populous nation in the world, behind China and India with a current population of 309 million. An estimated 4.3 million babies were born in the USA during 2007 and the population increased by an estimated 1.2 million people. According to the US Census Bureau projections, the US population could reach 422 million by 2050. The main growth in the population is through patterns of migration from Central and South America.[9]

As this century progresses, these massive changes in the numbers and distribution of the world's human populations will put intense pressure on natural resources, and especially water, on food supplies and its means of production, on energy and on the quality of air and the atmosphere. We will face bigger risks than ever from potential epidemics and new forms of disease. There will be profound effects on the structure of economic activity and trade. And, if the past is any guide, we will be at risk too from the persistent perils of cultural conflict and myopia.

Responding to these massive shifts in population will demand radically new ways of caring for natural resources, new technologies for generating energy, new and sustainable methods of food production and new approaches to both the prevention and treatment of diseases. Here, as everywhere, innovation is critical.

THE PERILS OF PREDICTION

It is all but impossible to predict the future of human affairs with any certainty. The forces of change create far too many currents and crosscurrents to chart them more than a little way ahead. Take the effects of technology, for example. The effects of transformative technologies are hard to predict for the very reason that they are transformative. To understand how hard it is to anticipate the future now, we need only think of how difficult it proved to predict the future in the past.

Getting the picture

On Sunday April 30 1939, the President of the United States, Franklin D Roosevelt, stood before an audience of over 200,000 people in Flushing Meadows, Queens, just east of New York City, and steadied himself at the podium. As he did so, an unusual camera was trained on him for the first time. His role that day was to open formally the 1939 New York World's Fair. The theme of the Fair was 'Building the World of Tomorrow' and during its two seasons of activity in 1939 and 1940 it attracted 45 million visitors. Among the hundreds of exhibits was the pavilion of RCA, the Radio Corporation of America. The pavilion featured demonstrations of the world's first commercial system of television. Roosevelt's speech that day was the first presidential speech to be televised. In addition to the audience at the Fair he was watched by about a thousand people gathered around a few hundred TV sets in various buildings in New York City. Ten days before the official opening of the Fair, David Sarnoff, the President of

RCA, gave a dedication speech for the RCA pavilion in which he heralded the system of television as the dawn of a new age of broadcasting. The pavilion attracted huge interest. But not everyone was convinced that the new medium would catch on.

An article in the *New York Times* concluded that, "Television will never be a serious competitor for radio." If you're listening to the radio, you can get on and do other things. To experience television, the *Times* argued, "People must sit and keep their eyes glued on a screen." Ironically, of course, this was to become the very attraction of the whole system. Nonetheless, it seemed clear to the writer that, "The average American family doesn't have time for it." Well, they found time. On average, the average American family went on to squeeze about 25 hours a week from their busy schedules to sit and keep their eyes glued on the television.

The fault line in the *Times*' assessment of television was to judge it in terms of contemporary cultural values where there seemed to be no place for it. In fact, television was not squeezed into existing American culture: it changed the culture forever. After the arrival of television, the world was never the same place again. Television proved to be a transformative technology, just as print, the steam engine, electricity, the motorcar and others before it had been.

Turning the page

As Johannes Gutenberg worked to iron out the technical wrinkles of his invention in 1450 in Mainz, Germany, I doubt that he anticipated the full consequences of the printing press that he was about to unleash on the world. A goldsmith by training, Gutenberg, blended existing technologies and added refinements of his own to develop a system of printing that was quick, adaptable and commercially efficient. His system made it possible for the first time to reproduce documents in volume and for them to be distributed far and wide across the continent and then the world. His printing press changed everything. His system opened up the world of ideas to everyone, and generated an unprecedented appetite for literacy and knowledge: an appetite that was to have seismic consequences for politics, religion and culture and that reshaped the world.

By 1500 there were printing presses rattling across Europe, pumping out millions of documents from pamphlets to books on every subject and from every religious, political and philosophical point of view, with significant ramifications – as I will explain in Chapter 4. In the sixteenth century, the English philosopher and politician Sir Francis Bacon developed the basic principles of the scientific method. He did so in a world that had been transformed by the proliferation of ideas and intellectual energy that had flowed from the printing presses of Europe. Towards the end of his life, Bacon commented that the advances in printing that Gutenberg had made had "changed the whole face and state of things throughout the world." Only now, almost 600 years later, is the future of the printed book under threat from e-technology, in the form of digital downloads.

Getting around

Created 400 years after Gutenberg's first printing press, the potential of the internal combustion engine was initially underestimated. It struck many people as an interesting innovation, but some struggled to see why it would replace horses and carriages, which seemed to do a perfectly good job of getting people around. One person whose curiosity was piqued by the new horseless carriages occupies an unfortunate place in the history of transportation. Her name was Brigit Driscoll. She was one of the first to be killed in an auto accident.

On 17 August 1896, Bridget, who was then aged 44, was visiting an exhibition at the Crystal Palace in London with her

teenage daughter, May. The exhibition included demonstration rides by the Anglo-French Motor Carriage Company.
As she was walking through the grounds, Mrs Driscoll was
struck by one of the vehicles and died of her injuries. The
case was highly unusual and was referred to the Coroner's
Court for proper consideration. The jury was faced with conflicting accounts of the exact circumstances of the accident,
including the actual speed of the vehicle. One of the witnesses
to the accident said that the vehicle had been moving at "a
reckless pace, in fact like a fire engine." The driver, Arthur
James Edsall, denied this and said that he had been traveling
at only four miles per hour. His passenger, Alice Standing,
said that the engine had been modified to make the car move
faster than four miles an hour, though an expert witness who
examined the vehicle contradicted this allegation.

After deliberating for six hours, the jury returned a verdict
of accidental death. Summarizing the case, the coroner, Mr
Percy Morrison reflected on the bizarre nature of this tragic
episode and said he hoped "such a thing would never happen
again." Well, it happened again. More than 20 million people
have now lost their lives in accidents involving motorcars.
Like the printing press, the motorcar changed the world in
ways that its inventors could not have imagined.

Making connections

In our own times, digital culture is changing the world just
as profoundly as these earlier technologies have done. And
the effects are cumulative. Radical innovations often interact
with each other and generate entirely new patterns of behavior in the people who use them. When Tim Berners-Lee
developed the original software for the World Wide Web
in 1990, his aim was simply to help academics research each
other's documents. He could not have foreseen the mushrooming expansion of the Internet and the viral growth of

social networking sites like Facebook and Twitter, with their profound effects on culture and commerce. The evolution of the Internet has been driven not only by innovations in technology but also by unleashing the imaginations and appetites of millions of users, which in turn are driving further innovations in technology.

New work for old

We can't predict the future. But some things we do know. One is that the nature of work will continue to change for very many people. Our children will not only change jobs several times in the lives but probably careers. In less than a single generation, the nature of work for millions of people has changed fundamentally, and with it the structure of the world economies. When I was growing up in the 1950s and 60s, the majority of people did manual work and wore overalls: relatively few worked in offices and wore suits. In the last 30 years especially, the balance has been shifting from traditional forms of industrial and manual work to jobs that are based on information technology and providing services. The dominant global corporations used to be in industry and manufacturing: many of the key companies today are in communications, information, entertainment, science and technology.

The emergence of e-commerce and Internet trading in the 1980s swept away long-established ways of doing business. The computerization of the financial markets and the synchronization of the global economies revolutionized financial services, including banks, insurance companies, stockbrokers and dealers. Since the so-called Big Bang in London in 1988, international corporations have swallowed up smaller traditional banks, retail stores have offered financial services of their own, and banks have become insurance and mortgage brokers.

At the beginning of the e-commerce boom, Lou Gerstner, Chief Executive of IBM, estimated correctly that companies would invest billions of dollars globally on e-business, not on hardware or software but on consultancy. In 2000, McKinsey claimed to have more than 60 percent of its London consultants employed on e-commerce projects. In 1998 it had been fewer than ten percent. Traditional business consultancies saw staff turnover rates rising rapidly as people defected to Internet-based companies. Turnover in some companies was as high as 40 percent. More venture capital in all categories was dispensed in the two years from 1998 to 2000 than in the previous ten. Along the way, some e-commerce organizations became extraordinarily valuable. Cisco Systems supplies networking equipment for the Internet. In November 2000 its stock market value was $400 billion, making Cisco worth more than the combined value of all of the world's car companies, steel makers, aluminum companies and aircraft manufacturers at that time.

On the other hand, some venture capitalists spent the three years from 1997 to 2000 pouring billions of dollars into Internet-based companies that soon disappointed their expectations. A great deal of this money was misplaced and lost, in part because in their frenzy to invest in the new forms of trading, many business people and investors alike overlooked some of the basic principles of business. The stock market soon loathed these companies and in time "99% of venture capitalists wouldn't even read their business plans, much less cough up money for them."

The heady expansion of the financial services sector in the five years from 2000 and its subsequent precipitous collapse in 2008 was a further illustration, if we needed one, that the course of human affairs, in business as elsewhere, usually defies prediction and often beggars belief.

Getting the idea

In the last 30 years too, there has emerged a powerful new force in the world economies. Often described as the intellectual property sector or sometimes as the creative industries, they include advertising, architecture, arts and antiques, crafts, design, fashion, film, leisure software, music, performing arts, publishing, software and computer services, television and radio. The intellectual property sector is even more significant when patents from science and technology are included: in pharmaceuticals, electronics, biotechnology, and information systems among others. All of these technologies are based on fundamental advances in the sciences and in engineering.[10]

The creative industries are labor-intensive and need many different types of specialist skill. Television and film production for example, draws on a variety of specialist roles in performance, in script writing, in camera and sound operation, in lighting, makeup, design, editing and post-production. As the financial significance of this sector grows, so does its employment base. The creative industries are also expanding in other countries, notably in the UK.

The communications revolution, and the new global markets it has created, has multiplied outlets for creative content and increased consumer demand. These new forms of work are creating a demand for new sorts of skill and aptitude. Unlike many other sectors, the creative industries continue to have high growth rates, mainly because they now encompass the fast-growing software, computer games and electronic publishing sectors.[11]

Old workers for new

Throughout the world, business and education are faced with a new generation gap. While the total number of people on earth

is increasing, there are profound differences between generations. As healthcare improves and life expectancy increases,
the boomers are continuing to boom in size and energy. In
the UK, for example, by 2020 the number of people over 50
will have increased by two million. Meanwhile, the number of
those under 50 will have dropped by two million. Employers
who look to young workers as their traditional source of labor
may find the spring is running dry. Fortunately, those now
passing 50 are not like their predecessors from generations
past. They account for 80 percent of the nation's wealth,
enjoy better health and are more inclined than the heavily
mortgaged parents of young children to take on new challenges and adapt to new ways of working. This makes them
highly effective new-economy workers.

As one study puts it: "Declining birth rates mean that
employers are going to have to become more creative if they
want to access the knowledge workers they need. And that
means abandoning the lazy prejudice of age discrimination."
In the United States, the numbers of workers paid for work at
home rose from 1.9 million in 1991 to 3.6 million in 1997.[12] A
report commissioned by the Trades Union Congress (TUC)
in the UK in 2010 estimates that as many as one in eight
people now earn a living from home. That's 12.2 percent of
the population, or an increase of 600,000 in three years.[13]

THE LEISURED SOCIETY?

Digital technologies are blurring the boundaries between
home and work, business and pleasure. The tendency to
communicate across time zones means that just as you're
going to bed someone has just arrived at their office and is
logging on. Emails pile up. The compulsion to answer the

cellphone implies that the incoming call is more important than the face-to-face conversation you were having. I don't know many people who are working less hard than they were ten years ago. Most are working faster with more to do and to shorter deadlines.

There is also an unprecedented deluge of news and information and an insistent pressure to keep abreast of it all. A well-known British journalist was reminiscing about his early days in radio news. He joined the BBC in the 1930s at a time when there was no regular news bulletin. In his first week, a bulletin was scheduled and he arrived at the studio to watch it being broadcast. The presenter sat at the microphone and waited until the time signal had finished. He then announced somberly: "This is the BBC Home Service from London. It is one o'clock. There is no news." The view of the times was that news would be broadcast if anything happened to warrant it.[14] Compare this with our own saturated processes of news reporting 24 hours a day on a multitude of channels and media. It isn't that there is more happening in the world now than there was in the 1930s. But there is now a ferociously hungry news industry, which generates, and sometimes manufactures, news stories around the clock to nourish its own bottom line. All of this adds to the general sense of crisis that permeates 21st-century culture.

A senior executive in a major oil company told me that the wind-down to Christmas used to begin in mid-December and the recovery might run on to the middle of January. Now people are fixing meetings in Christmas week and the whole operation speeds back in to action in the first week of the New Year. As he put it, "Standards of living are much higher than when I started out, but the quality of life is lower." Meanwhile many other people have no work at all. This is a different proposition that I will come back to in Chapter 3.

ANTICIPATING THE FUTURE

In 1974 Alvin Toffler published his groundbreaking book *Future Shock*. The idea of culture shock is well known to psychologists. It can happen to people who find themselves in an environment where all their normal reference points – language, values, food, clothes, social rituals – are gone. Political refugees and economic migrants can experience culture shock when they move to a new country. This experience can be profoundly disorienting and can lead in extreme cases to psychosis. Toffler saw a similar global phenomenon in the effects of rapid social change promoted by technology. He argued that being propelled too quickly into an unfamiliar future could have the same traumatic effects on people. The issue was not the fact of change: it is the rate and scale of it.

"Civilization is a race between education and catastrophe."
H.G. Wells

In our time we have released a totally new social force, "a stream of change so accelerated that it influences our sense of time, revolutionizes the tempo of daily life, and affects the very way we feel the world around us. We no longer feel life as people did in the past. And this is the ultimate difference, the distinction that separates the truly contemporary person from all others." This acceleration, he believed, lies behind "the impermanence, the transience, that penetrates and tinctures our consciousness, radically affecting the way we relate to other people, to things, to the entire universe of ideas, art and values." Interestingly, in the 1970s when Alvin Toffler was developing his apocalyptic views on the rate of social change, the personal computer wasn't available, let alone the Internet. He wrote *Future Shock* on a manual typewriter.

LOOKING FORWARD

In the 21st century humanity faces some of its most daunt-ing challenges. Our best resource is to cultivate our singular abilities of imagination, creativity and innovation. Our great-est peril would be to face the future without investing fully in those abilities. Doing so has to become one of the principal priorities of education and training everywhere. Education is the key to the future, and the stakes could hardly be higher. In 1934, the great Swiss psychologist Jean Piaget said, "only education is capable of saving our societies from possible collapse, whether violent or gradual." History provides many examples of his point. Over the course of humanity's relatively brief occupancy of the earth, many great societies and whole civilizations have come and gone. We build our own cultures not only on the achievements of those that have come before but on their ruins. The visionary novelist, H.G. Wells, put Piaget's point even more sharply: "Civilization," he said, "is a race between education and catastrophe." All the evidence is that he and Piaget were right. The problem is that too often, and in too many ways, current systems of mass education are a catastrophe in themselves. Far from looking to the future, too often they are facing stubbornly towards the past.

· 3 ·

THE TROUBLE WITH
EDUCATION

"Current systems of education were not designed to meet the challenges we now face. They were developed to meet the needs of a former age. Reform is not enough: they need to be transformed."

O NE OF THE MAIN REASONS that so many people think they are not creative is education. Picasso once said that all children are born artists: the problem is to remain an artist as we grow up. Creativity is not solely to do with the arts or about being an artist, but I believe profoundly that we don't grow *into* creativity; we grow *out* of it. Often we are educated out of it. Creativity is a multi-faceted process. It involves many ordinary abilities and some specialized skills and techniques; it can be fostered by many different ways of thinking, and it draws on critical judgement as well as imagination, intuition and often gut feelings. The dominant forms of education actively stifle the conditions that are essential to creative development. Young children enter pre-school alive with creative confidence; by the time they leave high school many have lost that confidence entirely. It is important to understand why and how this happens. There are ways in which adults can rekindle creativity in themselves and others. But if creativity is to become central to our futures, it first has to move to the heart of education.

REFORMING AND TRANSFORMING

As the technological and economic revolution gathers pace, education systems throughout the world are being reformed. These reforms almost always focus on 'improving' the existing system. Most countries have a dual strategy. The first is to increase access to education; especially the numbers of people who go to college. The demand for educational qualifications grows annually; education and training are now among the world's largest businesses.

The second strategy is to raise standards. Educational standards *should* be high and it is obviously a good idea to raise them. There is not much point in lowering them. But standards of what? Educating more people and to a much higher standard is vital. But we also have to educate them differently.

Education is not an impartial process of developing people's natural abilities and it never was. Systems of mass education are built on two pillars. The first is economic: they have been shaped by specific assumptions about labor markets, many of which are now hopelessly out of date. The second is intellectual: they have also been shaped by particular ideas about academic intelligence, which disregard other abilities that are just as important, especially for creativity and innovation. Perhaps the most powerful indicator of the need for transformation is the phenomenon of academic inflation.

ACADEMIC INFLATION

I went to college in 1968 and left in 1972. I did not look then as I look now. I was not the suave sophisticate that you will find on my website. I was deep into the heavy rock music of Led Zeppelin and, visually at least, I was channeling the lead singer, Robert Plant. I had shoulder length hair, wore jeans and a torn combat jacket, and was almost dangerously attractive to women. That was certainly my impression. I was 22 and considering my options. Should I get a job? Not yet, I thought. There was no rush. At that time, college graduates were virtually guaranteed a decent job and it didn't matter much what their degree was in. It could have been in Old Norse and it often was. Employers would still snap them up. "You can speak Viking," they'd say, "come and run our factory: your mind is obviously honed to a fine edge."

In the 1970s and 1980s, a college degree was a passport to employment. If you did well in school at that time, and especially if you went to university, you were assured of a secure job. If you had a degree and did not have a job, it was probably because you didn't want a job. And I didn't want a job. I wanted to 'find myself'. You could do this in the 1970s. So I decided to go to India, where I thought I might be. I didn't get to India, as it happens; I got to London (where, to be fair, there are a lot of Indian restaurants). But I knew that whenever I wanted a job I could get one, and soon enough I did.

In 1950, students with good high school qualifications expected a life of stable employment, perhaps staying with the same company until retirement. That is unlikely now. In some ways you are still better off with a degree than without one, but it will only get you started in the job market: it doesn't give you security once you are there. Graduates who find work in 2012 will not expect to be with the same company in 2050, or even that the company will still be around then. They may change not only jobs but also careers several times during their working lives.

There are many good reasons for gaining academic qualifications. The process should be inherently worthwhile and the best programs are. But academic qualifications are also a form of currency: they have an exchange rate in the market place for jobs or higher education. Like all currencies, their value can go up or down according to market conditions and how much currency is in circulation. University degrees used to have a high market value in part because relatively few people had them. The growth in population combined with the expansion of professional and administrative work means that unprecedented numbers of people are now going to college. In the 1970s, about 1 in 20 people in the old industrialized economies went to college. The current target is one in three, rising to one in two.

According to UNESCO, the number of people gaining formal educational qualifications in the next 30 years will exceed the gross total since the beginning of history. As a result, the market value of degrees is tumbling. Something more is needed to edge ahead of the crowd. Jobs that used to require only a first degree are now asking for masters' degrees, or even doctorates.

Several years ago, I was on a university appointments panel. I asked the chairman of the panel what we were looking for in the candidates. He mentioned the various qualities and qualifications that were essential for the job and then he said, "I think we're also looking for someone with a good PhD." I said, "A what?" He said, "A good PhD." "As opposed to what?" I said, "A dreadful one?" What he meant was someone with a PhD from a high-ranking university. There was a time when, if you had a PhD, you were in a tiny fraction of the population. All PhDs were regarded with reverence. Postgraduates were kept in a separate room and fed on plasma. Children were brought in to look at you and told this is what could happen to them if they didn't get out more. Now, we're getting picky. We want applicants to have *good* PhDs. What's the next twist on this spiral? Nobel Prizes? Will we eventually see Nobel Laureates applying for clerical jobs and being told, "OK, you've got a Nobel Prize, that's lovely. Can you also handle Excel? We need someone to sort out the payroll."

The current assumption is that by expanding education and raising standards all will be well. The end game assumes that when everyone has a PhD, there will be a return to full employment. But there won't. The markets will reconfigure as the currency rates fall and employers will look for something else. They are doing this already. The issue is not that academic standards are falling. The real issue is that the very foundations upon which our current systems of education are built are shifting beneath our feet.

TWIN PILLARS

The political impetus to develop national systems of education was not purely philanthropic or humanitarian: it was also economic. It arose out of the surging demands of the Industrial Revolution. The education systems that emerged were not only designed in the interests of industrialism, they were created in its image in terms of both structure and culture.

The factory floor

We now take it for granted that governments should provide mass systems of education; that they should be funded from the public purse; that all young people should go to school until they are at least 16 and that a high proportion of them should go on to college. As obvious as they may seem now, these assumptions are relatively new.[1] It was only from the 1860s onwards that countries throughout Europe, as well as many of the American states, began to establish mass systems of public education. The history of state education everywhere is an intricate tapestry of practical economic needs, individual philanthropic passions, of competing movements of social reform, and widely differing philosophical convictions. There were though, some common driving forces.

In many countries, the spread of industrialization in the nine-teenth century radically changed the face of the labor force and created entirely new social structures. Pre-industrial societies were dominated by the interests of the old aristocracies and the churches; which presided over largely illiterate, usually poor rural populations. Before the 1860s, the vast majority of Europeans were still illiterate. Only Prussia, some of the other northern German states, and the Scandinavian king-doms boasted widespread literacy.[2] The rise of industrialism generated enormous new streams of wealth and an entirely new social force: the wealthy and aspiring middle classes.

Education was seen as the essential route to social improve-ment and further economic opportunity. Education was also vital to generate the conditions for long-term economic pros-perity. The growth of public education was shaped around the interests the middle classes, and their ambition not only for themselves but also for the industrialized societies they were helping to create. For the first time, industrialism also provided the financial resources to pay for systems of mass education.

As millions of workers migrated from the countryside to the cities, to stoke the fires of industrialism in the factories and shipyards, a third social group began take shape: the urban working classes. For some pioneers of mass education, schools were a way to raise the aspirations of the working classes and to lift them out of poverty and despair. Others saw educa-tion as the best way to promote the values and opportunities that are meant to lie at the heart of healthy democracies. In the United States, Horace Mann saw education for all as the natural fulfillment of the principles of the Constitution. Oth-ers saw mass education less idealistically as the most efficient way of inculcating the working classes with the habits and disciplines that were essential to industrial production.

For all of these reasons, systems or state-supported and state-directed elementary schools sprang up throughout

Europe in the late 1860s, 1870s and 1880s. Such systems were inaugurated in Hungary in 1868; Austria, 1869; England, 1870; Switzerland, 1874; the Netherlands, 1876; Italy, 1877; and Belgium, 1879. According to Professor Gerald Gutek, by the time of the Civil War, "the common school movement in the United States had accomplished its aim of achieving popular systems of elementary schools in most of the states. After 1865, schools were established in the southern states. As various new states entered the Union, they too established common elementary school systems."[3]

Some skeptics argued that it was waste of public resources to attempt to educate the children of the working classes: such children were essentially uneducable and would not benefit from these efforts. They were wrong about that. Others feared the social and political consequences: educating the working classes would give them ideas above their station and lead to a social revolution. They were not wrong about that.

From the outset, education systems in Europe and North America were designed to meet the labor needs of an industrial economy based on manufacturing, engineering and related trades, including construction, mining, and steel production. Broadly speaking, industrialism needed a workforce that was 80 percent manual and 20 percent administrative and professional. This requirement had a deep influence on the structure of public education systems. Typically the educational model was shaped like a pyramid, with a broad base of elementary education funneling to a narrow peak of higher education. The vast majority of children went to elementary school and a smaller but still significant number went on to high school. The majority of young people left full-time education at 16, to find work. A small proportion went on to higher education. Those with strong academic qualifications went to universities, others to trade colleges or polytechnics.

In Europe, high schools were usually of several different types: academic schools for a minority of pupils who showed an aptitude for such work; and more practical or technically oriented schools for the majority who did not. Although national policies emphasized the value of all types of school, the academic schools, which fed the universities, had higher status, and so did the students who went to them. It was not that only a minority was capable of going to university: the supply of places was limited by the needs of the labor markets.

As these needs have changed, so the number of places in higher education has increased. In the United States and Europe, the expansion began in the 1960s, partly to accommodate the bulging population of baby boomers after the end of World War II. This trend has continued with the burgeoning demands of the so-called knowledge economy. From the beginnings of state education in the United Kingdom, the expansion of academic 'grammar' schools went hand in hand with the founding of new universities in the major industrial centers.[4] Between 1954 and 1966, the numbers of school leavers qualifying for university entrance rose from 24,000 to 66,000. During the 1960s, 23 new universities were established in the UK to meet the demands of the baby boomers, culminating in the creation of the Open University, which provided university-level education for all, via distance learning. Two-thirds of British universities were founded after 1960 when the polytechnics became eligible for university status.

There was a similar pattern of expansion in the United States. Some American universities such as Indiana, Madison Wisconsin and Ohio State are now the size of small towns and are turning out graduates in tens of thousands every year.

The number of young people capable of achieving university level education has increased over the last 40 years from one fifth to at least 50 percent. What happened during this period to account for this remarkable change in intellectual capacity? Is it the fluoride in the water or the rise of organic farming? The fact is that most young people have *always* been capable of higher academic study; but, until recently, graduates just weren't needed in such large numbers.

THE CULTURE OF EDUCATION

The rise of industrialism influenced not only the structure of mass education but also its organizational culture. Like factories, schools are special facilities with clear boundaries that separate them from the outside world. They have set hours of operation and prescribed rules of conduct. They are based on the principles of standardization and conformity. Students within the academic system are taught broadly the same material and they are assessed against common scales of achievement, with relatively few opportunities for choice or deviation. Typically, they move through the system in age groups: all the five-year-olds together, all the six-year-olds together and so on, as if the most important thing that children have in common is their date of manufacture. In high schools, the day is organized into standard units of time and the transitions are marked by the ringing of bells or buzzers. Teaching is based on the division of labor. Like an assembly line, students progress from room to room to be taught by different teachers specializing in separate disciplines.

Education systems also operate on the manufacturing principle of linearity; in that there are distinct sequential stages to the process. Each stage is meant to build logically on the one that precedes it; overall outcomes can be predicted with reasonable reliability. The idea is that if students progress in the prescribed way through the system, and especially if they complete college, they will emerge at the far end educated and prepared for whatever the world throws at them.

When I first moved to Los Angeles, I saw an egregious example of the linear principle in the form of a discussion paper for education entitled, "College begins in Kindergarten."

There's a lot more to say on this issue of linearity but let me simply say here that college *does not* begin in kindergarten. Kindergarten begins in kindergarten. The director of The Ark Children's Theatre in Dublin once made a wonderful comment on this theme. "A three-year-old," he said, "is not half a six-year-old. A six-year-old is not half a twelve-year-old." Three-year-olds are three. The obsession with getting to college is now pushing down through the system to distort even the education of pre-schoolers. In some urban centers the competition is so intense for places in the 'right' kindergartens that children are being interviewed – for kindergarten. What are the interviewers looking for, evidence of infancy?

Embedded in this principle of linearity is the idea that education is essentially a preparation for something that happens later on. It is for this reason that education is still mainly focused on children and young people. This system is sometimes called the front-loading model of education: you accumulate your educational resources at the beginning of your life and you eke them out gradually as you get older. I have also heard it called the gas tank model: you are filled up in your youth with an initial supply of education, which is meant to see you through the rest of life's journey. In practice, of course, most people leave school with half a tank; it's basic grade and there are too few gas stations if they run out en route.

It is worth pausing at the analogy with motorcars. Some policy makers talk about reforming education as if they were sorting out the auto industry. They emphasize the need to get back to basics and focus on the core business, to face up to overseas competition and to raise standards, improve efficiency, return on investment and cost-effectiveness. The difference of course is that motorcars and other lifeless products have no interest in how they are produced. People on the other hand are keenly interested in their own experiences in education. They have feelings and opinions, values and motivations, hopes and aspirations. Ignoring the human factor is at the root of many of the problems that industrial systems of education have created.

Education is not only a preparation for what may come later; it is also about helping people engage with the present. What we become as our lives evolve depends on the quality of our experiences here and now. Linear assumptions about supply and demand cut off many potentially valuable experiences on the grounds of utility. For most people there never has been a direct, linear progression from education to planned career. Our lives are too buffeted by the currents and crosscurrents of social forces and personal impulse. Life and work are shaped by an unpredictable mixture of events and opportunities, which make sense only retrospectively when writing a curriculum vitae. At which point the basic human urge for narrative takes over, turning the chaotic process of randomness and chance into a well-crafted account of your sleek trajectory through life.

The assumption that there is a direct linear relationship between general education and subsequent employment puts schools under pressure to prioritize those subjects that seem most relevant to the economy. It is argued that there is a need to produce more scientists and technologists. Consequently, science and technology are given higher priority and greater funding in schools, while provision for the arts and humanities is cut back to make way for them. This is the pattern in most developed countries. There are good reasons to doubt whether this policy is in the best interests of young people or of society in general; or even whether it is the best way to produce good scientists and technologists. In any case, it is a mistake to think of the relationship between education and the economy as a straightforward process of supply and demand, like producing motor cars. While industrial systems may be standardized, mechanistic and linear, human life simply is not. Our lives run on entirely different principles.

What's the use?

In almost all industrial systems there is the same hierarchy of disciplines in high schools, and increasingly in elementary schools too. At the top are mathematics, languages and sciences; some way down are the humanities – history, geography and social studies – and physical education; at the bottom are the arts. There is another hierarchy within the arts: art and music usually have higher status than theatre and dance. There isn't a school system in the world that teaches dance every day as a compulsory discipline in the way that mathematics is taught. The hierarchy shows itself in the amounts of time that are given to different disciplines; whether they are compulsory or optional and for whom; whether they are in the mainstream curriculum or after school; whether they are included in standardized tests and how much they feature in political polemics about raising standards.

The Council of Europe is an intergovernmental organization based in Strasbourg. It works with member states across Europe including many of the former Soviet Bloc countries. As part of a project that I directed for the Council of Europe, I surveyed education systems in 22 countries.[5] Someone has to do this sort of thing. There were many differences in education in these countries and many similarities. In all of them, the arts are on the edges of the school curriculum. Most systems include some art and music in the formal curriculum; very few teach drama and hardly any provide dance lessons. The pattern is the same in the United States, Canada, Mexico, Central and South America and in many parts of Asia. In fact, almost everywhere. Whatever the standards are that most countries want to raise, they don't seem to have much to do with what the arts teach. I know this from my own school experience.

When I was 14, my class teacher told me that I had a problem and sent me to see the head teacher. The issue was my choice of options for the next two years of school. I loved art and was very keen to carry on with it. I also wanted to take German. "Well, you do have a problem, Robinson," the head teacher said. "I'm afraid you can't do art and German." I was baffled. I'd seen films about Germany and there seemed to be pictures everywhere. "No," he said, "you can't do art and German here in this school. They clash on the timetable." I asked him what I should do. "If I were you," he said, "I should do German." I asked him why, and he said, "It will be more useful." I found this exasperating and still do.

I'd have understood if he'd said German would be more interesting; or that I had an obvious feel for languages, or that it would suit me better. But why is German more useful than art? I know it is useful, especially in Germany. Languages are very useful but is art not? Is it useless? The curricula of most school systems seem to divide into two broad groups: the useful disciplines and the useless ones. Languages, mathematics, science and technology are useful; history, geography, art, music and drama are not. When funding is tight or reform movements focus on raising standards, arts programs are usually cut.

In 2001, the Federal Government of the United States passed into law the Elementary and Secondary Education Act (ESEA) generally known as 'The No Child Left Behind Act, 2001' (NCLB). Its aims were to raise academic standards in all schools, to make teachers accountable for student achievement, to raise levels of college preparedness and in these ways to reinvigorate the economic competitiveness of the USA. The principal methods were to intensify programs of standardized testing for languages and mathematics and to link funding for schools to students' performance on the tests. NCLB was the result of a cross-party coalition; it was composed by serious people with the best interests of the country in mind and its intentions were admirable. In practice, it has largely failed to meet its own objectives and has been widely condemned for demoralizing teachers and students, for inculcating a numbing culture of teaching to the test, and for encouraging schools to adapt the testing systems to avoid financial and other penalties. Meanwhile students are dropping out and teachers are leaving schools at alarming rates, while overall achievement in literacy and mathematics has scarcely budged. In the process, provision for the arts and for the humanities in American schools has been devastated.

According to one study,[6] since NCLB was passed into law, almost half of the school districts have eliminated or seriously reduced their arts programs, and the associated teaching posts. Policy makers emphasize that devastating arts education was not the intention of the legislation. I'm sure it was not intentional. I don't imagine that serious politicians huddled in the committee rooms of Congress planning the downfall of the nation's piano teachers or deciding that dance educators were getting out of hand and had to be curbed. The arts suffered from collateral damage. The minds of the policy makers were focused on the disciplines at the top of the hierarchy. NCLB is a prime example of what some holistic doctors call the septic focus: the tendency to look at a problem in isolation from its context.

THE SEPTIC FOCUS

I had a friend, Dave, who was an actor. He was a large actor, weighing about 20 stone or 280 pounds. He liked to drink beer and had a particular taste for a brew called Abbot Ale. This is a powerful drink. You could run a small car on Abbot Ale, or a large actor. Dave regularly drank 12 pints of it a day. Some years ago he developed back pain and went to his doctor, who referred him to a kidney specialist. The specialist examined him and said that he had potentially serious kidney problems. Dave asked what could be causing it. "It could be a number of things," said the consultant. "Do you drink?" David said that he did, socially, and mentioned the Abbot Ale. The specialist told him he would have to stop drinking or face the prospect of renal failure. Dave said he couldn't stop drinking: he was an actor. "In that case," said the specialist, "why don't you change to spirits?" Dave said he thought that spirits could cause cirrhosis of the liver. "But you haven't come to see me about your liver," said the specialist, "I am concerned about your kidneys."

This is a clear example of septic focus. A holistic doctor would have recognized that the problem in Dave's kidneys was a result of wider factors in his overall lifestyle. Solving one problem by causing another is no solution at all. The septic focus is clearly evident in the education reform movements like NCLB that focus on certain parts of the system while neglecting the system as a whole.

Why *do* the disciplines at the top of the hierarchy get all the attention? Why does this hierarchy exist in the first place? The first answer is economic: some disciplines are simply assumed to be more relevant to the world of work and to command a higher rate of pay when finding a job. Generations of young people have been steered away from the arts with benign advice about poor job prospects: "Don't do art, you won't make it professionally as an artist." "Don't take music, you won't make a living as a musician." Benign advice maybe, but it is now profoundly wrong, as we will see. The arts are often thought to be important in schools for other reasons: as opportunities for creativity and self-expression or as leisure or 'cultural' activities. But when times are hard, many people take it for granted that the arts are not relevant to the hard-headed business of making a living.

We live in times when the sciences are strongly associated with truth and objectivity, fact and hard reality, and the arts with feelings, emotions and intuition. The arts are seen as disposable extras in education; something optional to do with self-expression, relaxation and leisure. I remember having an argument on television about this with a prominent British politician. He said that the arts are really important because they help to educate people for leisure. One of the many problems with this argument is that leisure is relative to work. If you have less work, you may have more leisure, but if you have no work, you are unemployed. That is quite a different feeling. At the time of our debate there were something like two million people in the UK who were unemployed. They were not organizing themselves, to the best of my knowledge, as the new leisure classes.

There is another reason for the hierarchy of disciplines. After all, children are not usually told, "Don't do math, you're not going to be a mathematician," or "Don't take science, you won't make it as a scientist?" The second reason is cultural. The disciplines at the top of the hierarchy are assumed in some ways to be inherently more important. This assumption is not to do with economics: it has to do with cultural ideas about knowledge and intelligence. These ideas have dominated our ways of thinking for the past 300 years. If one pillar of conventional education is industrialism, the second is academicism.

The ivory tower

In everyday language 'academic' is often used as a synonym for 'education'. Politicians talk routinely about raising 'academic standards' as if this means 'educational standards' in general. People use the term 'academic ability' to mean 'intelligence'. It is not the same thing at all. Academic work focuses on certain sorts of verbal and mathematical reasoning: on writing factual and critical essays, verbal discussions and mathematical analyses. These are all very important forms of ability. But if human intelligence was limited to them, most of human culture would never have happened. There would be a lot of analysis but not much action. There would be no practical science, no technology, no functioning businesses, no art, no music or dance, no theatre, poetry, love, feelings or intuition. These are large factors to leave out of an account of human intelligence. If all you had was academic ability, you couldn't have got out of bed this morning. In fact, there wouldn't have been a bed for you to get out of. Nobody could have made one. They could have written about the theoretical possibility of a bed, but not actually constructed the thing.

There is an interesting ambiguity in cultural attitudes to academic achievement. On the one hand academic achievement is thought to be absolutely essential to individual success and to national survival. If academic standards are thought to be falling, media pundits beat their chests and politicians become resolute. On the other hand, 'academic' is used as a polite form of abuse. Professional academics are thought to live in ivory towers and to have no practical understanding of the real world at all. An easy way to dismiss any argument is to say that it is 'merely' academic.

How have we become so enthralled by academic ability and so skeptical of it at the same time? As we shall see in the next chapter, the roots of this obsession lie deep in the Enlightenment: the massive expansion in European philosophy and practical science in the seventeenth and eighteenth centuries. This movement led to a view of intelligence that is dominated by deductive reason and ideas of scientific evidence. These ideas have been reinforced since by styles of formal education in schools and universities.

One reason why academic work has come to dominate general education is that the needs of universities have shaped the culture of mass education, both directly and indirectly. The requirements of university entrance have had a direct influence on the nature of the school curriculum and on forms of assessment and public examination. The universities have affected education in many indirect ways too, not least because the teaching profession is largely made up of university graduates. In many ways, the whole process of elementary and high school education is a protracted process of university entrance. Those who go to university rather than straight into work or vocational training programs are always seen as the real successes of the system.

If you were to stand back from education and ask, "What is it all for?" you might focus first on those who seem to benefit most from as its requirements and expectations. You might conclude that the primary purpose of compulsory education is to produce university professors, as they are the apotheosis of academic culture. I used to be a university professor and I have huge respect for academics and for academic life. But it is just another form of life. It should not be held up as the standard for other forms of human achievement. I know artists, business leaders, dancers, sportspeople, and many others, whose accomplishments, intelligence and humanity are as substantial as anyone I have met with a post-doctoral degree.

"Thinking of education as a preparation for something that happens later can overlook the fact that the first sixteen or eighteen years of a person's life are not a rehearsal. Young people are living their lives now."

Many highly intelligent people have passed through the whole of their education feeling they aren't and many academically able people who've been fêted by the system have never discovered their other abilities. Almost all of them have no real sense of their true creative potential. The waste of creative talent is a growing calamity.

The roles of education

Education has three main roles: personal, cultural and economic. A great deal could be said about each of these, but let me boil them down here into three basic statements of purpose, which I think are relatively uncontentious:

- **Individual:** to develop individual talents and sensibilities
- **Cultural:** to deepen understanding of the world
- **Economic:** to provide the skills required to earn a living and be economically productive.

It is essential to keep a constant eye on all three of these roles and to promote them equally and in relation to each other. Understanding how they interconnect is the key to transforming the education system into a 21st-century process that has creativity and innovation at its center. As things stand, the industrial/academic model of education is often failing miserably in all three areas. Let me give you some examples.

ECONOMIC CHALLENGES

Education has a critical role in developing the knowledge, skills and attitudes that are essential for economic vitality and growth. There is strong evidence that the current systems of education are causing problems in all areas of the labor market; affecting major companies, small and medium-sized businesses and public institutions alike. These problems affect everybody from the top of the labor market to the bottom of it: from people who are highly qualified to those with no qualifications at all.

The overqualified

Most national policies for education are dedicated to increasing the output of college graduates. The policies may be working but too often the graduates are not. In the last 30 years the number of graduates on the job market has more than doubled. The sheer volume of graduates has generated an unexpected crisis in graduate recruitment. It's not that there aren't enough graduates to go around: on the contrary, there are too many. In many parts of the world the numbers of graduates are not being matched by a similar rise in the numbers of graduate jobs.

Graduates in China, for example, face what Premier Wen Jiabao described in 2009 as a 'grim' job market, as the global recession took a grip on the Chinese economy. Many of China's six million graduates were struggling to find work because of falling exports, factory closures and a slowdown in consumer spending, which deterred employers from hiring them. For China, graduate unemployment is a highly sensitive issue. As part of its economic strategy, the government has encouraged students to go to university to stimulate skills and consumer spending. The families of millions of students have invested heavily in their education. But at the end of 2008 about one million of that year's graduates still had not found work. Desperate graduates were applying for routine jobs in rural areas; or were looking for posts as nannies and domestic helpers in more affluent regions such as Guangzhou. Quoting a housekeeping recruitment agency, the provincial govern- ment's newspaper, *Guangzhou Daily*, reported in January 2009, that 500 or 600 people were applying for domestic jobs every month, more than 90 percent of whom were university students; including 28 masters students.[7]

Graduate vacancies began to increase as the decade ended, especially in large companies, but the gap remains consider- able. In the United Kingdom, in the same period, there were about 20,000 graduate opportunities per annum and about 200,000 graduates a year competing for them. Many end up applying for jobs for which they were overqualified. During the recession of the early 1980s, around thiry percent of all graduates were in non-graduate jobs early on in their careers. Levels of overqualification are even higher now.

There is a further issue for graduates. Too few have what business needs. More complex economies demand more sophisticated talent "with global acumen, knowledge of different cultures, technological literacy, entrepreneurial skills, and the ability to manage increasingly complex organizations."[8] Employers say they want people who can think creatively, who can innovate, who can communicate well, work in teams and are adaptable and self-confident. They complain that many graduates have few of these qualities. It's hardly surprising. Conventional academic programs are not designed to develop them and often value the opposite approach: encouraging solo research rather than collaboration, preferring data to be presented in an accepted format, measuring success according to academic merit. Ironically, the demand for new skills is coming at a time when colleges are least able to adapt and provide them because growing student numbers restrict the time available for staff to offer personalized teaching.

Degrees originated at a time when colleges were select centers of learning, to which only a minority of people were admitted. Teaching took the form of large group lectures, small seminars and individual tutorials. The personal qualities associated with a degree – independence of mind, objectivity, and the capacity for abstract thought and reasoned debate – grew out of the ambience of the institution as much as from dedication to the study of the discipline. Nowadays, in most large universities, there are few opportunities for individual teaching. Students attend mass lectures by remote professors and large seminar groups run by poorly paid graduate assistants. Assignments are often graded with insufficient feedback to inform the student. The pervasive culture of standardized testing and multiple-choice assessment makes the process even more impersonal because the focus is on achieving performance statistics and retaining funding, rather than an interest in the individual's ability. It's little wonder that graduates lack the creative abilities that business urgently needs; or that, as the numbers of young self-employed entrepreneurs increase, fewer people are seeing the value of a university education at all.

THE WAR FOR TALENT

One of the consequences of the mismatch between education and changes in world economies is that companies and organizations everywhere are fighting a war for talent.[9] We live in a time when the ability to adapt is critical. In situations of high uncertainty, employers need to make decisions quickly in order to steer through change. Major companies are finding it increasingly difficult to find the people they say they need. And when they do find them, they often have trouble keeping them. Executives say there is a worsening shortage of the people needed to run divisions and manage critical functions, let alone lead companies. This problem has been building for some time.

The corporate consultancy company McKinsey has been working with the human resources departments of 77 large US companies in a variety of industries to understand their talent-building philosophies, practices and challenges. Their original study, published in 1998, was updated in 2008.[10] It included nearly 400 corporate offices and 6000 executives in the 'top 200' ranks in these companies. It also drew on case studies of 20 companies widely regarded as being rich in talent. Three-quarters of companies had said they had insufficient talent sometimes and all were chronically short of talent across the board.[11]

The study concluded that executive talent has long been an under-managed corporate asset. Companies that manage their physical and financial assets with rigor and sophistication have not made their people a priority in the same way. Few employees trust employers to provide useful opportunities for professional development. Most organizations take a short-term view of training needs. Only a third of employers provide training beyond the job. In a rapidly changing environment employers constantly fear that their best talent will be poached by other companies. They are wary of investing in developing their own talent since they fear it will primarily benefit their competitors. Staff turnover is often high and vacant posts are filled with outside talent. According to search professionals, the average executive will work in five companies; in another ten years it may be seven. The recent recession is having a further impact on these trends.

To win the war for talent, most companies choose to develop powerful recruitment and retention processes to get the 'right people' on board. In 1998 this meant identifying the top 20 percent: the best performers. The problem with the short-term model is that "it does nothing to prevent the exodus of the rest – those whose talents are undeveloped. It assumes a world with an unlimited supply of talent ... that does not mind working in businesses where development is not deemed a priority." The 2008 report suggests that there has been a gradual change in this strategy and a wider recognition in companies that it is essential to maintain a balance of talent across the board.[12] Even so, according to McKinsey, companies are engaged in a war for senior executive talent that will remain a defining characteristic of the competitive landscape for decades to come. Yet most are ill-prepared and even the best are vulnerable.[13]

The underqualified
The problems are serious enough for the highly qualified. They are deadly for the unqualified. The current system is failing millions of people even by its own standards. One index measures the high rates of dropout and withdrawal from compulsory education. In the United States an average of 30 percent of students who enter the 9th grade in school will dropout before the 12th grade and not graduate from high

school. In some areas the proportion is as high as 50 percent. In some Native American communities it's over 80 percent. Among those who stay the course, rates of underachievement and disaffection are often desperately high.[14]

It's wrong to blame the students for these numbers: they reflect a problem within the system. Any other standardized process with a 30 percent wastage rate, let alone 50 percent or 80 percent, would be condemned as a failure. In the case of education, it isn't a waste of inert commodities; it's a waste of living, breathing people. As matters stand, those who don't graduate from high school are offered few alternatives apart from low-income work if they can find it; or long-term unemployment if they cannot. The costs of unemployment create immense burdens for the economy while very many productive jobs that could be filled are not.

In May 2010 there were 23 million people unemployed in the European Union: nearly a third of them are under 25. According to one study, "One in three Europeans of working age has few or no formal qualifications, making them 40 percent less likely to be employed than those with medium-level qualifications. In the United Kingdom alone, 5.7 million adults of working age have no qualifications at all and 20 percent of all adults in England, around 7 million people, have serious problems with basic literacy and numeracy.[15] Most experts agree that the roots of Europe's jobs dilemma lie in an inflexible education system, high labor taxes and barriers to mobility.

As the 2010 report from the International Labor Organization shows, youth unemployment in particular is a global phenomenon and a deepening problem everywhere. In developed and some emerging economies, rising unemployment creates its own social hazards from the sense of alienation and prolonged inactivity. Ninety percent of young people live in developing economies, where they are especially vulnerable to underemployment and poverty. The ILO report estimates that in 2008, 152 million young people, or about 28 percent of all the young workers in the world, were in work but remained in extreme poverty; living in households surviving on less than US$1.25 per person per day. ILO Director-General Juan Somavia says that, "In developing countries, crisis pervades the daily life of the poor. The number of young people stuck in working poverty grows and the cycle of working poverty persists through at least another generation."[16]

The ILO study highlights the cost of unemployment among young people: "Societies lose their investment in education. Governments fail to receive contributions to social security systems and are forced to increase spending on remedial services." As Mr Somavia puts it, "Young people are the drivers of economic development. Foregoing this potential is an economic waste and can undermine social stability. It is important to focus on comprehensive and integrated strategies that combine education and training policies with targeted employment policies for youth."

The chronically high number of jobless, roughly half of whom have been out of work for more than a year, is more than an economic challenge; the long-term unemployed are part of a broad group who feel increasingly marginalized by the driving forces of social and economic change but powerless to become involved in making a difference. These groups tend to be concentrated in particular areas: lessening their shared chances of recovery. In the UK, the vast majority of unemployed people live on 2000 housing estates. In a work-driven society, being without work or the prospect of it can produce an aggressive counter-attack.

In the United States, as in many other countries there is a smoldering problem of social exclusion. In a growing number of urban centers the problems of gang[17] violence are growing, particularly among the alienated and disaffected. In major European cities gang warfare and violence have become an endemic feature of teenage life. One of the most troubling prospects is the emergence of a permanent underclass. If certain groups of inner-city residents are economically disenfranchised, they can become caught in an irrevocable cycle of crime, poverty and despair. There can be high price to pay in containing the anger and frustrations of those who feel marginalized and hopeless.

According to figures from the US Department of Justice, The United States has the highest incarceration rate of any country in the world. A report from the Pew Center in 2009 showed that a startling 1 in every 31 American adults is in the corrections system, which includes jail, prison, probation and supervision. That figure is more than double the rate 25 years ago when it was 1 in 77. During that period, prison and jail populations have grown 274 percent, to 2.3 million in 2008; while those under supervision grew 226 percent, to 5.1 million. Over the past 20 years, state spending on penitentiary systems has been the fastest-growing part of their budgets after Medicaid, the healthcare program for those with low income. In California in 2010, spending on the state correctional system was set to overtake spending on the whole of public higher education. Overall, state spending on criminal justice has increased more than 300 percent to an estimated record in 2008 of $51.7 billion.

Of those in the corrections system, 1 in 45 are on probation or parole, with 1 in 100 in jail or prison. The numbers are concentrated among particular groups. Just over nine percent of black adults in the US are in the correctional system, about four percent of the Hispanic population and two percent of whites. Within the mushrooming prisoner populations, there are disproportionate numbers of people who failed in education, who did not complete high school or who struggled with literacy or numeracy or otherwise underperformed in education because of undiagnosed learning difficulties.

The costs of incarceration are vastly higher than education. On average, keeping an inmate in prison costs $29,000 a year compared with an estimated $9000 a year for high school education.[18] Some policy makers clearly prefer to meet the costs of containment rather than invest in the talents of marginalized communities. Yet, developing the talents and aspirations of those who are in trouble is by far the best way to re-engage them in society and avoid the spiraling costs of recidivism. From every point of view: social, ethical and economic, it would make vastly more sense to invest in improving education in the first place and to give all citizens a proper start in their lives rather than underfund education and spend incomparably more on the consequences.

A 1996 symposium on creativity in America concluded that the result of the misplaced emphasis on the punitive rather than on the educational roles of government is that upward mobility, a staple principle of American life, is under assault and with it "the possibility of creative reinvention of the individual ... a fundamental aspect of the American imagination." As the symposium concluded, if this comparison between investment in education and in prisons shocks us, "it should also spur us into action because it reflects a change in the nation's priorities away from building the future and toward short-term solutions for the complex social and cultural problems we face."[19] Yet another example of the septic focus in action and its failure to treat causes rather than symptoms.

CULTURAL CHALLENGES

As technologies race forward, economies oscillate and populations shift, so too do values and behavior. Education systems everywhere now have to contend with massive waves of cultural change on every front. Some of these are the direct features of digital culture. Mark Prensky[20] and others make a distinction between digital natives and digital immigrants. This is not a hard and fast distinction but it does point to a significant generational shift. The proliferation of digital technologies has created what has been called the biggest generation gap since rock and roll. I often ask people at conferences to put their hands up if they are over the age of 30 and to keep them up if they are wearing a wristwatch. Usually it's the majority. When the current over 30s were growing up, digital technology was in its infancy. To keep track of the time you had to wear a watch. If I ask a roomful of teenagers the same question, very few of them keep their hands up. As a rule the current generation of teenagers do not wear wristwatches. For them, the time is everywhere, on their cell phones, iPods and games units. They see no need to wear a separate gadget just to tell the time.[21]

"Why would you?" they say. "It's a single function device. How lame is that?" I say, "No, it's not, it tells the date as well." But I know it's not a convincing case. Teenagers and younger children speak digital as their native tongue. Most adults speak it as a second language. Our children don't even consider these devices as technology. They are as natural to them as the air they breathe. Technology, as was once said, is not technology if it happened before you were born.

One of the consequences is that young people's minds are constantly engaged with the digital world: they are multitasking, connecting and creating content at a precipitous rate. For previous generations, one of the only ways to connect with the wider world of culture and ideas was to go to school. That's simply not true anymore. The pervasiveness of digital technology changes the whole equation for education and for the roles of teachers.

In the last 50 years many of the old certainties have also broken down; the nuclear family, patterns of religious involvement, gender roles and the rest. We live in a world in which cultural identities are increasingly complex, interwoven and contested. The growing inequalities of wealth and opportunity are opening even deeper divisions between cultural communities. In many countries, there is a worrying trend in disaffection and aggression among young people in schools. For example, in the United Kingdom statistics show that, in 2009, 17,000 pupils were excluded from schools for physical attacks on adults.[22] The sense of frustration and demoralization amongst teachers is strong. Sixty percent say they want to leave the school they work in. Half of the teachers surveyed said they wanted to leave the profession because of the poor level of discipline in schools.[23]

PERSONAL CHALLENGES

Young people who stay at school now find themselves under much more pressure from testing than my generation was. They work harder to get into college than we did; they work harder when they are there if they want a good result and, when they leave, their qualifications are worth less. This pressure begins when they are five, if not three, and continues throughout school. Instead of examinations and tests being an indicator of how they are progressing, they are like continually pulling up a plant to see how well it is growing.[24] For students who go to college, the pressure can become more intense. As academic inflation continues to rise, students put themselves under immense pressure to succeed. Many take performance-enhancing drugs like Ritalin and Adderall to keep them focused.

In addition to academic pressure, another pressure is to appear as laid-back as possible. In a study of suicidal behavior among students, Rory O'Connor and Noel Sheehy argue that students "are under pressure to be rounded, happy, successful, talented, bright young things and they want to fit in. ...They are under pressure not to appear under pressure." More and more of them are finding all of these pressures too difficult to bear and are suffering from the consequences.

The numbers of suicides at universities have highlighted the dangerously high expectations we now have for our children's academic success. Some student counselors are joining the call for schools to spend much more time on developing the basic communication and problem-solving skills that young people will need to cope later in life: "Only by getting young people to talk can we tackle the stigma associated with being unable to deal with stress and the reluctance to go to see anyone about it."[25]

As the pressures of education continue to intensify, many students are simply not learning the personal skills they need to deal with modern life and the increased pressures of continual assessment and being examined at every level: "We have always had some form of assessment but the emphasis has shifted. By assuming that academic success is the be-all and end-all of life, we are not teaching people how to deal with the fact that they may not reach the aspiration. We don't teach people how to deal with failure and this is a fundamental oversight."[26]

TAKING STOCK

The world is changing faster than ever and there are major problems facing all organizations in recruiting and retaining people with the creative abilities they need to engage with these changes. The lives of individuals and communities too are deeply diminished by the lack of these abilities. There are many complex factors at work, but the inherent deficiencies of industrial/academic systems of education are playing a major part. Despite the growing skills gap, the war for talent and the extraordinary pace of change on every front, many policymakers and others continue to chant the mantra about the need to raise traditional academic standards and scores on standardized tests. The reason, I believe, is that the assumptions underpinning these approaches to education have become so deeply embedded in their consciousness that many people are not even aware of them. They have blended into the everyday ideologies of common sense, as the way things have to be. Like a lot of common sense, they may seem obvious but they are wrong. The creative capacities of generations of people have been sacrificed needlessly to an academic illusion.

· 4 ·

THE ACADEMIC ILLUSION

"All truth passes through three stages:
First, it is ridiculed. Second, it is violently opposed.
Third, it is accepted as being self-evident."
Arthur Schopenhauer (1788–1860)

THE RATE AND SCALE of change engulfing the world is creating a tidal shift in how people live and earn their living. We now need to be equally radical in how we think of education. Raising academic standards alone will not solve the problems we face: it may compound them. To move forward we a need fresh understanding of intelligence, of ability, and of the nature of creativity. We need to rethink some of the basic ideas that we hold about education, intelligence and ourselves. Above all we need to awaken ourselves from what James Hemming (1909–2007) has vividly called, the "academic illusion".[1] It enthralls us more completely than you may think.

IMAGES OF INTELLIGENCE

How intelligent are you? This is not an easy question to answer. Intelligence is one of those qualities that we think we can recognize in people but when we try to define it, it slips from our grasp. If it's any consolation, there is no agreed definition of intelligence among the many specialists in psychology, neurology, education or other professional fields who devote a good deal of their own intelligence to thinking about it. There may be no agreed definition, but there are two ideas that dominate popular conceptions of intelligence that are embedded in the idea of academic ability. The first is IQ (Intelligence Quotient); the second is a memory for factual information.

Join the club

Mensa is an international association that promotes itself as one of the most exclusive clubs in the world. Membership is on the basis of "high intelligence" and Mensa claims to admit only two percent of the population to its ranks. The decision is based on applicants' performance in various 'intelligence tests' that ask questions like these:

1) What letter should come next?

   M Y V S E H M S J R S N U S N E P?

2) Details of items bought at a stationer are shown below.

   78 – Pencils

   152 – Paint Brushes

   51 – Files

   142 – Felt Tip Pens

   ? – Writing Pads

   How many writing pads should there be?

3) In which direction should the missing arrow point?

```
V   >   ∧   V   <
V   <   >   V   >
∧   >   ?   >   V
>   <   V   ∧   >
V   >   <   V   ∧
```

Questions like these test the ability to analyze logically the principles that govern a sequence of ideas.[2] Philosophers call this logico-deductive reasoning. Thinking 'logically' is an important part of the popular view of intelligence. The second is having a memory for information.

As a matter of fact

One of the best-known programs on British television is a quiz show called *Mastermind*. Each week four contestants take it in turn to sit under a spotlight in a darkened studio and face interrogation by the quizmaster. There are two 2-minute rounds of questions: the first is on a specialist topic chosen by the contestant; the second tests their general knowledge. The Mastermind of the Year emerges at the end of each series from an all-winners final, achieving recognition as one of the cleverest people in Britain. A long-running radio program called *Brain of Britain*, has a similar format and there is now a *Junior Mastermind* too. Contestants entering the phenomenally successful *Who Wants to be a Millionaire?* have the opportunity to win a fortune by giving correct answers to just twelve factual questions. Quiz programs like these draw on the ability to memorize factual information including names, dates and events and statistics. Philosophers call this propositional knowledge: knowledge *that* something is the case.

Academic ability is based on the two capacities for logico-deductive reason and for propositional knowledge. The term 'academic' derives from the name of a grove near ancient Athens called *Academeia*. It was there that, 400 years before the birth of Christ, the Greek philosopher Plato established an influential community of scholars. Plato's teachings drew from the methods of philosophical analysis that had been developed by his teacher, Socrates. Plato's most famous student was Aristotle, (who, in turn, was tutor to Alexander the Great). Aristotle further developed these ideas in his own work and teachings, which from there have grown systems of thought, of mathematics and of science that have shaped the intellectual character of the Western world. But apart from presumably having high ones themselves, Plato, Socrates and Aristotle had never heard of IQ or Mensa. So what is the link between the current obsession with IQ tests, mass education and the groves of *Academeia*?

MEASURING YOUR MIND

Like the motor car, television, the micro-processor and the Coca-Cola bottle, IQ is one of the most compelling inventions of the modern world. It is an idea in four parts. The first is that each of us is born with a *fixed* intellectual capacity or quotient: that just as we may have brown eyes or red hair, we have a set amount of intelligence. Second, how much intelligence we have can be calculated by a series of pencil-and-paper tests of the sort illustrated above. The results can be compared against a general scale and given as a number from 0 to 200. That number is your IQ. On this scale, average intelligence is between 80 and 100; above average is between 100 and 120 and anything above 130 gets you into Mensa's Christmas party. The third idea is that IQ tests can be used to predict children's performance at school and in later life. For this reason, IQ tests are widely used for school selection and for educational planning.

Finally, IQ is taken to be an index of general intelligence: that is, these tests are assumed to point to a person's overall intellectual capacities. Many people now seem to think that it is enough to roll out their IQ score for everyone to grasp how bright they are, or not. As a result of all this, the popular idea of intelligence has become dangerously narrow and other intellectual abilities are either ignored or underestimated. For all these reasons, since the idea of IQ emerged about 100 years ago, it has had explosive consequences for social policy and especially for education. Where did the idea come in the first place; how did it come to dominate the popular conception of intelligence; and is it a fair and accurate measure across all cultures?

Brave old world

The foundations of the modern intelligence test were laid in the mid-nineteenth century by Sir Francis Galton, a cousin of Charles Darwin. After reading *The Origin of Species* in 1859, Galton assumed that human life might follow the same principles of natural selection that Darwin had described in the rest of nature. Galton concluded that if heredity played a decisive role in human development it should be possible to improve the human race through selective breeding procedures.[3]

With that end in mind, he turned his attention to developing scientific ways of isolating and measuring "general intelligence" and of comparing it between individuals. He first used the word *eugenics* (with the meaning "good" or "well" born) in 1883. The modern intelligence test builds on Galton's work and more especially that of Alfred Binet.

At the beginning of the 20th century, Binet was working with children in elementary schools in Paris. As part of his work he wanted to identify children who might need special educational support. He began to develop short tests for children of different ages that could be administered easily.

His aim was practical and his method "was pragmatic rather than scientific."[4] By 1905 he had produced his first scale of intelligence based on a test of 30 items designed for children aged from three to twelve years. The tester worked through the items with each child until the child could do no more. Performance was then compared with the average for the age group to which the child belonged. If a child could pass the test expected of a six-year-old, say, the child was said to have a mental age of six. Binet used the difference between the mental age and the chronological age as an index of retardation.

In 1912, German psychologist William Stern proposed using the ratio of mental age to chronological age, to yield the now familiar intelligence quotient or:

$$IQ = \frac{\text{mental age}}{\text{chronological age}} \times 100$$

Within a few years translations were appearing in many parts of the world. The restricted uses for which it was originally designed were soon forgotten as it was applied in every sort of setting, especially in the United States.[5] One hundred years later, IQ remains the principal basis of selection for different forms of education, for many different types of employment and for roles in the military.

IQ has been used to support and to attack theories of racial, ethnic and social difference. Early IQ tests in the UK and the USA suggested that poor people and their children have low IQs and that the rich and their offspring have high IQs. It seemed that IQ somehow determined levels of affluence and of material success. An important variable of course is that poor people could not afford to educate themselves and rich people could, which is something of an oversight from a methodological point of view. For a time, these findings provided a powerful rationale for political initiatives based on eugenics, to 'improve' the human stock by selective breeding and population control. In the early 20th century, leading intellectuals including Winston Churchill and George Bernard Shaw supported the eugenics movement, arguing that the breeding of the poor should be carefully controlled. Some states in the USA legislated to sterilize people classified as 'idiots' or of low intelligence. With different motives, the Third Reich embraced eugenics as a key element in the Final Solution, with appalling ramifications.

A major controversy about the basis of IQ tests flared up in 1992 with the publication in America of *The Bell Curve* by Charles Murray and Richard Hernstein.[6] *The Bell Curve* argued that IQ tests do point reliably to vast differences in human intelligence. It argued that IQ is linked to low moral behavior and that there is a connection with the cultures of some ethnic groups especially Black and Hispanic communities. *The Bell Curve* was widely condemned as a racist tract and generated an inferno of debate, which is still smoldering.

From the outset, IQ has been a powerful and provocative idea, and it remains so, even though there is no general agreement on exactly what IQ tests measure, or on how, whatever it is they do measure, relates to general intelligence. Nonetheless these ideas of academic ability and of IQ have come to be taken for granted as the natural order of things, rather than as the product of particular cultural values and scientific assumptions, which they are. How has this happened? The answer lies in the triumph of science in the last 400 years and in its roots in the groves of *Academeia*.

THE TRIUMPH OF SCIENCE

Historians conventionally think of Western history in three main periods: ancient, medieval and modern. These periods are not separated by sharp boundaries or exact dates, but they are distinct phases in the cultural evolution of humanity. They are marked by different ways of seeing the world and by the very different worlds that were created as a result. They were based on different ideologies or paradigms.

The philosopher Susanne Langer (1895–1985) argues that intellectual horizons of a society, or of an historical period, are not set simply by events or human desires. They are set by the basic ideas that people use to analyze and describe their lives. Theories develop in response to questions. And a question, as Susanne Langer notes, can only be answered in a certain number of ways. For this reason the most important character-istic of an intellectual age is the questions it asks – the problems it identifies. It is this, rather than the answers it provides, that reveals its underlying view of the world. In any intellectual age there will be some fundamen-tal assumptions that advocates of all the different ways of thinking unconsciously take for granted. These deep-seated attitudes constitute our ideology and they set the boundaries of theory, by inclining us to this or that set of issues and ex-planations. If our explanations are theoretical, our questions are ideological.

"Copernicus, Galileo and Kepler did not solve an old problem: they asked a new question."

The term 'paradigm' was popularized in the 1970s by the American philosopher of science, Thomas Kuhn (1922–1996).[7] He used it to describe the seismic changes in human thought and culture that have marked the great scientific revolutions. A paradigm is an accepted framework of rules and assumptions that define established ways of doing things. In the history of science, a paradigm is not a single theory or scientific discovery, but the underlying approach to science itself, within which theories are framed and discoveries are verified.

Kuhn describes science as a puzzle-solving activity in which problems are tackled using procedures and rules that are agreed within the community of scientists. Kuhn was interested in the moments in history when there is a shift either in the problems or in the rules of science or both. He sees a difference between periods of 'normal science', when there is a general agreement among scientists about problems and rules, and periods of 'extraordinary science' when normal science begins to generate results that the accepted rules and assumptions cannot explain. If these anomalies accumulate there can be a loss of confidence in the accepted methods and a professional crisis in science, which can unleash periods of enormous creativity and invention. Periods of 'extraordinary science' create opportunities for completely new questions and for new theories about the nature and limits of science itself. These are times of scientific revolution.

A new paradigm may emerge when a new idea or method – what Susanne Langer calls *generative ideas* – runs with tumultuous force through existing ways of thinking and transforms them. Truly generative ideas excite intellectual passions in many different fields because they open up whole new ways of seeing and thinking. As Susanne Langer said, "a new idea is a light that illuminates things that simply had no form for us before the light fell on them and gave them meaning. We turn the light here, there and everywhere the limits of thought recede before it."[8] A paradigm change tends to run a characteristic course. It is triggered by new ideas that reconfigure our basic ways of thinking. Initially, there is a period of huge intellectual uncertainty and excitement as the new ideas are applied, stretched and tested against many different areas of inquiry. Eventually, the revolutionary ways of thinking begin to settle down and their real potential becomes clearer and more established. They become part of the new paradigm: the new way of thinking. Eventually, the ideas that gave birth to the new paradigm become drained of their excitement, leaving a residue of established ideas and of new certainties. They enter our consciousness as taken-for-granted ideas about the way things are and become part of the new culture.

The transition from one intellectual age to another can be traumatic and protracted. New ways of thinking do not simply replace the old at clear points in history. They often overlap and coexist with established ways of thinking for long periods of time. This complex and convoluted process of change can create many tensions and unresolved problems along the way. But eventually the new paradigm provides the framework for a new period of normal science.

Each major period of intellectual growth has been characterized by revolutionary new ideas that have driven forward the sensibilities of the times. In the ancient and medieval periods it was taken for granted that Ptolemy (c. AD 90–c. AD 168) was right: the sun orbited round the earth. There were two reasons for this belief. To begin with, that is exactly what it seemed to do: the sun came up in the morning, passed through the sky and went down again at night. It seemed obvious to everyone that it was the sun that was moving and not the earth. People weren't being flung off the planet on the way to work: there wasn't a network of ropes to cling to on the way to the shops. It was plain common sense that the sun was moving and they were not. There were religious reasons too for this assumption. In the medieval worldview, the earth was the center of creation and human beings were thought to be God's last word: the jewel in the cosmic crown. Theologians assumed a perfect symmetry in the universe. The planets, it was thought, revolved around the earth in perfect circular orbits.

Poets expressed this harmony in the rhythms of verse; mathematicians from the early Greeks developed elegant formulae to describe these motions; and astronomers based elaborate theories upon it. The problem was that there were worrying variations in these movements. The planets would not behave. Assuming that the earth was the center of things, astronomers worked out increasingly intricate variations in their theories to account for these variations.

As perplexed as everyone else, Nicolaus Copernicus (1473–1543) made a radical proposal. What if the sun wasn't going round the earth, he asked? What if the earth was going round the sun? This startling idea solved at a stroke many of the old problems that had plagued astronomers. Heliocentrism had arrived. Later, Johannes Kepler (1571–1630) showed that the planets did not move in circles but in elliptical orbits, a phenomenon that Isaac Newton (1643–1727) was to eventually explain by the effects of gravitational attraction.

The so-called Copernican revolution caused few ripples initially. But during his lifetime, Galileo Galilei (1564–1642) took a great interest in heliocentrism. His telescope enabled scientists to begin to see the truth of Copernican theories and the ideas began to take hold. These proposals amounted to heresy: an affront to God's design and to humanity's view of itself. Galileo was persecuted and put on trial twice in his lifetime for his views. Nonetheless, the theories were true and over time more and more people came to recognize that. Copernicus, Galileo and Kepler did not solve an old problem: they asked a new question and in doing so they changed the whole basis on which the old questions had been framed. The old theories were shown to be wrong because the assumptions on which they had been based were mistaken. They were built on a false ideology. As this realization spread, it ushered in a new intellectual age: a new paradigm.

The Renaissance of the fourteenth and fifteenth centuries marked a shift away from not only the theories of the medieval worldview but also from the ideologies in which they had been conceived. The insights of Copernicus and Galileo proved to be the dawn of a new age. The transition from Ptolemy's first century view of the universe with the Earth at its center, to the universe of Copernicus, repositioned not only the earth in space but also humanity's place in history.

The shock waves did not stop with astronomy: they rolled through all areas of cultural life including philosophy, politics and religion. Though they both denied being atheists, the arguments of Copernicus and Galileo raised serious doubts about many aspects of religious teaching. Five hundred years later, Darwin's theory of evolution was to issue an even more profound challenge to religious belief: a theory that was framed in the paradigm of objective science that had been heralded by the Copernican revolution.

The medieval world view that had been dominated by theology and faith was shaken apart and eventually replaced by a new one, based on logic, reason and evidence. This new dawn proved fertile for powerful generative ideas.

BORN AGAIN

The Renaissance was so called because it also marked a rebirth of interest in the methods of the ancient world, of Greek philosophy, literature and mathematics. The Renaissance saw the most extraordinary flowering of intellectual achievement on all fronts. In little more than 150 years, some of humanity's greatest figures were born and some of our greatest works produced: lives and achievements that have shaped the world that we now live in. Between 1450 and 1600 Europe saw the birth of Leonardo da Vinci, Michelangelo, Raphael, Galileo, Copernicus, Shakespeare and Isaac Newton. They produced works in art and literature of unsurpassed beauty and depth, and created the foundations of modern science, technology and philosophy.

The idea of a Renaissance person is one who is learned in a range of disciplines including the arts and sciences. The quintessential Renaissance figure is Leonardo da Vinci, a man gifted in painting, sculpture, mathematics and science. When Michelangelo was painting the Sistine Chapel he had in his room drafts of scientific theorems and of new technological innovations.

The Renaissance was also driven forward by a succession of technical innovations and accomplishments. Four in particular were to prove decisive: the printing press, the magnetic compass, the telescope and the mechanical clock.

Spreading the word

Before the invention of the printing press, only a small, literate elite had access to books, ideas and learning: an elite that was largely confined to the Church. The hold of the Church was based largely on its exclusive access to scriptures and through them the word of God. This gave the clergy unrivalled control over the people's minds. The Renaissance and the great cultural movements that flowed from it gradually shook loose the iron grip of the Church. As literacy spread, the flow of ideas increased and the supremacy of the Church declined. The printing and distribution of books unleashed a voracious appetite for literacy and learning which in turn challenged the authority of the literate over the illiterate. Printing disseminated ideas across national and cultural boundaries on a scale that was previously unimaginable.

The subsequent development of the portable book by Aldus Manutius (1450–1515) of Venice created the personal library and revolutionized for ever the control of knowledge. For the first time, the institution of the medieval library and the institutions behind it, notably the Church, began to be undermined and replaced by an independently published and commercial product. As Dr Juan F. Rada puts it: "A new technological and intellectual transition started, which reinforced the conditions of the scientific revolution and accompanied the great period of the discoveries. The portable book had a subversive impact, created the conditions for the Reformation, for the use of vernacular language, for the diversification of publishing and allowed for a great individual expression of authors and readers." The portable library also

created the instruments that were necessary for the development of complex bureaucracies and large organized states:
"Publishing became the vehicle for the transmission of ideas
and debate, for proselytism and for scholarly recognition. The
seeds for the Enlightenment were sown and with them the
belief in education and, in this century, the belief in universal
education and literacy."[9]

Getting our bearings

The Renaissance was indeed the great period of discoveries. The commercial fleets of the European powers began
to journey across the oceans on speculative expeditions of
exploration and colonization. These extraordinary forays into
the unknown were made possible by new navigational tools,
including the magnetic compass (developed originally by the
Chinese some 200 years earlier and only recently surpassed by
GPS), which revolutionized orientation, especially at sea, by
measuring points of direction with great precision. As some
explorers were mapping the earth, others took their lead from
Galileo and were surveying the heavens with a new sense of
scientific precision. The telescope made possible more accurate observations of the movements of the planets and of
the place of the earth in the heavens. All of these innovations
interacted with the evolution of new theories in science and
mathematics. So too did a more unlikely invention, which is
likely to have its roots in Chinese technology.

The mechanical clock, which gradually replaced the water
clock, made possible entirely new ways of thinking about
time. Interestingly for such a revolutionary idea, there is no
documented history of who invented the mechanical clock,
though it is likely that they first appeared in the 1200s. Reliable clocks released people from organizing their time by the
natural rhythms of day and night; a change that had profound
significance for patterns of work and industry.

The conventions of the clock have also deeply affected our conception of time. The idea that a day is divided into 24 equal segments of 60 minutes has become an inalienable part of daily consciousness. The clock also suggested new ways of thinking about the universe. In 1687 Isaac Newton published his *Principia* in which he set out his monumental theories about the workings of nature and of our place in the cosmos. In doing so, he conceived of the universe as a great clock-like mechanism, a philosophical idea that had a deep impact on subsequent developments in science and philosophy. Implied in this image were ideas about cause and effect and about the importance of external as against internal stimuli: ideas that now shape everyday thinking and behavior. As Alvin Toffler notes, the invention of the clock came before Newton published his theories and had a profound effect on how he framed them, though Newton himself warned against using his theories to view the Universe as akin to a great clock. He said, "Gravity explains the motions of the planets, but it cannot explain who set the planets in motion. God governs all things and knows all that is or can be done."[10]

The rise of the individual

Through the complex and interweaving changes of the Renaissance there emerged a new emphasis on the importance of individual experience. In the medieval period, Church and State were locked in a close embrace. The spread of literacy was one force that began to erode the power of the Church in the fifteenth century. Another was the growing unrest with the spiritual and political corruption of the Catholic Church.

In the early fifteenth century, the German cleric Martin Luther sparked a revolt against Rome: a movement that spread throughout Europe and split Christianity in two.

Luther argued that no third party and least of all a corrupt and self-serving Church should stand between individuals and

their relationship with their creator. The Reformation emphasized the need for individuals to reach their own understanding
of the scriptures and to deal directly with God. The emphasis
on empowering the critical judgment and knowledge of the
individual underpinned the growth of scientific method in the
seventeenth and eighteenth centuries in Europe; the period
now known as the Enlightenment.

Being reasonable

As the old certainties of the Church fragmented, philosophers
and intellectuals of the Enlightenment began to ask fundamental questions about the nature of things. Specifically, what
is knowledge and how do we know? They tried to take nothing
for granted. The aim was to see the world as it is; stripped of
superstition, myth and fantasy. Knowledge had to meet one
or both of two tests: to conform to the strict dictates of deductive logic or be supported by the evidence of observation. The
French philosopher René Descartes (1596–1650) argued that
nothing should be taken on trust. If a new edifice of knowledge
was to be constructed, it must be built brick by brick with each
element fully tested. He set out a logical program of analysis
where nothing would be taken for granted, not even his own
existence. His starting point was that the only thing he could
know for certain was that he was actually thinking about the
problems: *cogito ergo sum*. "I think, therefore I am." I must be
alive because I am thinking.

The Western world view has been deeply affected by this
principle of linearity. The rationalist moves through a logical
sequence, building one idea on another like bricks in a wall.
The empirical method similarly looks for patterns in events,
suggesting movements from known causes to known effects.[11]
Rationalism and *empiricism* were the driving forces of the
Enlightenment and they ran with irresistible force through
science, philosophy and politics, bowling over traditional

methods of thought and opening up vast new fields of adventure in science, technology and philosophy. They led in due course to the Industrial Revolution of the eighteenth and nineteenth centuries and to the dominance of science in all its forms in our own times. Along the way a fissure opened up between two ways of thinking that had previously been almost indistinguishable: the arts and the sciences.

Being human

The union of the arts and sciences gradually dissolved during the period of the Enlightenment. There was a powerful reaction in the late eighteenth and early nineteenth century, which took the form of Romanticism. Whereas the Enlightenment was represented by the great rationalist philosophers and scientists, including Hume, Locke and Descartes, Romanticism was carried forward in the powerful works of artists, poets and musicians, including Beethoven, Schiller, Wordsworth, Coleridge, Byron and Goethe. In contrast to the rationalists, the Romantics were focused on the quality of human experience and on the nature of existence.

The shaping of the modern world

Our present world view has been shaped by the extraordinary scientific, technological and cultural revolutions that emerged from this paradigm shift from the medieval to the modern world from the Enlightenment onwards. In the process, the explanatory powers of logic and of scientific evidence, and the intellectual authority of science as a whole have become firmly implanted as the accepted mode of thought. They are part of modern ideology and they interact powerfully with how we think and create theories in every field.

The achievements of the rationalist scientific world view have been incalculable. They include the extraordinary advances in medicine and pharmaceuticals and their impact on the length and quality of human life; the explosive growth in industrial technologies; sophisticated systems of communication and travel; and an unprecedented understanding of the physical universe. There is clearly much more to come as the catalogue of achievements in science and technology continues to accumulate. There has been a heavy price too, not least in the schism of the arts and sciences and the domination of the rationalist attitude, especially in the forms of education to which it has given rise.

THE RISE OF EDUCATION

Before the Industrial Revolution, relatively few people had any kind of formal education. In the Middle Ages in Europe, education was provided largely by the Church in what were known as grammar schools. Grammar schools of various sorts can be traced back to the ancient Greeks. The term 'grammar school' first appeared in English in 1387 in the form *gramer scole* but its Latin form *schola grammatica* was in use at least 200 years before that. The Kings School, Canterbury claims to be the oldest grammar school in England. It traces its origins to the coming of St Augustine in AD 597. The institutions themselves may have originated more than 1000 years earlier. Originally a grammar school was literally one that taught grammar and especially Latin grammar. Grammar with its alternative form *gramarye* and *glomerye* was highly revered by the uneducated who regarded it as a form of magic, a meaning that survives in our modern word 'glamour'.[12]

Many of the earliest grammar schools were founded by religious bodies. Some were attached to the larger or collegiate parish churches, others were maintained by monasteries. The purpose of these grammar schools was to educate boys for the Church, but medieval clerics followed careers in many fields. The Church was not one profession but the gateway to all professions including law, the civil service, diplomacy, politics and medicine. In the ancient and medieval schools, the principal focus was on learning Greek and Latin literature and the aim was to be fluent enough in these to enter professional life in law, politics or the civil service. Latin was the international language of the Church and fluency in it was a vital accomplishment.

Given their specialist functions, grammar schools have always been selective and provided some form of entrance test. By end of the fifteenth century there were 300 or more grammar schools in England and the Church was involved in most of them. As the fifteenth and sixteenth centuries unfolded and produced a deepening skepticism of religious doctrine, many non-religious organizations began to establish their own schools for their own purposes. Many of these were related to trade.[13] The growing influence of grammar schools of all sorts was accompanied by gradual changes in what they actually taught.

The curriculum of the medieval grammar schools was specifically classical. Classical education was based on the seven liberal arts or sciences: grammar, the formal structures of language; rhetoric, composition and presentation of argument; dialectic, formal logic; arithmetic; geometry; music; astronomy.[14] For centuries, the classics dominated the very idea of being educated and attempts at reform were resisted. During the Renaissance some pioneering head teachers tried to loosen the grip of the classics on the grammar school curriculum by introducing other subjects and a more practical approach to teaching them. Richard Mulcaster, the first headmaster of the Merchant Tailors' School from 1561 to 1586, tried hard to have English taught at grammar schools, arguing that it was essential to regulate its grammar and spelling. He pressed the case for drama in schools and his boys performed before Elizabeth I on a number of occasions. The curriculum

of Merchant Tailors' School came to include music and
drama, dancing, drawing and sport of all sorts – wrestling,
fencing, shooting, handball and football.

Francis Bacon (1561–1626) argued for the inclusion of
other subjects in the school curriculum, including history and
modern languages and especially science. The headmaster
of Tonbridge School published a book in 1787 arguing for
the curriculum to include history, geography, mathematics,
French, artistic training and physical training. In Britain, attempts to broaden the curriculum beyond the classics made
little progress until the mid-nineteenth century. Charles Darwin (1809–1882) went to school at Shrewsbury. Reflecting on
the experience, he said: "Nothing could have been worse for
my mind than this school, as it was strictly classical; nothing
else being taught except a little ancient geography and history.
The school as a means of education was to me a complete
blank. During my whole life I have been singularly incapable
of mastering any language ... The sole pleasure I ever received
from such [classical] studies was from some of the odes from
Horace which I admired greatly."[15]

The pressure for change eventually came from elsewhere.
Three developments in particular were to reshape public
opinion about schooling and to reform the grammar school
curriculum. The first was the growing impact of science and
technology, and the changing intellectual climate of which
they were part. Second, the rampant growth of industrialism
was changing the whole international economic landscape.
The Exhibitions of 1851 and 1862 vividly illustrated the rapid
industrial progress of other European countries, a process
that had begun in Britain but was now threatening to outrun
it. Third, new theories were developing about the nature of
intelligence and learning. The new science of psychology was
proposing new explanations about intelligence and how it
should be cultivated. These new theories challenged accepted
assumptions about how children learned, and questioned the

benefits of a strictly classical education rooted in learning grammar and formal logic. During the nineteenth and 20th centuries the classics became almost extinct in secondary education. In their place, the school curriculum settled into the now familiar hierarchy where languages, mathematics, science and technology are at the top and the arts and humanities are at the bottom. And so, as James Hemming notably put it, the academic illusion came to replace the classical illusion: "the idea that only those are educated who can read Horace in the original."

In 1870 the British Government passed an Act of Parliament to develop provision for primary schools. In 1902 it turned its attention to secondary education and began to establish county grammar schools.[16,17] Forty-two years later, at the height of World War II, the government passed the 1944 Education Act, which provided free secondary education for all. This was an enormous social advance and opened new routes to educational opportunity for millions who had been denied them. The Act was a deliberate piece of social engineering that was designed to meet the needs of the post-war industrial economy. It established three types of school: grammar, secondary modern and technical. The grammar schools were to educate the top 20 percent: the prospective doctors, teachers, lawyers, accountants, civil servants and managers of post-war Britain. It was assumed that they would need a rigorous academic education and that is what the grammar schools were intended to give them. Those who went to the secondary modern schools were destined for blue collar and manual work. They were given a more basic education that was really a watered-down version of the grammar school curriculum. Many European countries made similar sorts of provision.[18] Despite all the attempts to promote parity between academic and vocational courses, the attitude persists that academic programs were of a much higher status.[19]

THE IRRESISTIBLE RISE OF IQ

It was during the massive expansion of education in the post-war years in the United Kingdom that IQ took such a firm hold on the whole system. The large numbers of young people who were streaming into compulsory education had to be channeled into the various types of schools that were available. IQ testing was a quick and convenient method of decision-making.[20]

But like the SATs (Scholastic Assessment Tests) these tests took no account of social background or previous educational opportunity. They were also very limited. High scores relied to a large extent on standard verbal and logical operations. Success relied as much on knowing the techniques involved as on natural aptitude.

"Success relied as much on knowing the techniques involved as on natural aptitude."

Despite their obvious shortcomings, challenging the authority of these tests was never an easy matter. Then as now they had the backing of government and of the scientific establishment. They were assumed to be "above reproach or beyond social influence, conceived in the rarefied atmosphere of purely scientific inquiry by some process of immaculate conception."[21]

For all their popularity and sway over educational policies, IQ tests and SATS do not assess the whole range of a student's intellectual abilities. They look only for particular sorts of ability. The same is true of most of the conventional forms of education that they support. The most common form of assessment in schools is still the timed written examination, in which success mainly depends on a good short-term memory for factual information, at least until the examination is over. Some people need to work hard for months to pass these tests. Others can do the same work in a few weeks or days. There are considerable pressures for those with strong academic interests. But what about the others, whose real interests or abilities lie elsewhere? For them education has always been an alienating experience.

For generations, students have spent most of their time writing essays, doing comprehension exercises, taking tests of factual information, and learning mathematics: activities that involve propositional knowledge and forms of logico-deductive reasoning. Some lessons promote other sorts of ability. Most schools have art lessons and some music, perhaps playing an instrument or being in a choir; and sport. Some disciplines, including technology and the arts, have a practical element but they are typically at the margins of formal education. This pattern continues into higher education, and especially in universities: for most people the highest form of higher education. The arts are an important test case.

ARTS AND SCIENCES

The divisions of the Enlightenment and Romanticism are alive and well in contemporary attitudes to the arts and sciences. Typically the sciences are associated with fact and truth. The image of the scientist is a white-coated clinician moving through cold calculations to an objective understanding of the way the world works. In contrast, the arts are associated with feelings, imagination and self-expression. The artist is pictured as a free spirit giving vent to a turmoil of creative ideas. In education the impact of these assumptions has been far reaching.

The narrowing of intelligence

Practicing the arts as distinct from writing about them, is not part of the rationalist view of intelligence. Making music, painting pictures, involvement with drama, and writing poetry are not associated with academic ability. The clearest evidence of this view is in the universities. Some years ago, I was a member of a university promotions committee, which was a group of about 20 professors from the arts, sciences and social studies. A university lecturer is expected to do teaching, administration and research. A case for promotion has to include evidence of an acceptable standard in all three. One of my roles as head of my own department was to make recommendations to the committee about promotion. I had recommended an English lecturer who I thought was a sure case. The committee required members to leave the room when their own recommendations were being discussed. I thought this was a routine matter so I slipped out of the room and was back within a few minutes ready to rejoin the meeting. I was kept waiting for nearly half an hour: clearly there was an issue.

Eventually I was called back into the room and sat down expectantly. The vice-chancellor said, "We've had a few problems with this one. We're going to hold him back for a year," meaning that they were not approving his promotion. Members of the committee are not meant to question decisions that concern their own recommendations, but I was taken aback. I asked why, and was told there was a problem with his research. I wasn't prepared for this, and asked what was wrong with it. I was told there was so little of it.

They were talking about an English lecturer who, in the period under review, had published three novels, two of which had won national literary awards; who had written two television series, both of which had been broadcast nationally and one of which had won a national award. He had also published two papers in conventional research journals on nineteenth century popular fiction. "But there is all of this," I said, pointing to the novels and the plays. "We're sure it's very interesting," said one of the committee, "but it's his research we're worried about," pointing to the journal papers. "But this is his research too," I said, pointing to the novels and plays. This led to a good bit of shuffling of papers. By research, most universities mean papers in academic journals or scholarly books. The idea that novels and plays could count as research clearly hadn't entered the debate. But a good deal hangs on this. The issue was not whether these novels or these plays were any good, but whether novels and plays as such could count as research in the first place. The common-sense reaction was that they could not. But what is research? In universities, research is defined as a systematic enquiry for new knowledge. So I asked the committee whether they thought that novels and plays, as original works of art, could be a source of new knowledge. If so, does the same apply to music, to art and to poetry? Are we really saying that knowledge is only to be found in research journals and in academic papers? This question is vitally important, for a number of reasons. It relates particularly to the status of the arts and sciences in universities and in education more generally.

There's an intriguing difference in research in arts and science departments in universities. If you work in a physics or chemistry department, you work in a laboratory and you 'do' science. You don't spend your professional life analyzing the lives and times of physicists. If you are a mathematician, you don't spend your time scrutinizing the mood swings of Euclid or his relationships with his in-laws when he developed his theories. You do mathematics. But this is not what goes on in many arts departments.

Professors of English are not employed to produce litera-ture: they are employed to write about it. They spend much of their time analyzing the lives and drives of writers and the work they produce. They may write poetry in their own time: but they are not normally thanked for doing it in university time even though it may raise the profile of the university. They're expected to produce analytical papers about poetry. Producing works of art doesn't often count as appropriate intellectual work in an arts department: yet the equivalent in a science department, doing physics or chemistry, does. So why is it that in universities writing about novels is thought to be a higher intellectual calling than writing novels; or rather, if writing novels is not thought to be intellectually valid, why is writing about them? Universities are devoted to propositional knowledge and to logico-deductive reasoning. Academics can look at anything through the frame of academic enquiry: plants, books, weather systems, particles, chemical reactions or poems. It is the *mode of work* that distinguishes academic work, not the subject matter. The assumed superiority of academic intelligence is obvious in the traditional structure of qualifications. Traditionally universities have rewarded academic achievement with degrees. Other institutions give diplomas or other sub-degree qualifications. If you wanted to do art, to paint, draw or make sculptures, you went to an art college and received a diploma for your efforts. If you wanted a degree in art, you had to go to university and study the history of art. You didn't create art at university; you wrote about it. Similarly if you wanted to play music and be a musician you went to a conservatoire and took a diploma: if you wanted a music degree you went to a university and wrote about music. These distinctions are beginning to break down. Arts colleges do now offer degrees and university arts departments are beginning to offer practical courses. Though certainly in Europe and parts of Asia there is still resistance to the idea that degrees should be given for practical work in the arts.

CHANGING OUR MINDS

Our ideas can enslave or liberate us. Some people never do make the transition and remain resident in the old world view: their ideological comfort zone. As history has shown us, those who see the future and rush to meet it, like Galileo and Darwin, are often thought of as heretical, or worse. The modern world view is still dominated by the ideology that came to replace medievalism: the ideology of rationalism, objectivity and propositional knowledge. These ideas frame our attitudes and theories every bit as much as myth and superstition underpinned the painstaking calculations of the medieval astronomers. Just as their ideology created the framework for their questions, so does ours. We ask how we can measure intelligence. The assumption is that intelligence is quantifiable. We ask how we can raise academic standards but do not question whether they deliver what we need to survive in the future.

"Our ideas can enslave or liberate us. Some people never do make the transition and remain resident in the old world view: their ideological comfort zone."

We ask where we can find talented people but ignore the talents of people that surround us. We look but we do not see, because our traditional common-sense assessment of abilities distracts us from what is actually there. We ask how to promote creativity and innovation but stifle the processes and conditions that are most likely to bring it about. Like the medieval astronomer we continue to believe in the assumptions of mass education, despite all the evidence that the system is failing so many people within it.

The rationalist tradition has driven a wedge between intellect and emotion in human psychology; and between the arts and sciences in society at large. It has distorted the idea of creativity in education and unbalanced the development of millions of people. The result is that other important abilities are overlooked or marginalized. This neglect affects everyone. Children with strong academic abilities often fail to discover their other abilities. Those of lower academic ability may have other powerful abilities that lie dormant. They can all pass through the whole of their education never knowing what their real abilities are. They can become disaffected, resentful of their 'failure' and conclude that they are simply not very bright. Some of these educational failures go on to have great success in adult life. How many do not?

Human intelligence includes the capacity for academic activity; this does not mean that academic activity is the whole of intelligence. To educate people for the future, we must see through the academic illusion to their real abilities, and to how these different elements of human capacity enhance rather than detract from each other. But what exactly are these capacities and what should be done to release them?

KNOWING YOUR MIND

"Now, more than ever, human communities depend on a diversity of talents; not on a singular conception of ability."

H UMAN INTELLIGENCE IS MUCH RICHER than we have been led to believe by industrial/academic education. Appreciating the full range and potential of human intelligence is vital for understanding the real nature of creativity.

YOU'RE MORE THAN YOU THINK

Liz Varlow is a viola player with the London Symphony Orchestra and winner of the prestigious Frink Award. She was born in Birmingham, England, and started playing the violin at the age of eight. She won two scholarships to the Royal College of Music, and went on to win numerous prizes. Fellow musicians describe her as a very fine musician who has developed her musical sensitivity to the highest levels. What sets her apart is that she is profoundly deaf. Her hearing began to deteriorate at the age of sixteen. By the time she was nineteen, she had become deaf for reasons that have never been established. Nonetheless she has maintained her capabilities as an outstanding professional musician. How does she perform without hearing? "How does anyone play?" she says. "I know how to make sounds and also know how what I'm doing sounds. A 'normal' hearing player does this too. They make sounds and use hearing to check it. It's too late afterwards if the note is out of tune. With the benefit of a fine aural memory, a solid technique and a good sense of humor I have been able to deal with all professional situations and found deafness to be little handicap."

Dame Evelyn Glennie is one of the world's most accomplished percussionists. She travels the world giving virtuoso concerts to huge public acclaim. Her many CDs have sold millions of copies and she has won a variety of awards from professional music organizations including Musician of the Year. She is in demand worldwide to lead master classes on musicianship. She too is deaf. She became profoundly deaf at the age of twelve just as she was beginning to develop her musical abilities. She persisted in developing these abilities despite the lack of the one sense that most people would consider critical to their fulfillment. Such examples defy ordinary logic. How can someone who is deaf become an outstanding musician? The achievements of Liz Varlow and of Evelyn Glennie demonstrate the extraordinary flexibility and virtuosity of the human mind. It is these qualities that underpin the uniquely human capacities for creativity and innovation.

LIVING IN TWO WORLDS

One of the founding perceptions of modern philosophy is that we live in two distinct worlds. There is a world that exists whether or not you exist: the world of material objects, events and of other people. This world existed before you were born and, if all goes well, it will continue to exist after you have gone. There is another world that exists only because you exist: the world of your own private consciousness, feelings and sensations. Your world is one in which, as the psychologist R.D. Laing put it, there is only one set of footprints.[1] Your world came into being when you were born and it will end when you die. We share the first world with other people: we share the second world with no one. Recognizing the difference between *your* world and *the* world marks an important stage in the development of personal identity. How do we come to see the external world as we do? How do we know it's really there and not just in our minds? How do we get out of our minds?

Some of the philosophers of the Enlightenment worried about whether the outer world was as it seemed and even whether it was there at all. One of the most celebrated was the earnest Bishop Berkeley (1685–1753). His theory of idealism proposed that the whole world might be no more than an elaborate idea in the mind of God. His theory was greeted with amusement by the celebrated wit, Dr Johnson (1709–1784). One of the Bishop's supporters attacked Dr Johnson's flat rejection of idealism saying that Berkeley's theory "could not be refuted." Dr Johnson turned to a nearby boulder, kicked it with his foot and said, "I refute it thus." To Dr Johnson and everyone else, even idealist philosophers seem to carry on living in the world and doing their shopping despite their uncertainty about its existence.

The outer world may be an illusion but for everyday purposes we assume it is not: we simply accept that the people and things we see about us are real and appear to us all in the same way. However tantalizing these problems may be for philosophers, they're only problems if we think about them as such. For most of the time, we live our lives in what has been called the *natural attitude*.[2]

While some seventeenth and eighteenth century philosophers were busy dismantling public confidence in the material world, a new breed of scientists set about bringing it under our control. As Bertrand Russell (1872–1970) commented, the scientific outlook is not so much a rejection of philosophical doubts: it is more an illustration that in daily life, we assume as certain many things that on closer scrutiny we find to be full of apparent contradictions. How then do we bridge the gap between these two worlds?[3]

Consciousness and the brain

These days it is taken for granted that consciousness and brain are intimately related. This is a relatively recent idea. The ancient world saw only a tenuous link. The brain is an unpromising sight. It's a crinkled ball of flesh that has no moving parts and lives remotely from the rest of the body in a cage of bone. Normal human brains are about the size of a melon and look like a large walnut. The upper side seems to be in two halves or hemispheres and has a surface of convoluted folds. This is the cerebral cortex or new brain. It is thought of as being in four regions or lobes, *parietal, frontal, posterior* and *anterior*. A shaft of nerve fibers known as the corpus callosum connects the two hemispheres. Underneath the brain and to the back is a smaller cauliflower-shaped area called the cerebellum in an area known as the old brain. Coming out of that and connecting in to the spinal cord is the brain stem.

The functions of the mind that we now associate with the brain were thought by the ancient anatomists to be located in the heart and the lungs. The brain was thought to be the home of the soul that endured physical death and passed into the afterlife. The brain had no obvious functions otherwise. By the Middle Ages anatomists had concluded that the brain plays a more practical role in this life too. As anatomical studies became more sophisticated, they gradually revealed the physical connections through the spinal cord and nervous system between the brain and the rest of the body. The debate still rages about the nature of the relationship between the motionless grey substance that makes up the material brain, and the vibrant thoughts, feelings and desires that constitute human consciousness. The fact that there is a relationship between consciousness and the brain is easy enough to establish. Removing the brain does bring consciousness to an abrupt end. But how the conscious mind arises from the physical matter of the brain is not yet known. How is it that a ball of flesh the size of a melon can generate the insights of Isaac Newton, the music of Mozart, the dance of Martha Graham, the poetry of Shakespeare and the spiritual longings of Gandhi? How do we account for what has been called the ghost in the machine?

There is a common-sense distinction between mind and consciousness. In one sense, consciousness is what you lose when you go to sleep and regain when you wake up and become aware of your surroundings. Consciousness has a second meaning, that of understanding. It is in this sense that we talk of raising consciousness of an issue. Babies are born with a brain. They develop a mind as they grow, absorb and reflect on their experiences.

The brain has more on its mind that conscious thought. A good deal of the brain's activities are not apparent to the conscious mind. Much of its work is silent traffic within the rest of the body's automatic functioning: with the involuntary processes of bodily metabolism, glandular functions and the complex perceptions of taste, smell, touch, vision, hearing, and so on. Conscious thought accounts for only a proportion of what the brain is doing at any given moment. Although the relationship between the mind and the brain are still largely a mystery, much more is known than ever before about what the various parts of the brain do and how they relate to each other as they're doing it.

MAPPING THE MIND

Scholars have long thought that different parts of the brain have different functions. In the Middle Ages it was believed that the mind consisted of different faculties, and that each of these was located in a different part of the brain. These faculties included memory, imagination and logical reasoning. This theory was used as a justification for the classical curriculum of the grammar schools. Memory, it was thought, was trained by learning Latin vocabulary: logical reasoning by geometry, and imagination by poetry and music.[4]

Just as most human brains are similar in appearance, most skulls are the same general shape. On closer inspection they have distinctive bumps and hollows and individual variations in shape and size. In the eighteenth century, the Austrian scientist Franz Gall (1758–1828) studied the brains of hundreds of dead people and tried to match their shapes with the personalities of their former owners. From these he developed a detailed theory about personality, brain shape and the patterns of bumps on the skull, a theory known as *phrenology*; literally the 'study of the mind.' Gall identified 32 personality traits all associated with different patterns of bumps on the skull. The phrenologists believed that there was a direct link between specific functions, such as speech, and different regions of the brain. Gall's phrenological speculations were later discounted by more considered studies of the brain.

Studies of people with brain damage in the nineteenth century also showed that the idea of exclusive locations for particular brain functions was misleading. Modern research shows that the capacities of the brain are much more complex and dynamic than initial theories suggested. In the last 30 years there have been spectacular advances in the study of the living brain, using various techniques of brain scanning. These technologies can track the patterns of electrical activity and blood flow in the brain during different activities and have shed new light at two levels on how the brain works. There is a growing understanding of the functions of the different regions of the brain and of how they interact. There are also new discoveries at the molecular level about the synaptic and neural processes of the brain. Both areas of research suggest three crucial themes for understanding creativity. They are that human intelligence is highly *diverse, dynamic* and *distinct.*

DIVERSITY

The view of the Enlightenment philosophers was that knowledge of the world could only be derived from systematic logic and the empirical evidence of the senses. This approach has a powerful appeal to common sense. In practice though there are other factors to take into account. First of all, our senses are limited. We do not see the world as it is but as our particular human senses present it to us.

The nature of our senses determines our *field of perception*: what we are actually able to perceive and how. There is more to the world than meets the eye, or any of our senses. We experience the world as we do partly because of the way we are built. As human beings we are typically between five and six feet tall, we stand upright and our bodies are broadly symmetrical. Unprotected, our bodies can endure only small variations in heat. We have at least nine senses: sight, taste, touch, hearing, smell, balance, orientation, pain and temperature. Our eyes are at the front of our heads and we have binocular vision. We can see light that has a wavelength from about 400 nanometers (extreme violet) to about 770 nanometers (extreme red). Our ears can normally hear sounds in the range 20–15,000 Hz. We live in a rich sensory environment, surrounded by sights, sounds, smells, temperature and textures, but we perceive only some of it.

Other animals have different and often more specialized senses and consequently they inhabit very different sensory worlds. Some mammals such as bats can detect ultrasonic frequencies well above 15,000 Hz. Some animals and birds can detect infrasound or low-frequency sound. Pigeons can detect sounds as low as 0.1 Hz. Elephants communicate using sounds as low as 1 Hz. The result is that two animals living in exactly the same physical environment may have entirely different views of what's going on. Compare the lives of a seahorse and a killer whale, living in the same stretch of ocean; they may inhabit the same environment but they live in completely different worlds. One factor is their relative size and strength. But they are also equipped with entirely different sensory capacities.

Our senses are the channels through which information flows between the outside world and our own consciousness. If those channels were different, other sorts of information would flow through them and our view of the outside world could well be transformed. Your view of the world would be quite different if you could hear the sounds that bats hear; or see the world as cats do; or had the smell receptors of a dog; if you could see sounds, or breathe underwater, or fly.

Our physical configuration may determine what we *can* perceive of the world, but there are other factors that affect what we actually *do* perceive. These are cultural factors and they also have crucial significance for the development of creativity. Their importance is explored in Chapter 8.

The constitution of our senses, our bodies and of our brains deeply affects what we think about. It also affects *how* we think. This is the second caveat to the rationalist approach, which too often separates the mind from the body: a phenomenon known as Cartesian dualism. The rationalist view of knowledge is focused on the logico-deductive powers of mind. While this may seem reasonable in itself, there is more to consciousness than these particular powers. The brain is an organic entity that interacts with all the physical states and processes of our bodies. Our health, physical condition and appetites can deeply affect our states of mind. The academic life tends to deny the rest of the body. In many schools, students are educated from the waist up and attention eventually comes to focus on their heads, and particularly the left side. This is where many professional academics live: in their heads, and slightly to one side. They are disembodied in a certain way. They tend to look upon their bodies as a form of transport for their heads: it's a way of getting their heads to meetings. If you want real evidence of out of body experiences, sign up for a residential conference for senior academics and go along to the dance on the final night. There you will see it. Grown men and women, writhing uncontrollably, off the beat, waiting for it to end so that they can go home and write a paper about it.

In contrast, dancers exult in their bodies and in the forms of knowledge and expression that can only be experienced through physical movement. I used to be on the board of the Birmingham Royal Ballet in England and had the privilege of watching professional dancers at work. The rigor and precision of ballet and of all forms of professional dance is humbling. I mentioned earlier that dance does not have the same status in schools as mathematics and other academic subjects, but dance gives form to ideas and feelings that cannot be expressed in any other way. Martha Graham once said that dance is the hidden language of the soul.

There may be no agreed definition of intelligence, but we might agree here that intelligence includes the ability to formulate and express our thoughts in coherent ways. We can do this using words and in numbers. We can also visualize, we can think in sound, in movement and in all the many ways in which these different modes interact. Musicians are not trying to express in sound ideas that would be better put into words.

They are having musical ideas: ideas for which they may be no words. Visual artists think visually and have visual ideas.

Intelligence also includes the ability to engage effectively with the practical challenges of living in the world. Developmental psychologist Howard Gardner, best known for his theory of multiple intelligences, defines intelligence as the ability to solve problems in a given context. Consider a twelve-year-old Puluwat in the Caroline Islands, he says, who has been selected by his elders to learn how to become a master sailor: "under the tutelage of master navigators he will learn to combine knowledge of sailing stars and geography so as to find his way around hundreds of islands. Or consider the 14-year-old adolescent in Paris who has learnt how to program a computer and is beginning to compose works of music with the aid of a synthesizer." A moment's reflection, says Gardner, reveals that each of these individuals "is demonstrating a high level of competence in a challenging field and should by any reasonable definition of the term be viewed as exhibiting intelligent behaviour."[5] Gardner argues that there are least seven different types of intelligence. In later work he accepts that there are others too. The underlying point is that intelligence is multifaceted, rich, complex and highly diverse.

I mentioned earlier my reservations about Mensa, the organization for people with high IQs. My concern is not that there is an organization for people who are good at and enjoy IQ tests. I'm all for clubs and societies. It's good that people with common interests should get together and benefit from each other's passions. There are clubs for everything: cooking, chess, athletics, politics, philately, dog breeding, astronomy, you name it. Certainly there should be an IQ club. My problem is with the branding of Mensa. It's promoted as the club for the most intelligent people on earth. Really? If there were such a club, no doubt we'd all like to be considered for membership.

But shouldn't there be some other questions on the application forms? For example, can you compose a symphony? Could you play in an orchestra? Could you start and run a successful business? Could you write poetry that will move people to tears? Could you choreograph or perform in a dance that speaks to our inner humanity? All of these are examples of the inherent diversity of human intelligence and of the many ways in which we engage with each other and with the world around us. Shouldn't they count too in any conception of intelligence? And shouldn't people who are exceptionally good at any of these things be welcomed in the club that aims to celebrate the highest levels of intelligence? Human intelligence includes and goes well beyond conventional conceptions of academic ability and IQ. This is why the world is full of music, technology, art, dance, architecture, business, practical science, feelings, relationships and inventions that actually work.

DYNAMISM

Intelligence is not only diverse: it is highly dynamic. In the 1950s the American scientist Roger Sperry (1913–1994) conducted a series of ingenious experiments that involved people whose brain hemispheres had been separated by cutting the corpus callosum so that they operated independently. Sperry found that the 'split-brain' subjects could perform two unrelated tasks simultaneously; for example, drawing a picture with one hand while writing with another. He concluded that the two hemispheres of the brain fulfilled different but complementary functions. The left side of the brain was largely involved in logical procedures including language and mathematics; the right hand side of the brain was more concerned with holistic operations such as the recognition of faces and orientation in physical space.

This research provoked massive interest, not least in education. It suggested a physical correspondence in the brain to
the two great traditions in Western European culture. The left
hemisphere seemed to relate to the logico-deductive analysis
of the Enlightenment and the scientific method: the right
hemisphere to the Romantic impulses of beauty, intuition and
spirituality. Educational reformers were quick to argue that
the academic education system was in effect almost wholly
left-brained. James Hemming drew a striking conclusion.
Educating people entirely through the left-brain activities of
the academic curriculum was, he said, like training somebody
for a race by exercising only one leg while leaving the muscles
of the other leg to atrophy. Others went too far. I remember
reading an article by someone who had half-digested the implications of this research. She said she had written the piece
in blank verse because she had only used the right hand side of
her brain; a remark that suggested she hadn't used either side.
The point is not that the two halves should work separately,
but together.

Carl Sagan (1934–1996) captured this exactly. There is
no way to tell, he said, "whether the patterns extracted by
the right hemisphere are real or imagined without subject-
ing them to left hemisphere scrutiny." On the other hand,
"mere critical thinking without creative and intuitive insights,
without the search for new patterns is sterile and doomed. To
solve complex problems in changing circumstances requires
the activity of both cerebral hemispheres. The pattern to the
future lies through the corpus callosum."[6]

Brain-scanning techniques show that the brain lights up in
different configurations according to the activity in hand and
that even simple actions draw simultaneously on different
regions of the brain. Different areas of the brain are strongly
associated with particular mental functions but they participate
in other processes too. This is obvious in the effects of damage
to the brain. The right frontal lobe is focally responsible for

music and, if it is damaged, musical abilities are impaired. But if you were to remove this section of the brain and hold it in your hand it won't hum a tune. It relies on connections with the rest of the brain and body for its proper functioning. Speech is a particularly interesting example of how patterns of brain activity vary. When someone is speaking her native tongue her brain configures in one way: it configures in different ways when speaking a second language learned after infancy.

We experience these dynamics of intelligence constantly. Speech is usually accompanied by a dazzling variety of physical movements, facial expressions and gestures. Dance seems to be quintessentially a kinesthetic form of intelligence but choreographers design dances with a passionate attention to visual design and to the expressive qualities of the music, and often with mathematical rhythms and precision. For the audience dance is a visual art. Mathematics may seem to be wholly abstract but mathematicians often think visually too.

I remember watching a teacher in Hong Kong taking a Saturday morning class in mathematics. The children, aged between eight and twelve, each sat with an abacus on their desks. The teacher called out calculations for them to do: 1289 multiplied by 15822; 22348 divided by 4019. As soon as he finished calling the numbers, a forest of arms shot into the air. Every child had the correct answer. The children used only the abacus for their calculations; flicking the beads across the bars at lightning speed. Another boy was asked to use an electronic calculator for comparison. He lost every time. The teacher then asked the children to put the abacus away. The answers came just as quickly and always faster than the boy with the calculator. The children had clearly internalized the operation, visualizing the abacus in their minds' eyes and seeing the answers.

Perhaps the most extraordinary evidence of the holistic functioning of the brain comes from those who don't have a

normal range of sensory abilities. The extraordinary achievements of Evelyn Glennie and Liz Varlow illustrate the holistic,
dynamic operations of human intelligence. Evelyn Glennie
experiences the music with her whole being. Playing in bare
feet she absorbs the musical patterns, vibrations and rhythms
through her body in ways that transcend
ordinary concepts of sensory perception.
In this sense the mind itself may be likened
to an orchestra comprising specialist functions and sections but fulfilling its role by
dynamic interaction of these elements in
ways that make the whole much greater
than the sum of the parts. The brain is not
a mechanical object: it is an organic entity.
The mind is not a calculator: it is a dynamic
process of consciousness. The creative
process is not a single ability that lives in
one or other region of the body. It thrives
on the dynamism between different ways of
thinking and being.

> *"There is a vitality, a life-force, an energy, a quickening that is translated through you into action and because there is only one of you in all of time, this expression is unique. And if you block it, it will never exist through any other medium and be lost."*
> – Martha Graham

DISTINCTIVENESS

We each have great natural capacities, but we all have them in
different forms. Each of us is a unique moment in history: a
distinctive blend of our genetic inheritance, of our experiences
and of the thoughts and feelings that have woven through
them and that constitute our unique consciousness. Martha
Graham put it like this: "There is a vitality, a life-force, an
energy, a quickening that is translated through you into action
and because there is only one of you in all of time, this expression is unique. And if you block it, it will never exist through
any other medium and be lost."

People are so much more than either academic or non-academic. Each of us has a distinctive profile of intellectual abilities with different strengths in visual intelligences, in sound, in movement, in mathematical thinking and the rest. Does this mean that no one can be thought of as more intelligent that anyone else? Of course not. Some people have strong abilities in many areas, music, mathematics, verbal reasoning, visual thinking and so on. We typically think of such people as Renaissance-type figures. But high ability in one area does not entail it in others. A gifted mathematician need not be a gifted painter: a gifted poet may have no gift for dance. Consequently, we should hesitate to label someone with high academic abilities as more intelligent than a person with equally high abilities in music or dance.

This is not an argument against developing academic abilities: it is *for* an expanded concept of intelligence that includes but also goes beyond them. If we fail to promote a full sense of people's abilities through education and training, some, perhaps most, will never discover what their real capacities are. To that extent they do not really know who they are or what they might become.

I worked once with Robert Cohan the gifted partner of Martha Graham and founder director of the London School of Contemporary Dance. I asked him how he came to be involved in contemporary dance. In the early 1950s he left the US army and was living in New York. He had always enjoyed dancing and had had conventional training. A friend told him of a woman who was running dance classes downtown and suggested he might enjoy them. He went, and his life was changed. After the first three-hour session with Martha Graham, his body was shaking almost uncontrollably with excitement. He discovered in her methods and forms of dance a capacity in himself that he had never suspected. Through meeting Martha Graham he found himself and he spent his artistic life in the world he helped her eventually to create.

He went on to become her principal partner in dance and to promote her methods in Europe in the 1970s and 1980s as principal of the London School of Contemporary Dance.

Many people are diverted from their natural paths in life by the preoccupation in education with academic intelligence and the hierarchy of disciplines. It shows itself especially in the distinction between academic and vocational programs and the idea that doing practical work or studying for a trade is lower grade than taking an academic degree. And yet, the ability to construct buildings, to wire a house, to install plumbing systems, to make things grow, to make things that work, to provide practical services, is exactly what resonates with very many people and all these skills are fundamental to the vitality and sustainability of human life. Sometimes this is literally true.

I was in San Francisco recently for a book signing. One of the people in line was a man in his mid-30s and I asked him what he did for a living. He said he was a fireman. I asked him when he had decided to be a fireman and he said he'd always wanted to be a fireman. "Actually," he said, "in elementary school it was a problem because at that age everyone wanted to be a fireman. But I really did want to be a fireman and as I grew up I couldn't wait to leave school to join the fire service." He said that when he was in his senior year of high school one of the teachers asked his class what they were all planning to do when they left. Almost everyone talked about going to college: he said he was applying to join the fire service. The teacher said that he was making a big mistake; that he was academically smart and had a bright future and would be wasting his life if all he did was to join the fire service. The fireman said it was an embarrassing moment and he felt humiliated in front of his friends but he went ahead with his plans and has been in the fire service and loving it ever since. "But I was thinking about that teacher when you were talking just now," he said. "Because six months ago, I saved his life. He was in a car wreck and my unit was called out. I pulled him from the car, gave him CPR and saved him. I saved his wife's life too." He said, "I think he thinks better of me now."

Rethinking disability

One of the consequences of a narrow view of ability is a correspondingly wide view of disability. Some years ago, I was involved in a study of art and disability that was chaired by the film director, Sir Richard Attenborough, and funded by the Carnegie Foundation. The study celebrated the artistic capabilities of people with disabilities and argued for greatly improved provision. Some people with disabilities have difficulties with conventional forms of expression, in writing for example, or in speech, hearing or vision. Often they are branded by their disability: they are not seen as people with a disability but as disabled people. People with obvious disabilities, physical or otherwise, naturally have many other abilities that can be overlooked or undiscovered. Their real powers and true identities may lie in these unexplored territories of talent.

Identifying latent abilities is all the more important when conventional forms of communication are restricted. Striking evidence of this principle is given in a unique research initiative at the University of Sunderland directed by Dr Phil Ellis. Touching Sound was the title of a project concerned with music education and new technology and the name of a suite of computer programs incorporating vibroacoustic sound therapy, also known as visual music therapy: a new approach to sound therapy for children who have severe learning difficulties (SLD) and profound and multiple learning difficulties (PMLD).[7] Touching Sound uses low level laser beams and other technologies that are linked to sound synthesizers. When the beams are touched, sounds are automatically generated. Even minor movements can produce powerful responses. Touching Sound turns the computer into a new musical instrument, providing new ways of creating and shaping sound, of playing sound; overcoming, but not devaluing the barriers of traditional techniques. The iMuse (Interactive MUsic Streaming Engine) technology uses sensors that can be triggered by movements as small as the blink of an eye. This means even people with profound and complex needs can experience being in control of the music and visuals.

Sound therapy acknowledges the expressive potential of all sound with the aim of enabling and developing additional ways of communicating and expressing. Music in education can contribute to all areas of experience, including the mathematical, physical, technological, spiritual, the aesthetic, creative, and social. There are many skills of the mind that are developed in this process: imagining, formulating, discriminating, selecting, rejecting, evaluating, ordering, structuring.

The project has worked for children and others with severe learning difficulties, whose movements are limited to only a few muscles or even an eyelid. People with a normal range of movement take for granted the ability to affect their environment and to externalize their thoughts and feelings. Those with limited mobility and muscular control may spend their lives having other people do things to or for them, and have profound difficulties in expressing themselves. Touching Sound enables them to affect their environment and to be expressive. The feelings of liberation are palpable and the developmental effects can be dramatic. As Marie Watts, one member of the teams, puts it: "It allows the individual to take control of the environment. It's all about control and empowerment. The technology was also motivating for staff, as it enabled them to get instant feedback from the people they assist." (Dr Ellis' research has since led to an award for his work, which will result in the establishment of a Sound Therapy Centre in Sunderland.)[8]

More than we know

So-called *savants* are people who display extraordinary capacities in some areas of intelligence and below average abilities in others. Derek Paravicini was born in England in 1979, prematurely, at 25 weeks, weighing just a pound and a half. He is blind, autistic and an astounding musical prodigy. His blindness is thought to have been caused by oxygen therapy given in the neonatal intensive care unit. The therapy also affected his developing brain and caused severe learning disabilities.

He has absolute pitch, can recognize up to 20 notes played at once and can play any piece of music after hearing it only once. But he can also transform them seamlessly into the styles of different musicians. Asked to change into the style of another player, like Oscar Peterson, he will change style mid-song, playing 'My Favorite Things' in Peterson's distinctive style. "It's like he's got libraries of pieces and styles in his head," says Adam Ockelford, Derek's teacher. "He can just whip out a piece book and a style book and bring them together. It just kind of explodes." How Derek's fingers can do this but can't button a button or zip a zipper is not known. If he is asked how old he is now, he does not know.

He began playing the piano as a toddler, when his nanny gave him an old keyboard. His father says, "My daughter suddenly said one day, 'He's just played one of the hymns we heard in church this morning.'" Derek was three years old at the time. "And he didn't know, because he couldn't see, and no one had told him, that you're meant to use your fingers to play the piano. So he used karate chops and elbows, and even his nose, I seem to remember." At first he resisted any of Ockelford's attempts to teach him. But before long, he says, "Derek seemed to get it; this was not someone trying to take away his precious piano. This was someone trying to reach him. I think suddenly it clicked that he could have a conversation in sound. And suddenly he just blossomed," Ockelford explained. "From all this confusion that he must have experienced as a child, not understanding much language, suddenly here was a language that he could control, he could play with, he could dialogue. All the things that we normally do with words, Derek did with notes."

His progress was astounding. After three years of daily lessons, Derek was invited to play a few songs at a major charity fundraiser. It was there that Ockelford first saw the thrill Derek got from performing and from feeling the love of the crowd. Derek was trembling with excitement and elation and he has been performing ever since – in jazz halls, at benefits, in churches, connecting with audiences in ways most musicians are: taking requests, with a twist. He'll ask an audience member to select a song, then let a second audience member choose what key he'll play it in and then let a third select a style. At one event, Derek was asked to play 'Ain't No Sunshine' in B major in ragtime style. He executed it perfectly. "It's like having three computers all working at once and you could just put them together straightaway, without thinking," Ockelford comments. "Sometimes he does something quite funny musically. You can see a little sparkle. I think he's actually quite pleased with himself what he comes up with."[9]

Though autism is thought to be the source of Derek's extraordinary musical ability, his blindness may contribute. Because Derek is blind, the part of his brain that would normally be used for sight and light detection could be used for extra auditory ability. Other cases have been recorded of extraordinary visual capacities, of prodigious abilities in memory, or in mathematical calculation. In all of these cases the individual shows extraordinary capacities, well beyond any normal expectations, combined with a generally below average abilities in other areas.[10]

PLASTICITY AND POTENTIAL

Learning is associated with a growing complexity of the neural networks of the brain. It is estimated that at birth the human brain consists of about 100 billion brain cells. During infancy the child's brain is tremendously plastic. To begin with, each neuron has dozens of connections but these connections pare down to just a few strong ones as the brain develops and according to how it is used. Scientists at Harvard are engaged in a program of research to create a detailed map of the circuitry of the human brain. The research is part of a new field called 'connectomics'. A piece of technology called the automatic tape collecting lathe ultra microtome (ATLUM) cuts samples of brain tissue into very thin slices which are then placed under a scanning electron microscope to create images of individual cells and all their connections to other cells.

"As children grow, their brains are customized around the uses they make or do not make of them."

Jeff Lichtman, a Harvard professor of molecular and cellular biology, says that this technology "gives us an opportunity to witness this vast complicated universe that has been largely inaccessible until now." It's estimated that a full set of images of the human brain at synapse level resolution would contain hundreds of petabytes of information: about the total amount of storage in all of Google's data centers. One of the aims of this study is to understand the processes of neural growth and pruning. According to Lichtman, "Each baby nerve cell connects to 20 times the amount of nerve cells that it will have as an adult. We try to understand what the rules of pruning are. If the nerve cell has a hundred connections and needs to prune that down to five, the question is, which five?" The neurons fight to stay connected and each competition affects the outcome for the rest of the cells. "So to understand the competition's impact on one cell, you have to understand all the competitions." The net effect of all that new neural "hand-to-hand combat" is what we call brain development and it's what transforms a baby who can't walk or talk into a modern adult human being. It's this process that provides us with the flexibility that Lichtman calls "the magic of being human." When a dragonfly is born, he says, it has to know how to catch a mosquito. "But for us, none of this is built-in. Our brains have to go through this profound education that lasts until our second decade. What is changing in our brains?"[11]

The plasticity of the brain is evident in our use of language. If children are born into multilingual households, they learn all the languages they are regularly exposed to. Parents don't teach children to speak in the way they're taught languages in school. Mothers don't teach their babies the principles of grammar. They prompt and guide and teach particular words. But learning a language is so complex that teaching it formally to an infant would be impossible. Teaching them three or four languages would be unthinkable. Yet infants do learn three or four languages and more if necessary. They don't reach a point of saturation or ask for their grandmothers to be kept out of the room because they can't handle another dialect. They absorb them all. This is because they have a language instinct.

Research suggests, for example, that the relationships between speech, song and music are very strong in the process of learning to speak. The technologies of brain imaging provide strong evidence that the areas of the brain that are primarily concerned with music and language overlap considerably. Moreover, according to Diana Deutsch, Professor of Psychology at the University of California, "A person's native tongue influences the way he or she perceives music. The same succession of notes may sound different depending on the language the listener learned growing up."[12] As evidence, speakers of tonal languages including Mandarin are more likely than Westerners to have perfect pitch. In one study, 92 percent of Mandarin speakers who began the music lessons at or before the age of five had perfect pitch compared to 8 percent of English speakers with comparable music training. Research also suggests that babies are already familiar with the melody of the mother's speech, when they are born. Audio recordings from inside the womb at the beginning of labor revealed that the sounds produced by the mother can be heard loudly: "The phrases reaching the baby have been filtered through the mother's tissues, however, so that the crisp, high frequencies which carry much of the information important for identifying the meanings of words, are muted, whereas the musical characteristics of speech – its pitch contours, loudness variations, tempo and rhythmic patterning – are well preserved." In addition to forging a nascent connection between mother and child, early exposure to musical speech sounds may begin the process of learning to speak. After birth, the melodies of speech are also vital to communication between mother and infant, according to Deutsch. When parents speak to their babies, they use exaggerated speech patterns, known as 'motherese' which differ considerably between languages.

It isn't that multi-lingual households give birth by good luck to linguistically gifted children. All 'normal' children have the capacity to learn not only one but many languages. If a child is born into a home where only one language is spoken that is the language they learn. Learning a second language in adolescence becomes much more difficult.[13] By then our language capacities are less accessible.

Professor Susan Greenfield gives a startling example of the plasticity of the brain.[14] She tells of a six-year-old Italian boy who was blind in one eye. The cause of his blindness was that at a crucial period in his infancy his eye was covered with a patch. The result of this was that the neural networks, which facilitate sight from that eye, became redeployed, causing permanent blindness. As children grow, their brains are customized around the uses they make or do not make of them. If the language capacity is not used it may fade as the brain's neural capacities are turned to other uses. The same can be true of music or mathematics or any other capacities.

In the South Pacific many young children are accomplished underwater divers. They develop the ability to swim underwater for long periods so that they can gather

"Now, more than ever, human communities depend on a diversity of talents not on a singular conception of ability."

pearls; a vital skill for economic survival both for them and their families. In New York, most children do not have this ability. There are very few skilled pearl divers in the Bronx. There isn't the demand. But it's reasonable to assume that the average New Yorker translated at an early enough age to the South Pacific would learn the necessary skills. Living in the Bronx they may have the capacity but not the need and, as a result, not the ability.

DARRYL'S DANCE

In Chapter 2, I argued that conventional forms of education often fail to recognize and tap into the deep resources of talent and creativity that lie hidden within everyone. One result is that more and more people are alienated from the whole process. Statistically, the chances are higher that those who pull or fall out of education may fall in to the criminal justice system. The conventional strategy is to incarcerate offenders. This is usually seen as the logical, linear solution; even though it so often involves immense personal, social and economic costs and recidivism rates are so high (see also Chapter 3).

There are more creative approaches to education that are based on an implicit understanding that human ability is diverse, dynamic and distinct and that our strategies for dealing with disaffection and alienation should be equally sophisticated. One that I admire particularly, expresses a special irony in our current approaches to education. It brings together young offenders – those who have often been singularly failed by education; and dance – the discipline that lies at the lowest point in the hierarchy of educational priorities. The results are extraordinary and serve only to illustrate how often both the young people and the discipline are underestimated in education as a whole.

Dance United is a professional contemporary dance company based in Bradford in the United Kingdom. The company provides a dance-based education program called The Academy, as an option for young offenders within the local criminal justice system. The Academy is designed specifically for young people who have failed in conventional educational settings and who may be offenders or at serious risk of offending. The participants have included young people convicted of robbery, drug offences, burglary and assault. Referrals to The Academy are made by a range of agencies, currently including the Bradford Youth Offending Team (YOT) and Nacro (National Association for the Care and Resettlement of Offenders), who refer young people on Intensive Surveillance and Supervision Programmes (ISSP) or other community orders. Some referrals also come from school exclusion units.

The aim of The Academy is not simply to help young people to avoid re-offending; but to help them to discover their real potential and their innate capacity to succeed. The Academy aims for profound changes in the participants primarily by raising their beliefs in what they are capable of achieving. The program itself is based on methods that are used to educate and train professional contemporary dance artists. The physical and creative demands of dance itself are at the core of the program, which aims to promote work of a high artistic standard. The program helps them to learn to trust and support others too.

The Academy team is made up of professional dance artists and teachers working alongside support workers from the Bradford Youth Offending Team (YOT) and other agencies. Importantly, the young people on the program are treated not as offenders in remediation but as professional dancers in training.[15] The Academy program is very disciplined. For example, the ground rules include the requirement to dance in bare feet. Wearing jewelry, hats or other personal artifacts is not allowed.

The Academy works with up to fifteen young people at any one time on a program that takes 25 hours each week, for a period of twelve weeks. Each twelve-week cycle begins with an intensive, three-week performance project, at the end of which the production is presented in professionally staged performances, either in The Academy studio theatre, or at a local or regional theatre venue. From the fourth week, the program expands to include a broader dance and educational curriculum including jazz, African dance, capoeira, circus skills, choreography and more. The program also includes input from visiting artists, including photographers, filmmakers and musicians.

Many people greeted the idea of the Academy program with flat skepticism. How could dance possibly have any effect on people who had shown no regard for other people or property? Wasn't this just groundless romantic nonsense that pandered to the offenders? Surely, the obvious answer was prison. For Jim Brady, a professional member of the Bradford Youth Offending Team, who knows something about these issues, the obvious answer was wrong. "If prison worked," he says, "that would be the solution to youth crime. Unfortunately all the evidence suggests that prison doesn't work."[16] To begin with, his colleague, Dave Pope was skeptical himself about the power of dance. He says now that he has seen many other strategies for dealing with young offenders, but none that are as powerful or as effective: "I've seen offenders working on building sites, offenders joining in team sports, offenders doing offender behavior courses and I've seen offenders doing anger management courses. Contemporary dance, much to my surprise, has turned out to be the one thing where I've seen people make the most progress over the shortest period of time."

Why is this? Why should this program make such a difference where others have not? Tara Jane Herbert, the artistic director of Dance United is clear about what the program really does. Although the participants are treated as professional dancers and put through a comparable regimen, The Academy is not fundamentally about turning all of them into performers: "It's about giving those young people the opportunity to do something practical and the skills to be able to choose. Most of the young people that we work with don't make clear choices. They react. Dance training gives them the opportunity to actually think and then make an action. You have to be able to sit still before you make a choice, before you make an action." She says that typically the young people on the program do not know how to focus their own physical energy. The program teaches them how to focus. "They're very fidgety, or very floppy. They're not grounded. There's not a strength and a stillness behind them and that's what focus is about. It's about actually stopping before you begin something. It's like an orchestra. It's the silence before you begin playing and it's exactly the same in dance and in life."

The program helps to build their sense of self worth by facilitating real creative achievement. As one member of the team explains, "They've often been told they're worthless and can't really achieve anything. They learn here that they can. By getting up in the morning they've achieved structure, discipline, being able to take orders, the confidence in themselves to go out and approach difficult situations. It's not easy for some of them because they've never danced before."

Dance is a highly collaborative process. As Helen Linsell, one of the dance artists explains, "There are different people they have to get on with: people who are older, younger, and different members of staff that they might not connect with." Rhiana Laws, another of the dancers emphasizes that "There is no room for them to hang out or lean against the wall or sit down because they're tired, or giggle in the middle of an exercise because they did it wrong. We're absolutely rigid and that is what I experienced when I was training professionally."

Tara-Jane Herbert says that the public performance at the end of the first three weeks is a massive step. "We invite friends, family; and for most of them it's the first time that they'll be seen in a positive light. It's vital that the quality, the standard of work is excellent, so that they can shine. At the end of the performance their confidence has grown enormously and they suddenly understand why we've pushed for focus, why we've demanded cooperation and all the things that we've been pushing at them suddenly become clear."

One of the participants on the program was a young man named Darryl. When Jim Brady first met Darryl and his mother to consider his options as a young offender, it was hard to know what Darryl might have been thinking. "He didn't engage. He virtually didn't speak," says Brady. "Mom did all the talking. In among the menu of choices I said would be available, was dance." His mother said immediately that Darryl would not dance. Darryl said nothing. In the event, he went to The Academy. And Darryl danced. The results were remarkable, says Brady. "He's physically transformed by it. He's now concerned about nutrition and diet and general health. He's articulate and he's speaking. He carries himself very differently. He's confident and that all happened in the space of three weeks. That's quite a transformation."

Darryl himself is in no doubt. "You do one good session here," he says, "and you ache. But it's a good ache because you know you've done something good. After a few weeks you start to notice your body getting healthier, muscles are coming up and you can feel them growing. It makes you think that there is something you can do and enjoy and it passes time away." The physical and artistic rigors of dance have changed Darryl's view of himself. They have also changed his view of other people; "I've probably learned to consider what other people think," he says, "and look at things from the other person's point of view."

Darryl's father has noticed the difference too. "We really had a lot of friction with Darryl. Now we all have a really good relationship and we're just looking forward to the little spell at college and hoping he motivates himself that little bit more to try just that little bit harder."

The parents of one of the other young men on the program saw a change in him too. After the performance, they were a little overwhelmed. "He was just full of life," said his father. "He said it was brilliant and that he'd go back and do it again." His mother agreed. "He's a changed lad. I can't believe it's my son. I feel like that cloned him and made him good."

For the Chairman of the Youth Justice Board, Professor Robert Morgan, the moral of The Academy is clear: "We need to treat these young people as people with potential. Anyone who has observed the sort of work that is being done here realizes the huge untapped resources that we need to develop."

After a young lifetime of failure and conflict, Darryl sees the potential in very personal terms. "You can make a difference," he says. "Depending on how you look at it. If you want to keep an open mind and leave everything behind you, it'd be like a new world."

REALIZING WHO WE ARE

We all have great natural capacities, but we all have them differently. If we fail to promote a full sense of people's abilities through education and training, some, perhaps most, will never discover what their real capacities are. To that extent they do not really know who they are or what they might become. And now, maybe more than ever, human communities depend on a diversity of talents not on a singular conception of ability.

When we talk of realizing our potential, we should aim to do so in both senses of the word. We need to understand its range and variety. We also need to turn it into reality. This is where the idea of creativity assumes a central significance. The next chapter looks at what creativity means, how it relates to this idea of intelligence and how it can be promoted or stifled, in education, in business and beyond.

BEING CREATIVE

"When people find their medium, they discover their real creative strengths and come into their own. Helping people to connect with their personal creative capacities is the surest way to release the best they have to offer."

I SAID IN CHAPTER 1 that there are many misconceptions about creativity: that it's wrongly thought to be solely the domain of special people or special activities; that you're either creative or not; or that it's all about cutting loose and being uninhibited. What's wrong with these perceptions? What is creativity? How does it relate to intelligence? How does it work in practice? Let me begin with Las Vegas.

VIVA LAS VEGAS

My wife Terry and I have lived and worked together for over 35 years. She is a major fan of Elvis Presley. I can't over-emphasize what an understatement that is. There are three of us in the marriage. Fortunately, I'm alive. But it's only a marginal advantage to be honest. In 2007, it was our 25th wedding anniversary and we decided to renew our vows at the Elvis Chapel in Las Vegas. We went with 30 friends and family, including our two children, James and Kate. It was a great weekend. We had the Blue Hawaii package. There are others, but we liked this one. The package included the Elvis impersonator, four songs from a choice of ten, and smoke. As we came into the chapel there was a puff of smoke from a pipe near the altar, presumably to add to the air of mystery and sacredness. There was also a hula girl, who was optional. I had opted for her, for reasons I was rather pleased about in the event. For another $100 we could have had a pink Cadillac, but we thought that was bit tacky. It could have lowered the tone of the whole occasion.

After the ceremony, we had a reception at the Venetian Hotel, which is a huge place and includes, on the second floor, an indoor replica of San Marco's Square in Venice, complete with the Grand Canal, gondolas and gondoliers. I have been to Venice, and in some ways the Venetian Hotel is better. It's more authentic I feel, and it doesn't smell of sewage.

I mention Las Vegas for a reason. If you think of it, there is no reason for it to be there. Most other cities have a reason to be where they are. Some cities, like New York or Barcelona, are in natural harbors; so they're good for trade. Others are in fertile plains or valleys that are perfect for agriculture; or on major rivers, so they're good for transport and settlement; or on hilltops, so they're good for defense. None of these are true of Las Vegas. As far as I know, nobody is trying to invade Nevada. Las Vegas is in the middle of a desert. The area around it is an arid wilderness. It has no natural water supply, no local sources of agriculture and it suffers from extremely high temperatures. It's the most unlikely place on earth for a major city. Yet for years Las Vegas has been one of the fastest growing cities in America, with a reputation that is known all around the world. In one sense Las Vegas

"In one respect at least, human beings are radically different from the rest of life on earth. We have the ability to imagine. As a result we have unlimited powers of creativity."

really does occupy the most fertile place on earth: the human imagination.

Las Vegas began life as an idea. It proved to be such a compelling idea that it has generated a maelstrom of imaginative energy. I'm not asking you to approve of the idea of Las Vegas: simply to recognize that it is wholly and solely the product of human imagination. So too is every uniquely human achievement in every field.

IMAGINATION, CREATIVITY AND INNOVATION

Imagination is the source of our creativity, but imagination and creativity are not the same thing. Imagination is the ability to bring to mind things that are not present to our senses. We can imagine things that exist or things that do not exist at all. If I ask you to think of an elephant, your old school, or your best friend you can bring to mind mental images that are drawn from real experience. We wouldn't normally think of mental images of real experiences as *imaginative*. More accurately, they are *imaginal*. If I ask you to think of a green polar bear wearing a dress, you can imagine that too. But now you're bringing to mind something you haven't experienced; at least I assume not. These sorts of images are of possibilities composed *in* the mind rather than recalled to mind. They are *imaginative*. Sometimes we mistake imaginative experiences for real ones. These sorts of experience are *imaginary*. Imagination includes imaginal, imaginative and imaginary thoughts.

Imagination is the primary gift of human consciousness. In imagination, we can step out of the here and now. We can revisit and review the past. We can take a different view of the present by putting ourselves in the minds of others: we can try to see with their eyes and feel with their hearts. And in imagination we can anticipate many possible futures. We may not be able to predict the future but by acting on the ideas produced in our imagination, we can help to create it. The imagination liberates us from our immediate circumstances and holds the constant possibility of transforming the present.

Creativity is a step further on from imagination. Imagination can be an entirely private process of internal consciousness. You might be lying motionless on your bed in a fever of imagination and no one would ever know. Private imaginings may have no outcomes in the world at all. Creativity does. Being creative involves *doing* something. It would be odd to describe as creative someone who never did anything. To call somebody creative suggests they are actively producing something in a deliberate way.[1] People are not creative in the abstract; they are creative *in* something: in mathematics, in engineering, in writing, in music, in business, in whatever. Creativity involves putting your imagination to work. In a sense, creativity is applied imagination.

Innovation is the process of putting new ideas into practice. Innovation is *applied* creativity. By definition, innovation is always about introducing something new, or improved, or both and it is usually assumed to be a positive thing. Whether it is or not, in particular cases, is always a matter of judgment; and judgments can always vary. But the general intention of innovation is beneficial.

THE CREATIVE MIND

If you take your dog outside and point at the moon, the dog will look at your finger and then probably at you. If you take a young child outside and point a finger at the moon, the child will look at the moon. This developed skill is called *joint attention*: the ability to share words and a point of focus. As the brain develops, children learn to understand the idea that one thing can represent another. This ability is the foundation of the most significant achievement of the creative mind: the power of symbolic thought. Language is the most obvious example. When learning to speak, a child learns that the sounds can have meaning, and eventually, that letters represent sounds. Other animals have only a limited capacity for this.

If you say "fetch" to a trained dog, it will sit up and be ready to move. If you were to talk to it about the importance of fetching or great fetchers you've known, it will sit blankly until you throw the stick. Show it a picture of the stick and it will probably sniff it. The dog's abilities don't go far beyond the association of sounds with actions. They don't extend, as they quickly do for children, to sophisticated powers of thinking and communication.

The power of representation has given rise to intricate forms of language, mathematics, and the arts, which permeate human consciousness and frame our ideas and feelings about the world. We don't just look at the moon, we locate it within complex theories of the universe; we don't just have feelings for each other, we can capture them in music and poetry. We don't just live in communities: we construct elaborate political theories and constitutions.

"Creativity involves putting your imagination to work. In a sense, creativity is applied imagination."

SPEAKING YOUR MIND

There is a common-sense assumption that language is principally a system of communication: first we have our thoughts and then we find the words to convey them. Studies in linguistics and in developmental and cognitive psychology have long argued convincingly that while language is certainly a sophisticated way of communicating, its role in what and how we think is more complex.[2] The origin of the language we use affects what and how we think. A child quickly learns that things have names. But she does something more. She absorbs ways of thinking that the words make possible. These interpretations vary hugely between languages. For example, the word 'camel' in Arabic can be expressed is many different ways. As well as the standard Arabic word *djemal*, the spoken language uses several hundred other nouns, depending on local dialect. Having the words to describe the nuances makes it easier to see the differences between them.[3] But languages consist of more than the names of things. They are made up of grammatical structure, tenses, moods and syntax; and these also vary between languages, often profoundly. In some North American Indian languages, for example, the simple idea "I see a man" cannot be expressed without indicating with other parts of speech whether the man is sitting, standing or walking.[4] The Greek language has tenses and moods that are not available in English.

These differences illustrate the different 'natural' ways of thinking within different language communities. It is relatively easy for an English speaker to learn French or Italian, in part because many of the words are similar, but also because the conventions of these languages are similar. All three are part of the family of Indo-European languages. It can be harder for a European to learn Chinese, because the basic conventions are completely different.

Chinese is a monosyllabic and tonal language. Indeed, Chinese is tonal *because* it is monosyllabic. Each word is limited to one syllable and is represented by a single character in the written language. The number of similar sounding words would be unmanageable without some means of differentiating for meaning, which is where the voice itself comes in. Words are given a pitch: high, medium, low; and a tone or contour. The voice stays level or rises or falls as the word is pronounced. Almost literally, Chinese is sung. If you sing a wrong note the person you're speaking to will hear a different meaning altogether. The foreigner first learning to speak

Chinese cannot avoid frequent misunderstandings and gaffes; some more serious than others.

On the other hand, unlike English, French or Italian, Chinese does not use inflections to show agreement, tense or number; these have to be inferred from the context and word order. Written Chinese also differs from European languages in that there is no alphabet. Each word is a distinctive character, which has to be learned *in toto* without the benefit of letters to guide pronunciation. For this reason, a number of different dialects have developed over the centuries in China all based on a common written language. The result is that Chinese people from different parts of the country may have difficulty in understanding each other in conversation yet are still able to communicate in writing. An easy way to grasp this concept is to look at the keypad on a computer: whether English, French or Italian, everyone would understand the letters and numbers even though they would give the letters different words and sounds if they read them out loud.[5]

As they grow into their cultures, children absorb ways of thinking that are embedded in the particular languages they learn. In this way, languages play a central role in the growth of consciousness. Important as they are, words are not the only way in which we think. Words help us to think about some types of experience, but they are relatively useless in dealing with others. We use different modes of representation to express different types of ideas. It's said that the composer Gustav Mahler was sitting in his studio completing a new piano piece. As he was playing, one of his students came into the room and listened quietly. At the end of the piece the student said, "Maestro, that was wonderful. What is it about?" Mahler turned to him and said, "It's about this," and he played it again. If the ideas in music could be expressed in words, there'd be no need to write the music in the first place.

Some ideas can only be expressed in mathematics. As the Nobel physicist, Richard Feynman, put it: "If you're interested in the ultimate character of the physical world, at present time our only way to understand it is through a mathematical type of reasoning. I don't think a person can appreciate much of these particular aspects of the world, the great depth and character of the universality of the laws, relationships of things, without an understanding of mathematics. There are many aspects of the world where mathematics is unnecessary, such as love, which are very delightful and wonderful to appreciate and to feel awe about. But if physics is what are talking about, then not to know mathematics is a severe limitation in understanding the world."[6]

Mathematics is the best medium for some forms of understanding but relatively poor for others. If you want to describe the movement of electrons, you need algebra. If you want to express your love for someone you could use poetry. If someone asks you, "How much do you love me?" don't give them a calculator and say, "Here, you work it out."

The veil of conceptions

Our experiences of the world may be received through direct sensory perception, but how we interpret that information varies from person to person. The nature of our senses determines what we can perceive. But even though we have use of the same senses, people often see the same events differently. This is because they have different points of view. They may be in different physical places and literally have a different angle on what's going on. If there was no more to it than that, any dispute could be settled by comparing everyone's point of view and putting together an objective overview. In theory this is what is meant to happen in a court of law. In practice, gathering together everyone's points of view often deepens the details of the dispute. This is because our individual view of what is going on is deeply influenced by the ideas, values and beliefs through which we interpret our experiences. These affect what we actually perceive and what we make of it all.

Human intelligence is not just a process of perception but of selection. Otherwise there would be too much information coming in; like a radio tuned to an open frequency. When you look at a room, a landscape, the street; you don't pay equal attention to everything in your field of perception. You notice some things, not others. Two people standing in the same street may perceive it in completely different ways. A traffic warden may see a landscape of offenders; a window cleaner a land of opportunity. A bird fancier wandering through a wood will see it differently from a botanist interested in rare plants. If you drive a yellow car, you're likely to see yellow cars everywhere.

We see the world not as it is, but through a veil of conceptions. Some theories of intelligence argue that there is a direct line from the senses to the brain to the actions we take. The American philosopher of art, Susanne Langer, argues that there is an intermediate process. The brain she says, is like a great transformer: "The current *"We see the world not as it is, but through a veil of conceptions."* of experience that passes through it undergoes a change of character not through ... the sense by which the perception entered but by virtue of a primary use, which is made of it immediately. It is sucked into the stream of symbols which constitute a human mind."[7]

WHAT DO YOU MEAN?

Anything may be a symbol. A sunset may symbolize sadness for you and euphoria for someone else, according to personal associations or state of mind. These symbols are personal and psychological. Formal symbols are intended to mean something. Let me suggest a broad distinction between forms of symbolic representation that that are *systematic* and those that are *schematic*.

Systematic symbols

Words and numbers are examples of systematic symbolism. Systems of numbers are built from a small set of basic units that can be combined in an infinite variety of ways to express precise meanings. Just as numbers have accepted values, words too have conventional meanings that are definable in terms of each other; and rules that affect how they can be used and still mean something. In verbal language, one word follows another in sequences that are governed by conventions of syntax.

Systematic symbolism is governed by rules, which divide sense from nonsense very clearly, via agreed procedures. In such systems there are only certain ways in which the various elements can be composed and still have meaning. We may not be able to understand every word in a given sentence, but we can generally recognize that the sentence means something because we understand the rules of the system. If we meet a new word, we can look up the definition, and find its meaning described, using other words. In fact we don't always need to look up an unfamiliar word because what it means is often clear from its context.

The systematic nature of language is illustrated by the scientist and philosopher, Michael Polanyi, who asked what would happen if we were to replace each different sentence in the English language by a unique word. "We must first envisage," he said, "that from an alphabet of 26 letters we could construct 26^8 eight-letter words: that is about 100 billion." That number is roughly the number of neurons in a human brain, of course. This million-fold enrichment of the English language, "would completely destroy it not only because nobody could remember so many words but for the important reason that many would be meaningless. For the meaning of a word is formed and made clear by repeated use and the vast majority of our eight-letter words would be used only once or too rarely to acquire a definite meaning."[8]

Chemistry, for example, says that the millions of different compounds are composed of about 100 chemical elements: "Since each element has a name and characteristic symbol attached to it, we can write down the composition of any compound in terms of the elements it contains. To classify things in terms of features for which we have names, as we do in talking about things, requires the same kind of connoisseurship as the naturalist must have for identifying specimens of plants or animals. Thus the art of speaking precisely, by applying a rich vocabulary exactly, resembles the delicate discrimination practised by the expert taxonomist."[9]

SCHEMATIC SYMBOLS

Words and numbers work well for ideas that can be laid out sequentially. Pictures, on the other hand, present the whole pattern of ideas simultaneously. In visual form we can express thoughts that do not fit the structures of words. Paintings, poems, music and dance are examples of *schematic* symbols. Their meanings are uniquely expressed in the forms they take. If you want to understand the meaning of a painting you can't turn to a dictionary of colors to see what blue and green usually mean when they are put together. There is no manual of chords and harmonies that will tell us what a symphony is driving at and no dramatic codebook to tell us what a play means. There are no fixed meanings for the symbolic forms of art, to divide sense from nonsense. The meaning of a work of art is available only in the particular form in which it is expressed. The sound and feel of work in the arts is inseparable not only from *what* it means but from *how* it means. A painting, a play, a symphony, a novel are complex and unique forms created out of a sense of form and cultural knowledge rather than from systematic meanings.

Schematic forms may use systematic symbols. Plays, novels and poems are written in words, after all; and musical notation allows us to see each note in written form. But the score is not the music, just as the text is not the play. These are the symbols in which the schematic work is encoded and from which it must be interpreted either in performance or by the reader. Words can be used in a functional way to get the world's business done. Few of us spend much time refining a quick note or email to a friend or someone we work with. Our interest is in what is being said rather than in how it is expressed: in content rather than form. Poetry is a different matter. Consider this by W.B. Yeats:

When You Are Old
When you are old and grey and full of sleep,
And nodding by the fire, take down this book,
And slowly read, and dream of the soft look
Your eyes had once, and of their shadows deep;
How many loved your moments of glad grace,
And loved your beauty with love false or true,
But one man loved the pilgrim soul in you,
And loved the sorrows of your changing face;
And bending down beside the glowing bars,
Murmur, a little sadly, how Love fled
And paced upon the mountains overhead
And hid his face amid a crowd of stars.

W B Yeats (1865–1939)

Poets are concerned not only with literal meanings but also with the layered associations of words and of the rhythms and cadences of the poem as a whole. We don't only respond to a poem, or a play, or to music, line-by-line or note-by-note. The complete work is more than the sum of its parts. It is a feature of schematic symbols that we respond to them as a whole.

CREATING AND RECREATING

Human consciousness is shaped by the ideas, beliefs and values that we derive from our experiences and through the meaning which we derive from them. Our ideas can liberate or imprison us. In a literal sense we create the worlds in which we live; and there is always the possibility of re-creation. As psychologist George A. Kelly put it: "to make sense out of events we thread them through with ideas and to make sense of the ideas we must test them against events."[10]

He describes this process as one of successive approximations. The great generative ideas in human history have transformed the world view of their times and helped to reshape their cultures. We make the world we live in and we can remake it. This process of cultural evolution is probably what the comedian George Carlin had in mind when he said, "Just when I found out the meaning of life, they changed it."

What is true of the long cycles of creative change in a social culture is also true of the shorter cycles of creative work by individuals and groups. The creative process is also one of successive approximations.

THE CREATIVE PROCESS

"Creativity is the process of having original ideas that have value."

I define creativity as the process of having original ideas that have value. There are three key terms here: *process*, *original* and *value.* Creativity is a process more often than it is an event. To call something a process indicates a relationship between its various elements: that each aspect and phase of what happens is related to every other. Being creative involves several processes that interweave within each other. The first is generative. The second is evaluative.

Generating ideas

Being creative has similar features in all disciplines. The Nobel winning chemist Sir Harry Kroto is also a professional designer. I asked him what differences he experienced, if any, between creativity in the arts and sciences, in the studio and the laboratory. He said that for him the process is exactly the same, even though the outcomes are different (as we'll see in Chapter 7). In all creative processes we are pushing the boundaries of what we know now, to explore new possibilities; we are drawing on the skills we have now, often stretching and evolving them as the work demands. In the early stages, being creative may involve playing with an idea, doodling or improvising around the theme. It may begin with a thought that is literally half-formed: with a sketch, a first plan or a design; the first notes of a melody or the intimation of a solution to a problem. There may be several ideas in play and a number of possible starting points. Creativity does not always require freedom from constraints or a blank page. A lot of creative work has to work to specific briefs or conventions and great work often comes from working within formal constraints. Some of the finest poetry is in the form of the sonnet, which has a fixed form to which the writer must submit. Japanese haiku similarly makes specific formal demands on the poet, as do many other forms of poetic structure. These do not inhibit the writer's creativity; they set a framework for it. The creative achievement and the aesthetic pleasure lie in using standard forms to achieve unique effects and original insights.

As I mentioned earlier, being creative always involves *doing* something, so it will always involve using some form of media. These may be physical media, such as steel, wood, clay, fabric or food; they may be sensory media, like sound, light, the voice or the body; they may be cognitive media, including words, numbers, or notation. Whatever the media, there is an intimate relationship between the ideas that form and the media through which they take shape. This is true whether the process is focused on designing a building, developing a mathematical theorem, a scientific hypothesis or a musical composition. Creativity is a dialogue between the ideas and the media in which they are being formed. Robert Cohan has been a major influence in the world of modern dance. I asked him about the process of choreography. Dancers, he told me, think physically. It isn't that they begin from a verbal proposition and try to dance it. Choreography evolves in the making. It is a material process of movement and reflection on movement. Being creative is not just a question of thinking of an idea and then finding a way to express it. Often it is only in developing the dance, image or music that the idea emerges at all.

Making judgments

Creativity is not only about generating ideas; it involves making judgments about them. The process includes elaborating on the initial ideas, testing and refining them and even rejecting them, in favor of others that emerge during the process. Sometimes creative works arrive in the world more or less fully formed and need no further work. It's said that Mozart made few revisions to many of his compositions. The poet John Milton was blind. Each morning he dictated whole sections of his epic work *Paradise Lost* to his daughters and

"If you're not prepared to be wrong, it's unlikely that you'll ever come up with anything original."

made only minor changes to the text. Usually, creative work is more tentative and exploratory.

There are likely to be dead ends: ideas and designs that do not work. There may be failures and changes before the best outcome is produced. You can see examples of the iterative nature of the creative process in the successive drafts of poems and novels, of scholarly papers or in designs for inventions and so on. It is well known that Thomas Edison ran through dozens of ideas and designs for the light bulb before settling on the final version.

Terrance Tao is acknowledged to be the world's greatest living mathematician and he has been awarded many honors. In 2002, at the age of 31, he received the Fields Medal for Mathematics, which is the equivalent of the Nobel Prize. He says that discovery in mathematics is a constant process of trial and error: "You come up with a wrong idea," he says, "work on it for a month and realize it doesn't work and then you come up with the next wrong idea and then finally by process of elimination you come up with something that does work." I asked the renowned chemist, Sir Harry Kroto, how many of his experiments fail. He said about 95 percent of them. Of course failure is not the right word, he said: "You're just finding out what doesn't work." Albert Einstein put the point sharply: "Anyone who has never made a mistake, has never tried anything new." I don't mean to say that being wrong is the same thing as being creative but if you're not prepared to be wrong, it's unlikely that you'll ever come up with anything original.

Evaluating which ideas work and which don't, involves judgment and critical thinking. This can happen throughout the creative process and can involve standing back in quiet reflection. Evaluation can be individual or shared, involve instant judgments or long-term testing. In most creative work there are many shifts between these two modes of thought. The quality of creative achievement is related to both. Helping people to understand and manage the interaction between generative and evaluative thinking is a pivotal task of creative development.

Michael Polanyi makes a distinction between *focal* and *subsidiary* awareness. Whatever we're doing, we're aware of our actions on at least these two levels. If you're knocking a nail into a piece of wood with a hammer, the focus of your attention is on the head of the nail. You also have to be aware in a subsidiary way of the weight of the hammer and the arc of your arm. It is important that this relationship is the right way round. If you start to focus on what your arm is doing, you're likely to miss the nail. Polanyi continues: "Subsidiary awareness and focal awareness are mutually exclusive. If a pianist shifts his attention from the piece he is playing to the observation of what he's doing with his fingers while playing it, he gets confused and may have to stop. This happens generally if we switch our focal attention to particulars on which we had previously been aware only in their subsidiary role."[11]

In any creative process the focus of our attention has to be right. Although there are always points where criticism is necessary, generative thinking has to be given time to flower. At the right time and in the right way, critical appraisal is essential. At the wrong point, it can kill an emerging idea. Similarly, creativity can be inhibited by trying to do too much too soon or at the same time. The final phases are often to do with refining the detail of the expression: with producing the neat copy so to speak. But asking people to write a poem right away in their best handwriting can inhibit the spontaneity they need in the initial phase of generating ideas. They need to understand that creativity moves through different phases, and to have some sense of where they are in the process. In most situations,

"At the right time and in the right way, critical appraisal is essential. At the wrong point, it can kill an emerging idea."

trying to produce a finished version in one move is impossible. Not understanding this can make people think that they are not creative at all.

JUDGING VALUE

When I was a teenager, one of my cousins came to the house flushed with excitement. He'd thought of an invention that was going to make us all rich. He'd been walking down the road and was watching an elderly woman inching painfully along with a walking stick. In a moment of inspiration, he thought how much easier it would be if the walking stick had a little wheel on the end of it. Instead of lifting it every time she took a step she could just push it along. He couldn't believe that no one had thought of it before. We made him a drink and broke it to him gently. It was a good idea but for the one catastrophic flaw.

Judging the value of new ideas can be difficult. By definition, creative ideas are often ahead of their times. In the mid-1830s, Michael Faraday gave the first demonstration of electromagnetism at the Royal Institution in London. He stood in a gaslit lecture theatre before a distinguished audience of scientists and showed bright blue sparks leaping between two copper spheres. The audience was impressed but many of them were at a loss to know what to make of it all. "This is all very interesting, Mr Faraday," said one of them. "But what use is it?" "I don't know," Faraday is purported to have said, "What use is a newborn baby?" A world without electricity is now unthinkable. Our lives depend on it in almost every way, from food supplies to transport to heating, lighting and telecommunications. The nineteenth century saw few of the uses of electricity that we now take for granted. It was not as if people's homes were cluttered with dishwashers and televisions, simply waiting for Faraday to complete his experiments.

The applications of electricity only followed the harnessing of electricity itself. Faraday's discoveries helped to create circumstances in which these applications were developed. At the time, many people simply couldn't see the point of it. This is the often way with creative insights. They run ahead of their times and confuse the crowd.

Original thinkers are often appreciated more by subsequent generations because values change. Countless scientists, inventors, artists and philosophers were ridiculed in their own times, though their work has been revered by later generations. Think of Galileo, whose work on heliocentricism (placing the sun at the center of our solar system) was denounced as heretical and not considered science at all. Avant-garde artists are constantly asked, "But is it art?"[12] There are many examples of artists who died in penury, whose work now changes hands for fortunes. Equally, people who were thought of as visionary in their own times can be discredited by history for exactly the same reason. Think of phrenology. There are very few scientists who still take seriously the idea that personality can be interpreted by considering the shape of the human skull. However, in the mid-nineteenth century it was highly influential in shaping ideas about psychiatry (see Chapter 3).

Our view of the past is rarely settled. We live in a perpetual present tense. Our knowledge of other periods can never match their vast complexity as they were experienced and understood at the time. Our perception of the past is partial and selective. What we include and acknowledge is always open to change and revision. This is often because of changes in contemporary values. Individuals long forgotten or overlooked may be reinterpreted as key agents of cultural progress because of a shift in current fashion or political outlook. The strong sentiment and self-assurance of Raphael, for example, endeared him to many Victorians as the central figure in the Renaissance. There are those today who think more of Michelangelo, for his restless self-doubt, and build their image of the period around him. In these ways, our sense of history and of ourselves involves a continual selection and reselection of ancestors. History is not dead because the present is so alive.

Being original

Creativity is about coming up with new ideas. But what do we mean by new? Do we have to come up with something that has never been thought of before? Common sense suggests not – that a creative outcome can be original on different levels: for the person involved; for a particular community; for humanity as a whole. The towering figures of science, the arts, technology and the rest produced works of historic originality. Teachers don't expect that of young children. They try to encourage work that's original for the children themselves. Some may be capable of historic originality (think of Mozart and other prodigies).

"Creativity moves through different phases. Trying to produce a finished version in one move is usually impossible. Not understanding this can make people think that they are not creative at all."

MAKING CONNECTIONS

Creative insights often occur by making unusual connections: seeing analogies between ideas that have not previously been related. All of our existing ideas have creative possibilities. Creative insights occur when they are combined in unexpected ways or applied to questions or issues with which they are not normally associated. Arthur Koestler[13] describes this as a process of bi-association: when we bring together ideas from different areas that are not normally connected, so that we think not on one plane as in routine linear thinking but on several planes at once. Creative thought involves breaching the boundaries between different frames of reference. Some modes of thinking dominate in different types of activity: the aural in music, the kinesthetic in dance, and the mathematical in physics. They often draw on different areas of intelligence simultaneously. Mathematicians often talk of visualizing problems and solutions. Dance is closely related to musical understanding: visual arts draw deeply from spatial intelligence. The composition of music is often informed by an implicit understanding of mathematics.

FREEDOM AND CONTROL

Creative achievement is related to control of the medium. Simply asking people to be creative is not enough. Children and adults need the means and the skills to be creative. I can't play the piano. I don't mean I'm incapable of playing; I have just never learnt how to do it. To that extent, I can't be creative on the piano. I can make noises on it and give vent to my immediate feelings. In that sense I can be expressive. But I cannot be musically creative in the same way as those who can actually play it.

Many people have problems with mathematics. They see it as a sort of puzzle, the point of which is not wholly clear. Trying to appreciate equations if you don't speak mathematics is like to trying to appreciate a musical score if you don't read music. Non-musicians see a puzzle: musicians hear a symphony. Those who speak mathematics look through equations to the beauty and complexity of the ideas they express. They hear the music. For some of us, grasping mathematical beauty is like trying to read Proust with a French phrasebook.

Many adults say they cannot draw. They are right. They cannot. They are not incapable of it any more than I am incapable of learning the piano. They just do not know how. The problems they face are often of two kinds. The first problem is *perceptual*: we have to learn to look at things differently. Drawing is not a deductive process, like philosophy; it is a visual one. The problems that many people experience when drawing, arise from the logical/rational processes that tend to dominate and interfere with our modes of thought. We become intent on drawing an object in a photographic way, and find that we can't; rather than simply perceiving the object as it appears to us. The second problem is *technical*: knowing how to create on the page what the eye has learned to see. Given adequate hand–eye co-ordination, most people can learn to draw, but most people have not acquired the necessary skills. Like learning to write, learning to draw is a technical and cultural achievement not a biological one. Unless these things are taught, and learnt, the creative possibilities of drawing remain limited.

Most children's drawings follow a recognizable pattern up to the age of thirteen or so. At about the age of eight, for example, they begin to develop a sense of perspective. As they mature, they pay increasing attention to details and attempt more sophisticated pictures. Without good teaching, their drawing reaches a plateau, usually at about the age of twelve or thirteen. Many people give up drawing altogether at this point, often through frustration. They reach a stage where their creative ambitions have outrun their technical abilities. As a result, most adults have the graphic skills of a young adolescent. This is hardly surprising. Children don't develop these abilities just by getting older, any more than they wake up on their sixteenth birthday to discover they can drive a car.

This doesn't mean that people with limited skills cannot be creative. There are different levels and phases of creative development. Some people produce highly creative work with relatively undeveloped techniques. In general though, creative development goes hand in hand with increasing technical facility with the instruments or materials that are being used.

Here as everywhere it is a question of balance and synergy. Technical control is necessary for creative work but it is not enough. Being creative is about speculating, exploring new horizons and using imagination. Many highly trained people, musicians, dancers, engineers, scientists, are very skilled but not especially original. There are many possible reasons for this. They may not be working in their best medium. A musician may be competent in an instrument but not excited by it. There are other possibilities. One of them is bad teaching. I know many would-be musicians who endured the drudgery of practicing scales and harmonies only until they could put the instrument away forever. Facilitating creative development is a sophisticated process that must find a balance between learning skills and stimulating the imagination to explore new ideas.

THIS TIME IT'S PERSONAL

I find it helpful to make a broad distinction between general and personal creativity.

General creativity

Original thinking is possible in anything that we do. In the general run of our lives we settle naturally into routines of behavior and habits of thought. When we encounter a new problem or situation, our established habits can make it difficult to see novel solutions. There are various tools and techniques to help unblock conventional ways of thinking. These thinking techniques include divergent or lateral thinking.

In logico-deductive thought, ideas build on each another in carefully consistent steps and lead to a limited number of permissible answers; or sometimes to only one. Lateral and divergent thought works by making much freer associations:

often by thinking in metaphors or analogies, or even reframing the question itself to open up more possibilities. There are some tests for divergent thinking just as there are for IQ. Typically, you might be asked how many uses you can think of for a paperclip. An average score might be 10 or 15, all involving paper. People who are good at these tests might come up with over 100 ideas, and be able to see beyond the conventional use of a paperclip. They might consider a use for a paperclip that is 50 feet high and made out of rubber. The questioner didn't say it couldn't be.

Some of the most interesting breakthroughs in science, technology and the arts come from reframing the question, just as Copernicus and Galileo chose to question whether the earth was at the center of the universe. The questions we ask are often more important than the answers we search for. Every question leads to particular lines of inquiry. Change the question and whole new horizons may open up to is. The true value of a generative idea is that it leads to new sorts of questions.

These general techniques of creative thinking can be used to generate a flow of ideas and possibilities, especially in groups and committees. They include the repertoire of thinking skills developed by Edward De Bono;[14] and the concept of creative Synectics, developed by William Gordon and George Prince.[15] Used properly they can have genuine benefits in business, in the community and in our personal lives. Often they involve separating the processes of analyzing problems, generating solutions and evaluating the best options. These techniques also focus on giving positive rather than negative responses to people's ideas, and they emphasize the value of sharing multiple points of view.

Personal creativity

In addition to general capacities for creative thinking we all have unique talents and passions, and our own personal creative potential. It may be for a particular form of music or specific instrument, or music in general; it may be for mathematics or chemistry or contemporary dance; you may have a vocation for becoming a fireman, a homemaker, a physician or a teacher. We each have skills and abilities that can be developed. In my book, *The Element*, I talk about this personal dimension of creative achievement: the point where individual talent meets personal passion. Personal creativity often comes from a love for particular materials. A sculptor will feel inspired by the shape of a piece of wood or the texture of stone; musicians love the sounds they make and the feel of the instruments. Mathematicians love the art of mathematics just as dancers love to move; writers may feel inspired by a love of the expressive power of words; and painters by the potential of a blank canvas and their color palette.

Herb Alpert is one of the great popular musicians of his generation. If you listen to him playing the trumpet, it is as if he is speaking to you through it. In a sense, he is. His creativity as a musician is indivisible from his passion for the expressive qualities of the trumpet itself. He is now also a distinguished sculptor and painter. In each medium, his creative achievements have been inspired by his love and feel for the materials he uses and the possibilities he sees in them for creative expression. For other musicians, their best medium is the guitar, the piano, or the violin. There are many examples of people whose creativity is fired by particular media: not water colors but pastels, not mathematics in general but algebra in particular. I spoke once with a professor of physics from California. He described himself as a native speaker of algebra. When he came across algebra at school he had an intuitive feel for it. He said that English has become his second language. He now spends most of his life speaking algebra.

Discovering the right medium is often a tidal moment in the creative life of the individual. The composer and conductor, Leonard Bernstein, talked about the moment when he fell in love with music. When he was a young child, he came down-stairs one morning to find an upright piano in the hallway of his home. Evidently, his parents had agreed to look after the piano while some friends were out of the country. Bernstein's family was not especially musical and he had never been close to a piano before. With a child's curiosity he lifted the lid and pressed on the keys and felt the sounds vibrate from the instrument. A wave of excitement rushed through him. He didn't know why this happened but he knew then that he wanted to spend as much time as he could making such sounds. He had found his medium. In doing so he opened the door to his own creative potential.

Porcelain was introduced into Britain in the eighteenth century. Some of the most exquisite and valued pieces of porcelain were made in the Chelsea Porcelain Factory that was founded by Nicholas Sprimont in 1743. Before Sprimont discovered porcelain he was a silversmith by trade. He was a competent enough silversmith and made a good living. But he then came upon this new material and it fired his imagination. He loved the feel of it and the possibilities it held. Over the next 20 years he produced beautiful objects that far surpassed his achievements in silver. His creative energies and his accomplishments were driven by his relationship with the material itself; by the possibilities he saw in the medium he used.[16]

Creativity can be inhibited by the wrong medium. Some years ago, I worked with a very good literary editor on a book I had written. She was an excellent judge of style and added hugely to the quality of the book, as good literary editors should. She told me she had become a literary editor in her forties. Before that she was a concert pianist. I asked why she had changed professions. She said that she had been giving a concert in London with a distinguished conductor. After the concert they had dinner. Over the meal, he mentioned how good her performance had been and she thanked him. "But you didn't enjoy it, did you?" he said. She was taken aback. This hadn't occurred to her. She said she hadn't enjoyed it particularly, but then she never did. He asked why she did it and she said, "Because I'm good at it."

She explained that she had been born into a musical family. She had taken piano lessons and showed talent; she had gone on to take a music degree, then a doctorate of music and on to a concert career. Neither she nor anyone else had stopped to ask whether she wanted to do this or whether she enjoyed it. She did it because she was good at it. The conductor said, "Being good at something isn't a good enough reason to spend your life doing it." In the weeks that followed she wrestled with this idea and concluded that he was right. She finished the season of concerts, closed the piano lid and never opened it again. She turned instead to books, the art form she really loved.

> "The capacity for creativity is essentially human and it holds the constant promise of alternative ways of seeing, of thinking and of doing."

When people find their medium, they discover their real creative strengths and come into their own. Helping people to connect with their personal creative capacities is the surest way to release the best they have to offer.

CONCLUSION

I said in Chapter 5 that intelligence is diverse, dynamic and distinct. So too is the creative process. It can operate in the many diverse fields of human intelligence, it is about making dynamic connections, and the results are always in some way unique. Creativity is not a single power that people simply have or do not have. It involves many different mental functions, combinations of skills and personal attributes. We all have creative capacities but very many people conclude that they are not creative, when in truth they have never learnt and practiced what is involved. The capacity for creativity is essentially human and it holds the constant promise of alternative ways of seeing, of thinking and of doing. It means, as George Kelly put it, that no one needs to be completely hemmed in by circumstances: "No one needs to be the victim of their own biography."[17] Or as Carl Jung once said, "I am not what has happened to me. I am what I choose to become."

FEELING BETTER

"Being creative is not only about thinking: it is about feeling."

B EING CREATIVE IS NOT a purely intellectual process. It may draw on all areas of human consciousness: on feelings, intuitions and being playfully imaginative, as well as on knowledge and practical skills. Creativity often taps into areas of consciousness that are not regulated by conscious thought. Our best ideas sometimes come to mind without our thinking consciously about them at all. If we can't work something out, it is often better to sleep on a problem or put it to the 'back of our minds' where our subconscious mulls it over in ways that we can't control and may deliver a solution to us unbidden. Feelings, hunches, subconscious perceptions and intuitions can all play a central part in creative work, and not only in the arts. So too does a sense of aesthetics, of beauty, and sensuousness. This is true in all fields, from dance to calculus.

BEYOND THE NUMBERS

I once asked a professor of mathematics how he assessed PhDs in pure math. Actually, my first question was, "How long are they?" I used to supervise doctoral programs in the humanities for a university that had set a maximum length of 80,000 words for doctoral dissertations. This was essential because there came a point when people just had to be stopped. I once interviewed a candidate for a job who had just been given his PhD from a neighboring university. I asked him if there had been a maximum word length. He was startled by the very idea and said of course not. So I asked him how long the dissertations normally were. With a faint air of contempt for the question, he said that they were "as long they needed to be." I asked him how long *his* dissertation had needed to be. Arching his eyebrows as if stating the obvious, he said 370,000 words. That is roughly the same length as the Old Testament. I asked him the title and he said it was called something like, *Further education in Dombey: Some issues.* Dombey is a regional city in England with a population of about 270,000 people.[1] So, that is less than 1.5 words each. What he discovered there that merited over a third of a million words to explain, I was thankful never to find out. You will also note from his subtitle that this was not even a comprehensive study, merely a promissory note for a fuller work yet to be composed.

When I asked the professor of mathematics whether there is a maximum length for PhDs in pure math, he also said, "No, they are as long as they need to be." I asked how long they are typically and he said he had reviewed one recently that was 26 pages. That is page after page after page of math – but much shorter than 370,000 words – presumably with an equals sign at the end. I asked him how he assessed these dissertations. "Presumably they're always right," I said. (You would be fairly depressed if you had spent three or four years completing a PhD in pure math and it was marked "Wrong. Eight out of ten. See me.") "No," he said, "They're normally right." *Normally.* "So how do you assess one?" I asked. "Originality is a key factor," he told me. "Like all PhDs, they have to break new ground and tell us something we didn't know before."

In other words, a major criterion is how creative the work is. "But the other criterion," he said, "is aesthetic. It is the elegance of the proof, the beauty of the argument."

I asked him why that is such an important consideration. He told me that mathematicians believe strongly that mathematics is one of the purest ways we have of understanding the truths of nature. Since nature is inherently beautiful there is an equally strong assumption that the more elegant the proof, the more likely it is to correspond to the beauty of nature and to be true. He could have been discussing a sonata, or a poem or a dance, and in a way he was. Aesthetics is a powerful force in all forms of creative work: for scientists and mathematicians just as for musicians, poets, dancers and designers. It is one example of the many ways in which being creative may include, but always goes beyond, the confines of academic intelligence. Being creative is not only about thinking: it is about feeling.

"Aesthetics is a powerful force in all forms of creative work: for scientists and mathematicians just as for musicians, poets, dancers and designers."

THE EXILE OF FEELING

In the eighteenth and nineteenth centuries, the leading figures of the Enlightenment and of Romanticism drew clear divisions between intellect and emotion. The Rationalists distrusted feelings; the Romantics trusted little else. In their different ways, both saw intellect and feelings as separate realms of experience that should be kept apart from each other. The consequences of this division are still felt to this day. They can be catastrophic and they are everywhere.

Rationalist philosophers aimed to see through the illusions of superstition and common sense by a remorseless process of skeptical reasoning.[2] In the natural sciences (including physics and biology), feelings, intuition, values and beliefs were seen as dangerous distractions: the murky froth of an undisciplined mind. David Hume, a leading light of the Enlightenment, put it bluntly: "If we take in hand any volume of divinity or school metaphysics, for instance, let as ask, does it contain any abstract reasoning concerning quantity or number? No. Does it contain any experimental reasoning concerning matters of fact and existence? No. Commit it then to the flames, for it can contain nothing but sophistry and illusion."[3]

This meant, for example, that the biological sciences should make no metaphysical assumptions about the origins and functions of life. All of these should be explained in purely material terms. If there is a force beyond logic and evidence that is responsible for life on earth, science should make no presumptions about it and take no interest in it. Darwin's theory of natural selection met these materialist conditions with persuasive elegance and clarity and its effects are still pulsating through global belief systems.

In the human sciences, there was a similar rejection of religious ideas and of all forms of transcendentalism. Pioneering psychologists, including Ivan Pavlov (1849–1936), J.B. Watson (1878–1958) and B.F. Skinner (1904–1990), set out to examine human behavior in ways that set aside all ideas about immaterial spirits or souls. In their various ways, they looked at human behavior wholly in terms of social conditioning, of learned responses to experiences and of meeting the practical needs of survival. Behaviorism was a theory developed by B.F. Skinner in the 1920s. It suggested that people could be conditioned into particular forms of behavior. There is of course some truth in this. Much of our behavior is predictable and conditioned. Pavlov's experiment with dogs came to a similar conclusion. Pavlov rang a bell whenever he gave food to the dogs in his laboratory. Eventually the dogs would salivate at the sound of the bell alone. Pavlov called this a conditioned response. Human beings can show conditioned responses too.

However, in the past 100 years there has been a huge amount of experimental research inside and outside laboratories in all aspects of human behavior. It has not pointed to an ultimate theory of human behavior that can reliably predict how all people will act in any given circumstances.

Sigmund Freud (1856–1939) conceived of the mind as a mental apparatus for engaging the individual with the outside world. He distinguished between *the id*: the basic instinctual drives of human behavior, which operate on the pleasure principle; *the ego*: the conscious mind, which operates on the reality principle and manages our thoughts, executive functions and relationships in the world; and *the super ego*: which is the seat of moral values, a sense of higher purpose, of spirituality and of conscience.

According to Freud, the ego exists in a constant state of tension as it strives to manage the more primitive impulses of the id, the moral tendencies of the super ego and the competing demands of the external world. Keeping a rational mind depends on controlling the complex interactions of these different psychological drives. Consequently, and in many ways, Freudian psychology presents the emotions as potential sources of disturbance to a balanced personality.

Despite the huge influence of these ideas in the human sciences and in popular culture, by the mid-20th century growing numbers of academics and therapists alike were rejecting these mechanistic approaches to human behavior. In 1960, Jerome Bruner and Frank Miller established the Center for Cognitive Studies at Harvard University, in an explicit attempt to move beyond the behaviorist paradigm and to explore the intrinsic nature of mind and consciousness. The great developmental psychologist, Jean Piaget, had long argued for more qualitative approaches to understanding how children and adults learn and experience the world. Both his and Bruner's work had profound influence on theories of education.

Many psychologists and therapists also objected to what they saw as essentially negative conceptions of feelings and emotions that came from the rationalist and behaviorist traditions; what R.D. Laing called "the negative psychology of affect." Many, like Laing, saw rationalist models of psychology as symptoms of a larger problem: "that our civilization represses not only the instincts, not only sexuality, but any form of transcendence."

From the beginning of the 20th century there had been radically alternative theories of human well-being and emotional health. William James (1842–1910), Viktor Frankl (1905–1997), Carl Jung (1875–1961) Abraham Maslow (1908–1970), Carl Rogers (1902–1987) and many others had argued in their own ways for more harmonious conceptions of feelings, spirituality, mind and body. Some, like Alan Watts (1915–1973) and Aldous Huxley (1894–1963), drew on ancient Eastern teachings where the divisions between mind, body and spirit had not been so sharply drawn in the first place. By the 1960s a complicated cultural reaction against rationalism was beginning to gather pace, a reaction that manifested in far-reaching changes in what the cultural historian, Raymond Williams, would have called the "structure of feeling" of the time.

"The two touchstones of personal growth are individuality and authenticity."

The personal growth movement

The personal growth movement began in the 1940s and mushroomed during the 1960s first in America and then in Europe. 'Personal growth' refers to various sorts of group encounter activities that aim to explore the relationships between people and increase their knowledge of themselves and each other. Encounter or T-groups encouraged members to see the world through the eyes of others and to rethink their own perceptions of themselves. These encounters often made use of role-play techniques, of art and other 'creative' activities; they drew on the alternative theories of psychoanalysts such as Jung and Rogers; and often integrated Eastern techniques of meditation and of physical relaxation including yoga. The principles and practices of the personal growth movement have continued to grow and are now the basis of coaching, mentoring and publishing programs around the world.

The two touchstones of personal growth are individuality and authenticity. An individual desiring a personal growth experience, "may consider himself less emotionally, physically, or sensually spontaneous than he would like. He may be lonely and find it difficult to communicate honestly with another. The values of sensitivity training and group encounter are honesty and the presentation of the authentic self."[4] Although it developed out of academic studies into personality and behavior, group encounters attracted large numbers of paying customers to the search for more authentic relationships. The personal growth movement is also impelled by a hunger that many people feel to connect with their own natural strengths and with their own creativity.[5]

According to Carl Rogers, the burgeoning of personal growth was stimulated by the decline of organized religious beliefs and the need to find alternative sources of meaning in existence. Victor Frankl believed that unknown numbers of people were suffering dangerously from what he called the "existential vacuum": the loss of an ultimate meaning to existence that would make life worthwhile. As Frankl saw it, "the consequent void, the state of emptiness is at present one of the major challenges to psychiatry."[6]

Carl Jung agreed. During his long professional practice as a psychoanalyst, he was consulted by people "from all the civilized countries of the earth." Among all his patients in the second half of life, "that is to say over 35, there has not been one whose problem in the last resort was not one of finding a religious outlook on life. It is safe to say that every one of them fell ill because he had lost that which the living religions of every age have given their followers, and none of them has been really healed who did not regain his religious outlook."[7]

However that may be, holistic therapists all argued for systems of analysis that addressed a person's total being in the world, including the authentic expression of personal feelings. The implicit ethic is to live for the moment, in the here and now. The parallel with an existential point of view is clear-cut. But rather than being wholly existentialist, the counter-culture, as it came to be known, was and is rooted as much in metaphysical interests. Rethinking materialist values and the search for experiences of transcendence, especially through alternative religions, are at the heart of these movements. As traditional religious structures have been eroded, esoteric beliefs, fundamentalist religions and cults of all sorts have proliferated enormously. So too has interest in the so-called para-sciences, in extrasensory perception and in alternative states of consciousness.

Emotional disturbance

Despite the best efforts of the counter-culture, the mainstream culture of mental health continues to focus on remedies for emotional disturbance, to the undoubted delight of the pharmaceutical industries. For most of the last 100 years, the entire complex edifice of mental healthcare has been has been built on the concept of emotional ill health. There is now a worldwide industry in helping people to cope with their emotions. Counselors, therapists, psychologists and psychiatrists of every sort are kept in business by a constant tide of people suffering emotional disturbances, problems of self-image, relationship or trauma across a scale from short-term depression to complete breakdown. The problems are not confined to the clinically disturbed. Many people feel out of touch with their feelings. Consultancies and publishing houses have sprung up around the need to help often highly qualified professional people, to improve their communication skills, to restore their self-confidence and to help them relate to other people.

Soft skills

In recent years, there has been a growing movement in what is now called positive psychology and in particular in the study of happiness. There is also a growing recognition of the importance of what Daniel Goleman has called emotional intelligence, or EQ. Emotional Intelligence includes a range of personal and interpersonal qualities: being able to understand and express personal feelings; being able to get along with other people, to communicate clearly and with empathy for the listener; and responding positively and with sensitivity to new situations. These so-called 'soft skills' are now seen as crucial factors in productive relationships at home and in the workplace, and in emerging styles of leadership. People with high emotional intelligence are more likely to emerge at the top of organizations and to be able to lead them into an uncertain future. These are creative leaders who are more likely to coach and mentor their staff, rather than direct, in order to encourage them to develop their unique skills and abilities.

Business leaders often say that people currently entering the workforce seem weaker in these areas than earlier generations. The 'exile of feeling' may be more pronounced that ever. Goleman reports on a survey of pupils and teachers that shows "a worldwide trend for the present generation of children to be more troubled emotionally than the last: more lonely and depressed, more angry and unruly, more nervous and prone to worry, more impulsive and aggressive."[8] People around the world, he says, are facing the same kind of problems.

There are many factors to take into account. In the developed economies especially, the nuclear family is disappearing rapidly. Fewer people are getting married and among those that do, divorce rates are at historically high levels. Adults are spending longer hours at work, and give less time to their children. Whatever their home circumstances, many young people spend large amounts of time bonding with computers of various sorts rather than physically playing with other children. Parents' fear of crime means that few children are allowed out to play unless accompanied by an adult and, according to Goleman, miss out on the "games that used to be commonplace in residential streets that furnished children with all sorts of life skills such as an ability to control anger and settle disputes."[9]

Somewhat closer to home, the fact that we are embodied beings and not just beings in bodies was made clear to me when our son James was twelve and preparing for important end-of-year examinations at school. A few weeks before they were due to take place, he asked whether, if he did well in the examinations, he could have a games computer. We said no. He asked what his incentive would be in that case, and we said that we would be very pleased with them. He was not impressed. As it happens, he did well and a few weeks later he raised the subject of the computer again. This time we relented, mainly because by then, I wanted one too. We went into town together and bought the computer, together with a set of games. I spent an hour setting it all up and left him to try it out.

Downstairs in the kitchen, our daughter Kate who was then eight, was standing with a length of old rope that she had found in the garden shed. She asked me if I would make her a swing. I found some wood for a seat and wrapped the rope around a bough of an apple tree and left her swinging happily backwards and forwards.

A couple of hours later, James came downstairs, saw her on the swing and dashed out to join her. They spent the rest of the day together on the swing and then the whole of the next day and virtually the entire summer. They invented games, new moves, tricks, circus routines and fantasy situations, all of which revolved around that swing. They laughed, argued, made up and carried on, and eventually wore a deep groove in the ground beneath it. Being outdoors and playing physically opened their imaginations and gave them much more pleasure than the hundreds of dollars worth of computer that was left on its own upstairs. Though I doubt that James would have been particularly motivated, had I said to him a few weeks earlier, that if he did really well in his examinations he could have the piece of old rope that was in the shed.

Many students, at all levels, now spend more hours on desk study and using computers than on physical activities and engaging face-to-face with their peers. The regimens of standardized testing in many countries mean that they also work under increasing pressure of competition. Many school systems have cut back on practical programs in the arts and the opportunities they offer for engaging with feelings. Significantly, there have been severe cuts too in physical education programs and all that they offer in connecting physical and mental energies.

But not every factor in education is new. The cultivation of feeling has long been marginalized by academic education. In the 1970s, Dr Anthony Storr, a lecturer in psychotherapy at Oxford University, said that he saw many examples of what he called "the Oxford neurosis," which he described as "intellectual precocity combined with emotional immaturity."[10] While it would be rash to attribute all forms of emotional disturbances to an excess of education, there is no question that formal education and training have played a part, at times a major part, in the exile of feelings from Western culture. The conventional academic curriculum largely ignores the

importance of developing the 'soft skills' such as an ability
to listen and to empathize. This is not a coincidence or an
oversight. It is a structural feature of academicism.

TWO TRADITIONS

For the past 150 years there has been a tension between the
world views that emanate from the Enlightenment and those
that come from Romanticism. A common theme is a commitment to individualism: though these two great cultural
movements offer different views of how a person becomes
an individual. I distinguish them as the 'rational individual'
and the 'natural individual'. Both views tend to compound
the division of intellect and emotion and they have different
implications for education and for creativity.

The rational individual

In the rationalist worldview, the individual possesses certain
qualities of mind, and these are what education should
promote. Many differences in systems of philosophy and
scientific investigations have evolved through the rationalist
view of the world. For all their differences they have some
common characteristics: the powers of logic and deduction
are the true hallmarks of independent thought; these powers
are the most reliable source of knowledge of oneself and of the
material world; true knowledge is objective and independent
of cultural values and personal feelings.

Approaches to education based on rational individualism
make common assumptions: Education should focus on
processes that promote a rational state of mind, especially
through cultivating the powers of logico-deductive reason.
A rational mind is developed through absorbing the various
bodies of knowledge that these logico-deductive powers have

generated. One of the main roles of teachers is to transmit
bodies of knowledge. In this sense, education is a form of
initiation.

The natural individual

Natural individualism makes completely different assumptions. In this view, every child is by nature a unique individual
with innate talents and sensibilities. Education should draw
out these qualities rather than suppress them with the values and ideas of the adult world. Education should not be
knowledge-based but child-centered. Naturalist models of
education make the following assumptions:

- Education should develop the whole child and not just their
  academic abilities. It should engage their feelings, physical
  development, moral education and creativity.

- Knowledge of the self is as important as knowledge of the
  external world. Exploring personal feelings and values is
  essential and so are opportunities to exercise imagination
  and self-expression.

- One of the main roles of teachers is to draw out the individual in every child. In this sense, education is a process of
  self-realization.[11]

Like those of rational individualism, the cultural roots of
natural individualism run deep. At the center of eighteenth
century Romanticism was the idea of the natural world. In
1780, Jacques Rousseau published *Emile*, in which he argued
for a new approach to education that was based on play, games
and pleasure. He wanted forms of education that cherished
childhood and did not impose adult values on young minds.
Over the next 200 years, many other pioneers of 'child-
centered' education argued, from different perspectives, for
the importance of play and creativity. Some developed their

own proprietary systems to promote it. They included: Johann Pestalozzi (1746–1847), Friedrich Froebel (1782–1852), Maria Montessori (1870–1952), Rudolf Steiner (1861–1925), Carl Orff (1895–1982) and John Dewey (1859–1952). For all of them, it was vital for education to encourage the development of children's natural abilities and personalities. They argued in different ways that children should be allowed to follow a natural pattern of development rather than a standard course of instruction. Like a sculptor, the teacher should follow the unique grain of each child's personality slowly revealing the individual within. In natural individualism there is a concern not only with intellectual development but also with emotional, spiritual and physical growth. Above all, naturalists wanted to address the whole child: mind, body and spirit.

The value of physical and imaginative play has been recognized by philosophers back to Plato and Aristotle, but the nineteenth century added a new perspective. Darwin's theories of evolution made human development a subject of scientific study. All human behavior was assumed to relate to the survival of the species. As babies and children spend so much time playing, play was now assumed to have a biological function. In the 1920s and 1930s, developments in the psychology of play combined with 'progressive' theories of education to influence mainstream education policy.

Throughout the last 100 years there has been a continuous line of people pressing for more creative approaches to education. In the USA, John Dewey developed new methods of teaching at his Laboratory School. At the Dalton School in New York and the Porter school in Missouri, teachers were encouraging 'learning by doing'. These ideas were part of a broader movement in the 1930s to encourage creativity and self-expression in schools. While John Dewey and others were promoting more liberal approaches to education, A.S. Makarenko (1888–1939) was developing his own system in Russia. The revolution had left millions of children orphaned and homeless. Makarenko devised a system of education based on practical work and collective responsibility. Recognizing the appalling emotional suffering of the children, he found tremendous value for them in creative activities, beauty and pleasure and organized an influential program of music groups, and productions of plays and dance. A report on elementary school education in the UK in 1931[12] said that education had to look to the whole child. It emphasized the importance of play, self-expression and creative activities, which "if the psychologists are right are so closely associated with the development of perceptions and feelings." The dominant tendency to see the school curriculum as a jigsaw of separate subjects had to be questioned and so too did presenting work to children simply as lessons to be mastered. Education had to start from the experience, curiosity and the awakening powers of children themselves.

Naturalist attitudes gained ground in education during the 1950s and 1960s, partly because they were seen as representing a more egalitarian approach to education. Naturalists argued that academic education marginalized feelings, intuition, aesthetic sensibility and creativity – the very qualities that make human beings human. In the 1960s and 1970s, the argument for self-expression and creativity in education was rooted in a concern to promote the life of feeling. This concern connected with far-reaching cultural developments in the personal growth movement outside formal education.

EDUCATING THE EMOTIONS

The various pioneers of naturalist approaches in education did not share a single philosophy or promote common practices, any more than all proponents of rationalist philosophies had a single point of view. They sometimes differed profoundly. Each offered their own highly nuanced conception of human development and their own sophisticated method of teaching and learning. As their ideas and approaches filtered down into the broad practices of public education, the general ideals of rational and natural individualism came to represent two distinct options: a choice between a traditional, subject-based, academic education and progressive, child-centered education. In their extremes, they seem to have little in common; but in two respects at least, they do share common ground.

First, they promote the idea of the individual breaking free from the constraints of culture. For the rationalists, the individual becomes independent of cultural influences by the power of rational, objective thought. Since objective knowledge exists independently of people and culture, the rational individual is free of cultural bias and sees the world just as it is. For the naturalist, the aim is to liberate the individual spirit from the pressures of culture and reveal the authentic self. Since every person is unique the authentic self will emerge like the butterfly from the chrysalis provided there is enough creative space in which to grow. In this respect, both of these ideals are *a*cultural.

Second, they reinforce the division between intellect and emotion. Personal Growth and natural individualism were reactions against *objectivism*: against treating knowledge as impersonal. I come back to this idea later. The danger lies in moving too far the other way, towards *subjectivism*: to thinking of individual consciousness as completely independent from the world of others.

Laing describes as *schizoid* the person who experiences a rent in his or her relationship with the world and in relationships with herself. The schizoid is thus unable to experience herself together with the world but rather in despairing isolation from it. If this exaggerates the dangers of subjectivism, the underlying principle still applies: that, if a person does not exist objectively as well as

"Feelings are a constant dimension of human consciousness. To be is to feel."

subjectively but only as a subjective identity, "he cannot be real." In other words, there has to be a healthy and positive relationship between our knowledge of the external world and our knowledge of ourselves. So what is the real relationship between knowing and feeling and what does it mean for being creative?

KNOWING AND FEELING

Descartes said, "I think therefore I am." As Robert Witkin pointed out, an equally powerful starting point would have been, "I feel therefore I am."[13] Feelings are a constant dimension of human consciousness. To be is to feel. Feelings encompass a wide range of subjective states, from calm intuitions to raging physical furies. In all cases, feelings are forms of perception. How we feel about something is an expression of our relationship with it. In that sense, feelings are evaluations: for example, grief at a death, elation at a birth, pleasure at success, depression at a failure, disappointment at unfulfilment.[14] We experience a wide range of feelings precisely because of the complexity of our perceptions: of events, other people and ourselves. For example, fear differs from anger because seeing something as threatening differs from seeing it as thwarting. These varied perceptions have different consequences both physiologically and in the behaviors that result.

In general terms, emotions are *intense states of feeling* that involve strong physiological responses. Two people falling into a canal may experience very different emotions. A good swimmer may feel angry or frustrated. Someone who cannot swim may panic. In both cases, they experience a strong emotional *arousal*. These are related to but different from emotional *attitudes*.

In fear or anger, the release of adrenaline primes the body for vigorous activity, to deal with the causes of the danger. Blood flow is diverted from the digestive system to the muscles; the heartbeat quickens, sugar is released by the liver, the sweat glands are stimulated, and so on. The emotional arousals we experience when faced with danger or extreme circumstances drive us to the necessary action, literally without thinking: to either 'fight' or 'take flight'. The floods of hormonal changes are not conscious decisions but ancient instincts that are born out of the need for survival. Our emotions have a powerful role in enabling us to anticipate threats, dangers, pleasures and opportunities that are essential to our sense of well-being.

If the physical action for which these changes prepare us does not happen, or is suppressed, we are left with a physical feeling of pent up anger or energy. The increased hormonal levels in the body, which would have been used up by those actions, must be slowly dispersed as our systems calm down. Emotional arousals subside as the situation changes and our physical condition settles; the pent up feeling will persist until this process is over.

If the incidents that provoked the arousal are repeated often enough – if you are continually bitten by dogs or frequently fall in canals – you may develop a general fear of dogs or canals; a latent feeling that can flare up when they are near or brought to mind. These feelings are a form of perception. We feel the feelings because of the way we think. The memory of the previous event will trigger a repeat response.

Research suggests that the seat of many of our emotional responses lies deep within the parts of the human brain that were among the first to evolve. This area of the 'old' brain includes the amygdalae: almond-shaped groups of nuclei in the medial temporal lobes of the brain that are part of what is sometimes called the limbic system. The older regions of the brain have fundamental roles in regulating the basic bodily functions that sustain life, including breathing and the metabolism of other organs. They are involved in controlling stereotyped reactions and movements and do so without reference to the slower processes of conscious thought. Rational, abstract thought developed at a much later stage in the evolution of the brain and is strongly associated with the neo-cortex, the convoluted folds lying across the surface of the two cerebral hemispheres, and the development of the frontal lobes.

The old brain does not think or learn in the usual sense. As Goleman notes, it is a more a set of pre-programmed regulators that keep the body running and reacting in ways that ensure survival. This does not mean that feeling and reason are separated and insulated from each other. All areas in the brain are connected through intricate neural circuitry. There is a "continual dance between intellect and emotions, feeling and reason, which is essential to the proper functioning and maintenance of both."[15] In a sense we do have two different ways of knowing the world and interacting with it, the rational and the emotional. This distinction roughly approximates to the folk distinction between heart and head; "knowing something is right in your heart is a different order of conviction, somehow a deeper kind of certainty, than thinking so with your rational mind."[16] There is a steady gradient in the ratio of rational to emotional control over the mind; the more intense the feeling, the more dominant the emotional mind becomes and more ineffectual the rational. This is an arrangement that seems to stem from "the eons of evolutionary advantage to having emotions and intuitions guide our instantaneous response in situations where our lives are in peril, and where pausing to think over what to do could cost us our lives."[17]

As we mature, the balance between reason and emotion changes, or should do. Newborn babies are convulsed by their emotions, by feelings of hunger, distress, or contentment. They express them through noises, facial expressions and movement. Toddlerhood and adolescence, the two periods of acute developmental transition from babyhood to childhood and from childhood to adulthood, are famously times of turbulent emotions and mood swings. As the adult emerges from the child, there is a normally a growing control of emotions. Consequently, we are alarmed if adults act like infants, howling in meetings or crying in frustration at not getting their own way; and we are right to be disturbed by adults whose emotions are out of control.

But growing up and becoming mature is not about suppressing feelings, or discounting their importance. In the intricate ecology of consciousness, "the emotional faculty guides our moment-to-moment decisions, working hand-in-hand with the rational mind, enabling or disabling thought itself."[18] Likewise, the thinking brain plays

"The relationships of thinking and feeling are at the heart of the creative process in all fields, including the arts and the sciences."

an executive role in our emotions, except in those moments when emotions surge out of control and the emotional brain runs rampant. The intellect cannot work at its best without emotional intelligence. Maintaining a balance between them is essential to a balanced personality. The relationships of thinking and feeling are at the heart of the creative process in all fields, including the arts and the sciences.

ARTISTS AND SCIENTISTS

Among the legacies of the Enlightenment and Romanticism are many common-sense but mistaken assumptions about the differences between the arts and sciences. The sciences are thought to be about knowledge, facts and objectivity: the arts about emotions, self-expression, being, and subjectivity. The sciences apparently lead to pure knowledge, the arts to personal introspection: the sciences are useful, the arts dispensable.[19] Scientists are pictured as methodical, clinical and objective; artists as expressive, impassioned and creative. In reality there are many similarities in the creative processes of the arts and sciences and much closer connections between them than is commonly thought. Both have objective and subjective elements: both draw on knowledge, and feelings, intuition and non-logical elements. Both involve personal passions and both can be highly creative. Science as well as the arts can have considerable influence on how we feel about the world and on the world we have feelings about. These features of arts and sciences have implications for how we should think about creative processes and for how they should be provided for in education and training.

Discussing the arts and sciences opens up complex issues of definition. Science covers an enormous range of disciplines and fields of interest, from the natural sciences to the physical, to the study of human personality and social systems. The arts, too, cover a wide range of practices, styles and traditions both historically and in different cultures: from the fine arts, to craft and design, to traditional folk arts. For the sake of this discussion, let me compare the extremes of each spectrum: the physical sciences, which are concerned with the inanimate world, and the fine arts, which are concerned with human sensibilities.

The work of the sciences

The main process of science is *explanation*. Scientists are concerned with understanding how the world works in terms of itself. Science aims to produce systematic explanations of events, which can be verified by evidence. The implicit assumption is that it is possible to develop 'a theory of everything' and that individual scientists are contributing to a collaborative mosaic of explanatory ideas. Scientists aim to stand outside the events they are investigating and to produce knowledge that is independent of them: knowledge that would be true for whoever repeated their observations. The dominant mode of scientific understanding is logico-deductive reasoning and the production of propositional knowledge.

It is sometimes assumed that the sciences are "above reproach, beyond social influence, conceived in the rarefied atmosphere of purely scientific inquiry by some process of immaculate conception."[20] The reality is rather different. Science is the work of living, breathing human beings. The apparently impersonal process of scientific inquiry involves a very personal commitment by the scientist in four ways: the choice of problems; the methods of scientific inquiry; personal judgment; and standards of objectivity.

Whose problem is this?
One of the scientist's first moves is to identify an area of inquiry, a set of problems, which engages his or her interest. This decision may be wrapped in a web of personal interests and motivations. The history of science is one of individuals becoming passionately engaged in specific issues that draw their personal energies. Michael Polanyi talks of the intellectual passions of science. Passions are expressions of value. Positive passions mean that something is important to us. People who have achieved great things in a given field are generally driven by a love for it, a passion for the nature of the processes involved. The term 'flow' has been used to describe times when we are immersed in something that completely engages our creative capabilities and draws equally from our knowledge, feelings and intuitive powers. These peak performances typically occur when someone is working in their element at the peak of their performance. The excitement of the scientist making a discovery, "is an intellectual passion telling us that something is precious and more particularly that it is precious to science."[21] This excitement is not a by-product of scientific investigation but part of the process itself: an essential personal commitment to the issues being investigated.

The scientific method
Scientists, like everyone else, are rational only to the extent that the conceptions to which they are committed are true. Descartes wanted to see through common-sense assumptions about the world to achieve a more rational sense of reality. His method was to substitute one set of assumptions with another, in this case the principles of deductive reasoning of mathematics and geometry. He wrote in his *Discourse on Method*: "The long chains of simple and easy reasoning is by which geometers are accustomed to reach their conclusions of their most difficult demonstrations lead me to imagine that all things to the knowledge of which man is competent are mutually connected in the same way."[22] Just as Descartes accepted the assumptions of mathematics and geometry, all scientists accept the legitimacy of certain methods and modes of procedure. They identify themselves with particular frameworks of interpretation and rely on their reliability. The astronomer "presupposes the validity of mathematics, the mathematician, the validity of logic and so on."[23] The whole framework of scientific inquiry would collapse if these structures were proved faulty. And this does happen. The great paradigm shifts in scientific understanding described by Thomas Kuhn (see Chapter 4) have come about precisely when the existing, dominant structures of thought have proved inadequate.

Personal judgment
Although scientists accept such frameworks, they do not determine the course of any particular scientific inquiry. Scientists need to formulate hypotheses and to design experiments. In doing so, they exercise considerable personal judgment. And when all the statistics have been coded and calculated, the columns and data carefully set out on the computer screen, there is still a need to analyze and interpret them – to give them meaning. At the heart of all scientific undertakings there is an element of personal judgment, which cannot be eradicated:

nor should it be. The capacity for personal judgment is probably the most sensitive instrument a scientist has.

I remember when I was in my final year at school, having various arguments with a friend, Allen. Like Mr Spock in *Star Trek* he often contradicted an argument by saying that it wasn't logical. I asked him one day why he had such confidence in logic. He was stumped. He couldn't say. He had simply come to think of logic as the only way to think. It is often assumed that this is the case and that science and mathematics are the best practical examples. But do scientists *limit* themselves to logical analysis? Logic is one of the methods that scientists use at key points in the process of scientific inquiry. But there are others that are not logical at all. Intuition can be equally important to scientific investigation.

There is a point in scientific inquiry where logic is not the best instrument. Discovery in science often results from unexpected leaps of imagination: the sudden jumping of a logical gap, in which the solution to a problem is illuminated by a new insight, a new association of ideas or a vision of unforeseen possibilities. Many of the great discoveries were made intuitively. Scientists do not always move along a logical path. They may sense a solution or discovery intuitively before an experiment has been done and then design tests to see if the hypothesis can be confirmed or proved wrong. Every attempt is then made to be as methodical as possible. But although rational analysis plays a part, it is only part of the real process of science.

Successive approximations
Objectivity is no guarantee of truth. Scientific arguments may be objective: they are not necessarily true. It is perfectly possible to be objective and wrong. In the Middle Ages, scientists and the population believed that the sun moved round the earth. They saw it happen every day. Their conclusion was perfectly objective and completely wrong. Objective meanings

are those that are tested using criteria that are agreed by particular communities. Scientists use methods and criteria that are agreed within the communities of science. This does not mean that objective meanings are impersonal; nor can they be. They are not *im*personal: they are *inter*-personal. This does not guarantee that they correspond with the way things are. The reason is that, "the world of objective knowledge is man-made."[24]

Scientific knowledge is subject to revision as new evidence comes to light or new ideas emerge. Scientific understanding is the product of the creative mind. The essential process of science is argument and debate, of challenging or building on existing knowledge in the light of new ideas or evidence. This is the intellectual excitement and creative impulse of science. It is concerned not only with facts but also with what count as facts: not only with observation but also with explanation and meaning. In all of these respects, creativity is at the heart of science.

The work of the arts

The main process of art is *description*. Artists are involved in describing and evoking the *qualities* of experience. The poet writing of love or melancholy is trying to articulate a state of personal being: a mood or sensibility. A composer may try to capture a feeling in music and to invoke it in the listener. Artists are concerned with understanding the world in terms of their own perceptions of it: with expressing feelings, with imagining alternatives and with making objects that express those ideas.

At the heart of the arts is the artifact. Artists make objects and events as objects of contemplation. Composers make music, painters make images: dancers make dances, and writers produce books, plays, novels and poems. In its materials, sensuous and aesthetic qualities, the form of the work embodies the meaning. The artist is not concerned with systematic explanation but with producing unique forms of expression that capture the qualities of his or her personal insights and experience.

Artists deal with ideas on any topic that interests them. These may be social or political ideas, especially in drama, film or literature, because these deal directly with the actions of people and their motivations. They may be interested in formal questions and ideas about their own disciplines. This was one of the driving concerns of modernism in music, theatre, literature and in painting. Formalism, conceptualism and cubism, and all the rest, were concerned with exploring the nature and limits of art forms themselves.

There is a difference between expressing feelings through the arts and simply giving vent to them. The process of the arts is centered on making things. Artists are not just expressing feelings, but ideas about feelings; not just ideas but feelings about ideas. In doing this, they can draw from all areas of their being. The writer E.M. Forster said that in the creative state, we are taken out of normal ways of thinking: we let down a bucket into our subconscious and may draw up something that is beyond the reach of our conscious minds. An artist, says Forster, "mixes this thing with his normal experiences and out of the mixture he makes a work of art. The creative process employs much technical ingenuity and worldly knowledge; it may profit by critical standards, but mixed up with it is this stuff from the bucket, which is not procurable on demand."[25] The process of the arts is to give shape, coherence and meaning to the life of feeling.

"It is not what interests artists or scientists that distinguishes them from each other, but how it interests them."

Artists do not generally spend their days in states of emotional ferment. Artists do produce original work and at their best they are highly creative. But the daily work of the arts can involve a huge amount of practical routine. Watch a dance company in rehearsal or a musician practicing an instrument. Writing novels and composing poems is as much a diligent craft as a process of inspiration. Creativity in the arts, as in the sciences, requires control of materials and ideas and great discipline in honing exact forms of expression.

Meaning and interpretation

Responding to works of art and trying to make sense of them for ourselves is also a creative process. In watching a drama, the audience is not faced with reading something that it can unravel systematically by reading off its meaning like a computer print out. Like the actors and director, the audience is involved in interpreting what it sees. A play is open to interpretation on two levels: what is expressed in the play and what is expressed by the play. We interpret what is being expressed in the play as it unfolds before us, by following piecemeal the actions of the characters. It is only when the play is over that we can make our sense of the play as a whole.

I say our sense because what the play means for us may be quite different from its meaning for the actors, the dramatist or the director. The rich three-dimensional world that the dramatist seeks to invoke exists on the page in an abstract form from which it is impossible to derive the performance itself purely by logical means. Giving the world of the drama a living form involves the director and actors in a sustained effort of interpretation, which draws heavily on intuition, skill and cultural knowledge. It is for this reason that memorable performances are indelibly stamped not only with the original creative work of the dramatist but with that of the actors who bring it to life: Gielgud's Hamlet, Warner's Hamlet and so on.

A written play suggests a performance; it does not determine it. Jerzy Grotowski (1933–1999) observed that all great texts represent a sort of deep gulf for us: "Take Hamlet. Professors will tell us that they have each discovered an objective Hamlet. They suggest to us revolutionary Hamlets, rebel and impotent Hamlets, Hamlet the outsider etc. But there is no objective Hamlet. The strength of each great work really exists in its catalytic effect. It opens doors."[26]

There are often deep disagreements over the judgments people make about works of art, which differ according to personal tastes and cultural values. The significance of a work of art cannot be measured with a slide rule. This doesn't mean that it cannot be judged at all. There is a difference between unsubstantiated personal opinion and reasoned judgments. Objectivity means that judgments are being made according to criteria that are publicly available and with reference to evidence in the work itself. In this sense, it is as legitimate to talk about the objective processes of making and understanding art as it is about anything. To assume that artistic judgments are simply personal opinion is as mistaken as assuming that all scientific opinion is undisputed fact. Meaning and interpretation are at the heart of all creative processes.

Although discoveries are often associated with particular scientists, they are not seen as unique to them in the way the paintings are to the artist who produced them. In 1959, Watson and Crick discovered DNA and described its structure as the building blocks of life. Although they were the first to discover DNA, they were not responsible for it being there in the first place. Any scientist who follows the same route of inquiry and calculations as another will reach the same conclusions. If not, there would be concern about the evidence or procedures. The same is not true of the arts. Two or more artists would almost certainly produce different outcomes from the same starting point. Mathematicians or scientists may be the first to produce particular intellectual work: painters, poets or dancers are the only ones to produce the work. It is always unique to them.

Artistic work is personal in a sense that is not true of equations and calculations in mathematics, where the ability to replicate results fundamental to the validity of the work. This not the case in the arts and it is because artists' works are unique to them that biographical enquiries are interesting to academics.

A work of art can be about anything at all that interests an artist; just as a scientific experiment or theory can be about anything that interests a scientist. Artists and scientists can be interested in the same subject: painters and geographers may share the same passion for the physical landscape; novelists and psychologists for human relationships; poets and biologists for the nature of consciousness. It is not *what* interests artists or scientists that distinguishes them from each other, but *how* it interests them. The difference lies in the types of understanding they are searching for, in the functions of these processes and in the modes of understanding they employ. Artists and scientists are not always different people. In the Renaissance the individuals roamed freely over both the domains that we now think of separately as arts and sciences.

The recognition of common creative processes in the arts and the sciences has led to a wide range of collaborative projects and to the early dawning of what may prove in our own times to be a new Renaissance. It is a Renaissance based on a more holistic understanding of human consciousness; of the relationships between knowing and feeling; and of how all that we think and feel is part of the creative process of making sense of the world around us and of the worlds within us.

CONCLUSION

A world without feelings would be literally inhuman. Our most damning criticisms are focused on people who lack human sensibility. Yet our education systems do far too little to address this human dimension of our personalities. Louis Arnaud Reid puts it this way: "The neglect of the study of feeling and of its place in the whole economy of the mind has been disastrous, both in philosophy and in education. Sensitiveness plays far more part in understanding of many kinds than is generally understood and acknowledged."[27] Being sensitive to oneself and to others is a vital element in the development of the personal qualities that are now urgently needed, in business, in the community and in personal life. It is through feelings as well as through reason that we find our real creative power. It is through both that we connect with each other and create the complex, shifting worlds of human culture.

"It is through feelings as well as through reason that we find our real creative power. It is through both that we connect with each other and create the complex, shifting worlds of human culture."

YOU ARE NOT ALONE

"Individual creativity is almost always stimulated by the work, ideas and achievements of other people."

THE LONE GENIUS?

THE POPULAR IMAGE OF CREATIVITY is of the lone genius swimming heroically against an oppressive tide of convention pursuing ideas that no one has had before. There are numerous examples of iconic figures who have made groundbreaking contributions in their own areas of work. I have mentioned some of them in previous chapters; including Galileo, Isaac Newton, Martha Graham and others. But the image of the lone genius can be misleading. Original ideas may emanate from the creative inspiration of individual minds, but they do not emerge in a cultural vacuum. Only in the most exceptional circumstances do individuals live apart from and wholly unaffected by culture. Individual creativity is almost always stimulated by the work, ideas and achievements of other people. As Isaac Newton famously said, if he saw further than others, it was because he stood on the shoulders of giants. Even working alone, as some people do, there is an essential cultural dimension to creative work that is of profound importance for developing creative abilities.

DEFINING CULTURE

We live in two worlds, the inner world of personal conscious-ness and the outer world of material circumstances. In practice, our own ways of seeing the world are deeply influenced by our dealings with other people, not least by using shared forms of representation that we have created together, such as the languages we speak. We each have our own lives, but much of what we create is in common with each other. What we create in common is our culture. To use a phrase from the anthropologist Clifford Geertz (1926–2006), all human lives are suspended in "webs of significance" that we ourselves have spun. Creativity is the process by which these threads are formed and it is in our interactions with others that they are woven into the rich fabrics of human culture. Creativity and culture are the warp and weft of human understanding.

I define creativity as the process of having original ideas that have value. What does culture mean in this context? Like cre-ativity, the term culture is used in various ways. Since the late eighteenth century, culture in one sense has meant a general process of intellectual or social refinement. It is in this sense that a person might be described as cultured. Being cultured is associated particularly with an appreciation of the arts. By extension, culture also means the general field of artistic and intellectual activity.[1] A distinction is often made between high art and popular culture. 'High art' normally means opera, classical music, ballet, contemporary dance, fine art, serious literature and cinema. 'Popular culture' means commercial music, popular cinema, television, fashion, design and popular fiction and other forms that have mass appeal. It is this meaning of culture that economists usually have in mind when they talk about the cultural industries.

The term 'culture' is also used in a more general social sense to mean a community's overall way of life; including its patterns of work and recreation, morality, intellectual practices, aesthetics, belief, economic production, political power and responsibility. It is this broader social definition of culture that I will be using here. By culture I mean *the values and forms of behavior that characterize different social communities*.

I argued in Chapter 4 that human intelligence is diverse, dynamic and distinct. So too are human cultures. Each of these characteristics is significant for understanding the intimate relationships between creativity and culture.

A MATTER OF TIME AND DIFFERENCE

Our physical senses affect what we can perceive of the world but there are other factors that influence what we actually *do* perceive. Many of these factors are cultural. Different cultures commonly perceive the world in radically different ways. Some cultural differences are obvious, such as the languages people speak, the clothes they wear, the food they eat and the sorts of dwellings they inhabit. Other differences are harder to detect because they are deeply embedded in different ways of thinking. One example is cultural variations in the sense of time.

In 2001, my family and I moved from Stratford on Avon in England to live in Los Angeles, California. We found a very different sense of time. In Europe, a century is not considered to be a long time: in Los Angeles it is. Our home in Stratford on Avon was built in 1870 and was one of the newer properties in the area. It was still too soon to know if the neighborhood would really catch on. Our house in Los Angeles was built in 1937. In LA terms it is almost a heritage property. In Los Angeles, a century is a very long time. This may be why Americans use the word 'decade' a lot; similar to the way the British use 'century'. It must meet a yearning need for a sense of tradition. I heard a great example just after we relocated to LA. I was driving on the freeway listening to the local radio station and heard a commercial for a local car dealership. I missed the name of the company but caught the slogan: it was, "Proudly serving Los Angeles for almost half a decade!" That's what? Four years, maybe?

By way of contrast, in Asia, a millennium is not a big deal. On my first visit to Beijing, I had dinner, perhaps unsurprisingly, in a Chinese restaurant. It was a memorable meal in several ways. As a starter I chose 'black chicken soup'. I had assumed that 'black' was a figurative term that referred to broth or to the style of cooking, rather than to the condition of the chicken. I was wrong about that. The pieces of chicken were black all through; a color in meat that I usually associate with putrefaction. I was not wrong about that. For my entrée, and to the strong approval of the waiter, I chose a steamed garoupa fish. He took the order to the kitchen and a few moments later he reappeared with a round bamboo basket. He lifted the lid and gave me a look of eager inquiry. Inside was the fish in question still alive and flopping around with a look of confused panic in its eyes. I knew if I approved, I would be passing a death sentence. I know that animals do need to die if we are to eat them and that being squeamish like this is a feeble hypocrisy. Some cultures, including China, quite properly do not indulge in these ambiguities. Even so, I'm just not used to meeting my entrée.

I nodded weakly and fifteen minutes later the fish was back in front of me; steamed, garnished and reproachful. To delay eating it, I said to the waiter, truthfully, how much I generally enjoy Chinese food. I do; particularly if I have not been socializing with it beforehand. He thanked me but said that this was not really a Chinese dish. The Mongols, he said, had introduced this method of cooking fish into China 900 years ago. Clearly, in Asian terms, it was too soon to know if it would really catch on. It was barely a millennium. This could be a fad: a passing form of nouvelle cuisine.

Cultural differences in the sense of time can have profound consequences for how people live their lives and for politics. In 1972 President Richard Nixon was preparing for his historic visit to China. Evidently, his Secretary of State, Henry Kissinger, told him that the Chinese Premier and Foreign Minister, Chou En-Lai, was a student of French history. During his trip, Nixon asked Chou what he thought had been the impact of the French revolution in 1789 on western civilization. Chou En-Lai thought for a few moments and then said to Nixon, "It's too soon to tell." To an American President concerned about the next day's headlines, this panoramic sense of cause and effect could hardly be more different.

Human cultures are shaped by many factors, including geography, patterns of populations, access to natural resources and technology; and by political events, including wars, invasions and conquests. All of these interact with the various forms of shared understanding that their communities evolve over time to make sense of their lives. All cultures also consist of multiple elements within themselves; including their systems of government, of justice, education, social class, occupations, economic production and the arts, and whether these concepts even apply.[2] They include many subsets, cliques and countercultural groups that hold alternative sensibilities within the dominant culture. Human cultures are complex and diverse because human intelligence is in itself both rich and creative; like intelligence, cultures are not only diverse, they are highly dynamic.

"Human cultures are complex and diverse because human intelligence is in itself both rich and creative; like intelligence, cultures are not only diverse, they are highly dynamic."

DYNAMIC CULTURES

Culture, in the biological sense, implies growth and transformation. This is true of social cultures. The rate of change
varies enormously in different cultures and at different times.
In our own lifetime we are seeing exponential changes within
many cultural communities across the earth, as culture becomes ever more globalized and connected.

Just as individual intelligence is dynamic and interactive,
so too are the processes of cultural change. There are 'hot
spots' for certain brain functions: for language, recognition
of faces and so on. But in any activity many different areas
of the brain are used in concert with each other. The same
is true of the social culture. We can talk separately about
technology, the economy, legal systems, ethics and work, but
the lived experience of a culture can only really be understood
in terms of how all of these elements interrelate and influence
each other.[3] One example is the interaction of the arts with
technology.

The arts and technology

New technologies facilitate new forms of creative work. William Shakespeare is generally recognized as one of the greatest
writers to have ever lived. He was extraordinarily prolific and
gifted. But his work was entirely in the forms of plays and
poetry. He did not write novels. Why not? It would seem
the natural form for one of the world's greatest storytellers.
Shakespeare did not write novels because the idea probably
had not occurred to him. He was writing in the sixteenth
century. The novel only began to develop fully as an art form
in the eighteenth century. It germinated in the cultural conditions that evolved in the wake of the spread of printing. These
conditions included the means of print reproduction and
distribution that printing made possible and the consequent

emergence of a large literate class with an appetite for extended narrative. As literacy spread and methods of printing improved, the form of the novel gradually emerged. In the literate societies of the 21st century, the novel is one of the most popular art forms of all.

The modern orchestra is a musical apparatus that makes possible certain types of music. The classical tradition in western European music evolved with the advance of the orchestra and its constituent instruments of metal or wood. Classical music would not have developed as it did without the string, brass, and woodwind instruments, and the sounds that these instruments made possible for composers and musicians alike.

At the end of the nineteenth century a virtual earthquake disrupted the visual arts. For centuries, painters and sculptors had recorded the likeness of people, places and events. It was one of their main roles, and sources of income. The invention of photography broke their monopoly. It provided a quick, cheap and faithful method of visual record. The new technology caused agonies of debate; some centered on the Royal Academy in London, analyzing the status of this new technology. Some artists worried that photography would be the death of painting. Others argued that this was unlikely since a photograph could never be a work of art.

Within the context of established ways of thinking, the question was, "Could a photograph be a work of art?" In fact, photography was challenging the establishment with a more profound question about the nature of art. It was breaking the mould in which established ideas of art had been formed. As Walter Benjamin (1892–1940) put it, the issue was not whether a photograph could be a work of art, but what the development of photography meant for the definition of art itself.[4] As photography evolved in the 20th century into an art form in its own right, it came to be seen not so much as a threat to the visual arts, as a form of liberation.

Freed from the confines of figurative and representational work, painters explored new possibilities: from the expression of personal feelings to extending the limits of visual form through abstract and conceptual art. Technological innovations in the production of paints and pigments also opened up new creative horizons in painting. Impressionism was facilitated in part by the invention of flexible metal tubes for transporting paint, which made it easier for painters to work outdoors and capture the fleeting moments of light and landscape. Just as painters feared that photography would be the death of painting, theaters feared that film would be the death of their art form. Neither of these proved to be true. In the medium term, theater was released into a new period of great invention and innovation, from the 1920s to the 1950s in particular.

All technologies are neutral. What counts is who uses them and what they use them for. Any material, any tool in the hands of an artist, can result in a work of art. The fountain pen or a word processor in the right hands can result in sublime literature or a list of groceries. A camera in the hands of an artist may produce art that is as poignant and penetrating as anything produced with brushes and oil paints.

"It is an interesting feature of cultural change that, for a period of time, new technologies tend to be used to do the same old thing."

It is an interesting feature of cultural change that, for a period of time, new technologies tend to be used to do the same old thing. The early photographers tended to compose their subjects by mimicking the formal portraiture of oil painting. As the technology evolved, photographs gradually made possible other forms of visual record. Photography made it possible to capture real moments and events that painting could not. The introduction of the cheap, portable Brownie camera by George Eastman in 1900 made photography available to the masses and literally transformed the image of popular culture. Early moving pictures were like visual records of existing forms of theater: the directors simply pointed a stationary camera at a conventional melodrama. As cameras became lighter it was possible to move them to different angles. The invention of the movable focus made it possible to zoom in and out of the action and to create more intimate images. As filmmakers experimented with these new technical possibilities, the language of film began to emerge and, with it, the movies became a distinctive and legitimate field of artistic expression.

The interaction of creativity and technology is a two-way process. New technologies present fresh possibilities for creative work: and the creative use of technologies leads to the evolution and sometimes transformation of technologies. Cameras and pigments evolved as artists invented new techniques in using them. The same is true of the evolution of musical instruments and the techniques of recording.

Digital technologies are now putting in the hands of millions of people everywhere, unprecedented tools for creativity in sound, in design, in sciences and in the arts. Simultaneously they are providing completely new ways of distributing ideas and of collaborating in their development. In the process, the users are generating countless new networks and applications that are interacting with the design and production of software and hardware at every level. As the digital revolution gathers pace we can expect even more radical modes of creative production to emerge, whose consequences are as hard for us to predict now as those of photography were for the Victorian members of the Royal Academy.

Perhaps one of the most vivid examples of the dynamic nature of culture is the rate at which spoken languages evolve. All living languages are dynamic. New words and expressions emerge continually in response to new situations, ideas and feelings. *The Oxford English Dictionary* occasionally publishes supplements of new words or forms of expression that have entered the language. Some people deplore this kind of thing and see it as evidence of deteriorating standards and as a drift from correct English. But English has been in a constant state of evolution since its inception. It was only in the eighteenth century that any attempt was make to formalize spelling and punctuation of English at all. The language we speak in the 21st century would be virtually unintelligible to Shakespeare, and so would his way of speaking to us. Alvin Toffler quotes an estimate that of the 450,000 words in general use in the English language now; Shakespeare would have understood perhaps 250,000. That means, if Shakespeare were to materialize in London or New York today he would be able to understand on average only five out of every nine words in our vocabulary. As Toffler engagingly puts it, if he were to be here now, "the Bard would be a semi-literate."

"If Shakespeare were to materialize today he would be able to understand on average only five out of every nine words in our vocabulary."

DISTINCT DIFFERENCES

Human culture consists of ideas and beliefs that constitute what some philosophers call 'Weltanschauung', or world view. Different world views give rise to different ways of evaluating experience and to different forms of behavior. You see examples of Weltanschauung in the discrete worlds that are portrayed in novels, films and theater. Within each play and every genre, only certain sorts of behavior make sense: the same behaviors in another context might be incomprehensible. The playwright, Nicholas Wright, argues that the job of the writer, director and actors is to define the world that the play inhabits and within which the action is plausible. In Middleton and Rowley's Jacobean tragedy *The Changeling*, for example, the only alternative that the heroine Beatrice Joanna sees to marrying her unwelcome suitor is to murder him: "Today young women would see other possibilities. But these possibilities don't have a place in a production of the play. It's the job of the director to present a social world where no other choice is open to her, and it's the job of the actress to present a woman who can't imagine one."[5]

Cultures are essentially systems of permission. All cultures have their own codes of conduct. Being in a culture depends on understanding these codes and knowing what counts as acceptable and unacceptable in the forms of language, dress, behavior and observance. Cultural approval and rewards are given for some forms of behavior and disapproval and sanctions for others. These systems of permission can be formal: enshrined in laws and enforced by judicial punishment. They may also be informal: embedded in social attitudes and expressed in tones of voice and body language. Since individual identity is so often linked to cultural acceptance, breaking the conventions of the group can take genuine courage and in some instances can carry the constant threat of social penalties and exclusion.

If we look at the codes and conventions of other communities, especially those that are distant from us in place or time, we can describe objectively the ways in which they are different; whereas it is much more difficult to grasp the subjective experience of being part of them. Cultures are infused with sensibilities values and feelings. What strikes us when reading novels and plays written in other times is not only the differences in practical circumstances in which people live but also in their sensibilities: how they saw things, what mattered to them and the feelings they had and expressed.[6] It is for this reason that factual accounts of other cultures cannot capture their full living complexity. If you want a real sense of the lived experience of other times and communities it can be more effective to listen to their music, eat their food, absorb the imagery, hear their poetry and move with their dances. It is in these forms of expression that the feeling of a culture is most tangible.

Very many people now live within interweaving cultural communities. Those who migrate physically to a new country or to a different region may find themselves in quite different cultures. The children of immigrant families often have lives that are bicultural or multicultural: speaking two or more languages or dialects; one with friends at school or work, another at home with family. They need constantly to recalibrate their cultural sensibilities as they move between these different groups and be mindful of their different codes and customs.

The processes of cultural reinforcement are fundamental to the stability of the community. The socialization of the young arises partly from the need in society, "to reach a basis of stable expectation from today. That stability depends upon the same expectations being constantly realized despite changes in personnel." This is not to say that these conventions do not evolve. They do, especially from one generation to another. Although one generation may train its children in social character, new generations develop their own structures of feeling which are transmitted via their peers and the social norms of the time, which may differ in fundamental ways from those of their parents. It is here most distinctly that the new generation responds in its own ways to the unique world it is inheriting, reproducing many aspects of the culture, "yet feeling its whole life in certain ways differently and shaping its creative response into a new structure of feeling."[7]

"Human cultures are constantly evolving through the thoughts, feelings and actions of the people who live in them."

LIFE IS NOT LINEAR

In some senses, culture is an organic term that suggests living processes of growth and development. Human cultures are constantly evolving through the thoughts, feelings and actions of the people who live in them. Like the course of each individual life, the broader processes of cultural development are not linear; nor are they easy to predict. They are dynamic, organic and complex. The processes of cultural change are often hard to understand with hindsight and impossible to plan in advance. Let me give three short examples.

In the 1950s and 1960s, rock and roll swept through the Western world like a tidal wave. In its many forms, it galvanized a generation of baby boomers and outraged the sensibilities of many of their parents. The stars of rock and roll drew from a huge variety of cultural sources: the blues, country and western, jazz and swing, traditional folk music and many forms of dance. It is impossible to imagine the course of rock and roll being planned out in advance by a government cultural committee: an earnest group of civil servants listening to scientifically calculated variations on three chords, with a plan of action plotted against a statistical graph of the baby boomer generation. No one did or could have predicted the cultural influence of rock and roll. On the contrary, the policymakers who thought about it at all tried to ban it. The phenomenon caught fire as it did because it fed on a highly combustible mixture of creative energy and cultural rebellion. You might say that rock and roll succeeded because it challenged the dominant Weltanschauung and expressed a new Zeitgeist: a new philosophy and spirit of the times.

Interestingly, the great surge in rock music in Britain in the 1960s and 1970s owed little if anything to music education in schools or colleges. Some of the most notable figures in rock music at that period attended higher education. But they did not choose go to music schools. They went to art colleges. The pedagogic traditions in art schools provided an atmosphere of experimentation, personal creativity and hip culture that was totally lacking in the formal conservatoire atmospheres of the music schools. In all these respects the art colleges provided an unexpected breeding ground for rock culture: another example of the non-linear nature of cultural trends. A second example is the escalating growth of social media in the present day. When Bill Gates and Paul Allen were developing their fledgling company, Microsoft, in the 1970s; when Steve Jobs and Steve Wozniak were building their alternative personal computer in the 1980s; when Tim Berners-Lee was wondering in Switzerland if he could connect the databases of computers into a world wide web; not one of them had in mind the phenomena they would facilitate in the early 21st century. Google, Twitter, Facebook, Flickr and thousands of other forms of social media are now spreading virally throughout global culture. These extraordinary movements are being driven by a primal human impulse to connect with each other and share ideas and information. Even the most sophisticated technologies only change the world when they connect with basic human instincts. When they do, their impact is unstoppable.

A third example of non-linearity is the fate of the cell phone. In the last decade or so, the cell phone has been the dominant platform for digital communications. Since the advent of the iPhone and its many imitators, thousands of applications have been added that have converted the cell phone into a digital cornucopia of new experiences and possibilities. For a generation of young users, the musical, visual, and gaming capabilities of smart phones leaves little time or inclination for making actual phone calls. Young people currently prefer to text each other rather than speaking on the phone. The result is that in the two years from 2008, there was a 30 percent drop in the use of phones for voice calls and a corresponding fall in the revenues of the phone companies who were so keen to encourage the sale of the phones in the first place. As with many cultural trends, it was impossible to predict.

CULTURE AND CREATIVITY

We are all "suspended in webs of significance" and cannot help but be deeply influenced by the ideas of other people. Cultural knowledge is a complex web, about which each of us knows only a relatively small amount. There are some areas in which we can each claim to be relatively well informed or even expert. But there are many others in which we are amateur or plainly ignorant. We depend on the knowledge of other people for much of our own understanding of the world. We are laced together in networks of knowledge. In large communities and organizations these networks are highly complex.

"Creativity is about making connections and is usually driven more by collaboration than by solo efforts."

Most of our own knowledge comes from other people and it comes in many forms: from stories, anecdotes, theories, systems of belief, and so on. While some of our conceptions are based on first-hand observation, an increasing proportion of them are based on messages from other people, directly and through a variety of media. This was always the case, but the store of human knowledge is now doubling every ten years and the rate of expansion is accelerating.

One result is the increasingly intensive specialization in all disciplines: a tendency to know more and more about less and less. As knowledge expands, greater specialization is inevitable. The risk is that we lose sight of the larger picture, of how ideas connect and can inform each other. The output of modern science is so fast, for example, that any individual can properly understand only small sections of it. Individual mathematicians can usually deal competently with only a small part of mathematics. It is a rare mathematician who fully understands more than half a dozen out of 50 papers presented to a mathematical congress. According to Michael Polanyi, the very language in which the others are presented, "goes clear over the head of the person who follows the six reports nearest to their own specialty. Adding to this my own experience in chemistry and physics, it seems to me that the situation may be similar for all major scientific provinces, so that any single scientist may be competent to judge at first-hand only about a hundredth of the total current output of science."[8]

The creativity of a culture depends on how open these networks are and how easily we can access knowledge. Creativity is about making connections and more often than not, as we will see in the next chapter, it is driven by collaboration as much as, if not more than, by solo efforts.

For this reason, cultures that enforce strict boundaries between specialisms can inhibit potentially valuable forms of innovation. The division of arts and sciences in Western cultures, and especially in education is a case in point. Fortunately, there are now many ways in which artists and scientists are beginning to collaborate and to discover common ground. Two examples are new methods in the social sciences and innovative schemes linking the arts and the natural sciences.

'Thick description'

Early psychologists aimed to produce objective explanations of human personality and behavior. The hope was that they might even come up with rules and explanations for why people behave as they do, just as physicists were explaining the behavior of magnets and the laws of gravity. In the physical sciences, understanding these laws can be used to predict future events. Magnets do not behave as they do only now and then, or on Tuesdays. They do what they do.

The early pioneers of the social sciences, especially in anthropology, also modeled their work on physics and chemistry. They tried to behave as if they occupied a culture-free, scientific zone from which they could draw neutral conclusions about the people that they studied. Their research tended to picture other cultures, and especially little-known ones in Africa, Asia and America, as culturally primitive with incomprehensible and apparently childish belief systems. In the last 30 years, leading social scientists have moved in other directions. They have recognized that in some key respects the human world is not at all like the inanimate world of the natural sciences.

The geographer charting the movement of tides along a coast is not trying to fathom the tide's motives for this behavior. The inanimate world does not have reasons for what it does. It just does it. Scientists in these fields try to understand *how*, not *why*. People, on the other hand, do have reasons for what they do, even if they don't understand those reasons themselves. The social world is driven by purposes, feelings and values. It is composed of ideas and interpretations. The work of the social sciences is complicated for that reason. Scientists have their own values and preconceptions as ordinary human beings, which can color what they actually see.

The physical world owes no allegiance to any particular set of interpretations. Despite the successive reformulations of scientific theory, the physical universe just carries on being itself. What changes is how we make sense of it. This is not true of the social world. We construct that in a much more literal way through the institutions we create and the relationships we enact. For Clifford Geertz, the task of the social scientist is essentially one of description and interpretation. Understanding human cultures, he says, "is not an experimental science in search of laws but an interpretive one in search of meaning."[9] Alongside conventional methods of statistical analysis, social scientists are increasingly using ethnographic techniques and forms of narrative description; what Geertz calls 'thick description', that mirror the skills of travel writers and novelists.

Arts and sciences

There is an increasing interest in direct collaboration between the arts and sciences. Many scientists have a deep interest in the arts: and a growing number of artists are taking inspiration from scientific ideas. They are also using advanced technologies to produce new forms of artistic expression. Scientists too are finding inspiration in the creative processes of the arts and in working with artists. One example is a highly acclaimed collaboration between fashion design and biological sciences.

Primitive streak

Between fertilization of the egg and the appearance of the recognizable human form, a single cell divides many times to produce millions of cells. Unchecked, cell proliferation leads to cancer, but the regulation of cell production during the development of the embryo ensures that the right kinds of cells form in the right place at the right time. Exactly how this happens is one of the most important questions in biology today. In the Primitive Streak project, fashion designer Helen Storey and her sister Kate Storey, a developmental biologist, worked together on a fashion collection chronicling the first 1000 hours of human life. The collection and associated research materials were eventually exhibited throughout Europe and the United States and in China, in art houses and science facilities. It attracted tens of thousands of visitors and challenged the commonly held belief that science and art are unable to communicate with each other. Helen Storey said later that the most notable feature of the many groups who visited the exhibition was their sheer diversity: young and old, those with a love of the arts, those with a life dedicated to science, and almost anyone in between.[10]

THE POWER OF IDEAS

As Victor Hugo said, "nothing is more powerful than an idea whose time has come" and there can be a powerful relationship between theory and popular culture. Most people do not have much time for theory. Yet their lives are constantly permeated by it. Ideas that originate in the laboratories of scientists, the studies of philosophers and the studios of artists sometimes seep deep into the culture, often without our realizing it.[11] Contemporary language is peppered with the jargon of psychology, for example. Bar room conversations refer to ego, sex drives, the Oedipus complex and other Freudian ideas as if these were simple facts of life rather than nineteenth-century theoretical propositions. Mothers bring up their babies according to the fads and fashions of developmental theories: breast-feeding or not, playing with them or not, stimulating them with music or pictures, depending on the seepage rate of theory into culture.Sometimes, the trickle becomes a tsunami.

In the 1960s, a disparate group of women, including Gloria Steinem and Germaine Greer, helped to trigger a social earthquake with the publication of a series of books on the principles of feminism. For very many people, not least men, feminism was a trauma. It hacked at the very foundations on which people had built their understanding of themselves, their families, their partners and their lives. It attacked some of the most cherished ideas about normal life: that men were the dominant sex; that a woman's place was in the home; that sex was a male pleasure and a female duty; that men had great ideas and that women cared and wept. These ideas ran rampant, as generative ideas do, through many different fields. They coursed through academic life, helping to recast the history of the arts and sciences. Academics revised the achievements of many men and women and the achievements of others were discovered for the first time. Feminist ideas challenged the structure of working life that propelled men to the top and kept women at the fringes of corporate life; they affected attitudes to relationships in the community and at home.

Over the next 30 years, a new wave of feminism followed the classic track of a great generative idea: huge initial excitement, followed by progressive refinement and specialization and eventually to increasingly narrow debates and contradictions about increasingly obscure points of interpretation. It gave way in the 1990s to a new phase of post-feminist thought in which some of the basic principles of the early writers were reviewed and recast. Along the way some of the most revolutionary early ideas had entered the cultural bloodstream and had become taken for granted as the natural way of seeing things. The word feminism itself, the need for equal rights and the concept of sexual harassment, have now entered the language and are taken for granted.

New ideas are not always new, and they rarely come out of the blue.[12] Many others had expressed the core ideas of the feminist movement of the 1960s, at many other times. From the suffragettes of the 1920s to the writings of Mary Wollstonecraft in the eighteenth century, many had contributed to the development of feminist perspectives long before they were recognized as such. The work of many of these women has been lost in the canons of the dominant male culture that they set out to criticize. Feminist ideas took hold when they did because of the particular sensibilities and cultural conditions of the time. They emerged from these conditions and helped to shape them. The idea of sexual liberty has more practical application when cheap and effective forms of contraception put women in charge of their own fertility. Before then, the advancement of women was held in check by the uncertainties of pregnancy and motherhood. Feminism developed hand in hand with technological advance. But it was also part of the general politics of liberation of the 1960s and 1970s that interacted with movements in civil rights, anti-authoritarianism and the expression of the individual: the emergence of the 'me' generation. In presenting a powerful intellectual analysis, feminist theorists helped to articulate a new structure of feeling. What are the real implications of 1960s feminism for civilization? It is still too soon to be certain.

THEORY AND IDEOLOGY

The rationalist view of the world is that is that human knowledge moves forward confidently on the basis of new theories building systematically on the old. This is not what happens at all. In practice, theories are as subject to social fashion as the length of skirts or the cut of lapels. A good deal of theory stays in relative oblivion. Throughout the world there are scientists, artists and philosophers producing new ideas of every sort. Yet certain ideas can suddenly capture popular imagination, despite the fact that at any moment there may be a multitude of theories all addressing the same issue. Each might be consistent with the observed facts and be as plausible as the next one. Political theories are a useful example of this. How do some rise to dominate the others? It's not always because they are better thought out.

"Theories are taken up not just because they are available but also because they meet a need."

Intelligence testing has held the attention of politicians and many educators against all comers from the 1900s to the present day despite the many conceptual and methodological flaws and the high social costs of these systems. Whatever principles govern theoretical fashions they are not simply a consequence of progressive development of better ideas. Other factors are at work. Theories are taken up not just because they are available but also because they meet a need.

Clearly theories are intended to be explanatory. But they are often taken up for other reasons too. Naturalist theories of education were influential in the 1950s and 1960s, not only because they were consistent with the facts of education as they then appeared, but because they *"Human cultures* expressed a mood among a generation of *are the outcome of* teachers. In the same way psychometric *human creativity."* theories previously tallied with the selective interests of public education. The significance of theory is not only explanatory: it is ideological. In an important sense, theory is expressive. It is part, but only part of the complex, organic web of human culture.

Human cultures are the outcome of human creativity. Even so, creative thinking and achievement thrive in certain cultural conditions and can be stifled in others. What does this all mean for leading a culture of creativity in specific organizations, including schools and businesses?

BEING A CREATIVE LEADER

"Creating a culture of innovation will only work if the initiative is led from the top of the organization. The endorsement and involvement of leaders means everything, if the environment is to change."

WHAT SHOULD LEADERS DO to promote creativity and innovation in organizations? There is no single strategy or template, mainly because all creative cultures are unique; but there are principles that apply to the most effective creative organizations. This chapter looks at the practical implications of the arguments I have presented throughout *Out of Our Minds* and identifies nine principles on which to develop a systematic culture of creativity and innovation.

LEADING A CULTURE OF INNOVATION

Organizations usually talk more about innovation than about creativity and there is a distinction between the two. In practice, a culture of innovation depends on cultivating three processes, each of which is related to the others.

- The first is *imagination*: the ability to bring to mind events and ideas that are not present to our senses.

- The second is *creativity*: the process of having original ideas that have value.

- The third is *innovation*: the process of putting original ideas into practice.

Innovation may focus on any aspect of an organization's work: on the introduction of new products, of new services or new systems. Innovation may be the aims, but the process of getting to it has to begin with imagination and creativity.

Aiming straight for innovation without developing the imaginative and creative powers on which it depends, would be like an athlete hoping to win a gold medal at the Olympic Games but with no intention of exercising beforehand. Just as success in athletics depends on building physical fitness, a culture of innovation depends on the processes of imagination and creativity that give rise to it. As Theresa Amabile of Harvard Business School puts it, "Creativity by individuals and teams is a starting point for innovation: the first is a necessary but not a sufficient condition for the second."[1] So what is involved in leading a culture of innovation?

Creating a culture of innovation will only work if the initiative is led from the top of the organization. The endorsement and involvement of leaders means everything, if the environment is to change. I was once asked to advise a major company that needed to improve communication between the senior management team and the front line staff who dealt with the clients. Evidently the staff had a lot of creative ideas for improvements in customer service, which the leadership was not taking seriously. I asked the person who wanted to hire me what the CEO thought of the situation. He said that the CEO did not think there was problem, but that the company would be appointing a new CEO in six months. In that case, I said, call me when you have the new CEO. In my experience, if the CEO does not think there is a problem that may well be the problem. In fairness, many leaders do have well-founded anxieties about promoting innovation. The first is that they will have to lead the way by coming up with a constant slew of new ideas. The good news is that the principal role of a creative leader is not to have all the ideas: it is to nurture a culture where everyone can have new ideas. The second anxiety is that unleashing creativity will lead to chaos and loss of control. The good news is that creativity is not a synonym for anarchy. Creativity and innovation work best where there is a balance between the freedom to experiment and agreed systems of evaluation. These anxieties about innovation are often born of the command and control mindset of leadership. Creative leadership involves more and also less than command and control. The starting point is to adopt a new metaphor for human organizations to replace the outdated idea of employees being mechanized cogs in the wheel of the business machine.

"Organizations are not mechanisms and people are not components. People have values and feelings, perceptions, opinions, motivations and biographies, whereas cogs and sprockets do not."

Mechanisms and organisms

In 1900, Frederick Taylor's *The Principles of Scientific Management* revolutionized the structure of organizations. His premise was that human organizations should work like machines and that the main role of leadership is to improve profitability by increasing productivity. Each worker should have clearly differentiated roles, and each task should be honed to make the best use of time, effort and company resources. At the heart of Taylor's approach were the principles of standardization, set routines and the division of labor.

Meshing as they did with the expanding interests of industrial production, Taylor's theories had profound effects on how organizations everywhere were run. It was based on these principles that Henry Ford developed the hugely successful manufacturing process for the Model T. 'Fordism', as it was known, went on to become the dominant template for industrial production for most of the 20th century and it has infused the cultures of many other types of organization too. Taylorism and Fordism continue in various guises to influence corporate cultures to the present day; from the Total Quality Management (TQM) movement of the 1980s to Motorola's Six Sigma strategy, which is still used widely today.[2]

The influence of the mechanistic metaphor remains deeply embedded in the mindsets of management. The management charts of many organizations bear close similarity to the motherboard of a computer. They consist of patterns of boxes, arranged in hierarchies, with horizontal and vertical lines indicating the directions of power and responsibility. These images add to the impression that organizations really are like machines. Especially in times of recession, there is tacit acceptance that fine-tuning the mechanistic model is acceptable: making optimal use of time and resources and paring away excess capacity in the interests of greater productivity. All of these may be good and necessary things in themselves, but the basic conception of the organization as a complex machine is fundamentally inimical to fostering the culture of innovation upon which the future of most organizations now depends.

Taylorism of course is not the only game in town. In the last 40 years, the principles and practices of organizational culture have become the focus of increasingly intense study. There are now myriad alternative schools of thought; many of them challenging the mechanistic metaphor. The groundbreaking works of Peter Drucker, Jim Collins, Warren Bennis, Tom Peters, Charles Handy, Rosabeth Moss Kanter, Clayton

Christensen, Meg Wheatley, Theresa Amabile and many others, have shed powerful light on the complexities of human organizations and of different styles of management and leadership. Business schools everywhere have generated a trove of research and a burgeoning library of management journals and books on every aspect of corporate culture. More and more companies and institutions are embracing the need for systematic innovation. There are many approaches, according to the size and nature of the organization. Implicitly or explicitly, they are all embracing a very different metaphor of organizational culture.

However seductive the machine metaphor may be for industrial production, human organizations are not actually mechanisms and people are not components in them. People have values and feelings, perceptions, opinions, motivations and biographies, whereas cogs and sprockets do not. An organization is not the physical facilities within which it operates: it is the networks of people in it. If a fire alarm sounds and all the staff head for the car park, there is no organization left in the building: it is all in the car park. Human organizations consist of people, relationships and energies. They are living, breathing communities that exist only in the actions and purposes of the people who populate them. For all of these reasons, human organizations are not like mechanisms: they are much more like organisms. Leading a culture of innovation depends on understanding the differences between these two metaphors and on shifting from one to the other.

Two cultural challenges

I defined culture earlier as the values and forms of behavior that characterize different social communities. Leading a culture of innovation means engaging with two cultural challenges: external and internal. In the natural world, successful organisms live symbiotically with their environment, drawing

nutrients and energy from it while at the same time helping to
sustain the environment in the process. This is not always true
of course. Some parasitic organisms destroy
their host environment by sucking the life
out of it. This is famously true of some
companies too. But let us assume we are
talking here of organizations that are ethical
and which conduct forms of business that
are sustainable and mutually beneficial.
If they are to survive, let alone flourish,
organizations need to have a vibrant internal culture, which
evolves symbiotically with the changing cultural environment
in which they are aiming to grow. The task of a creative leader
is to facilitate a resilient relationship between the *external* and
internal cultures.

*"The task of a
creative leader is to
facilitate a resilient
relationship between
the external and
internal cultures."*

The challenges of the external culture include technological
innovations, population change, new patterns of trade, fluc-
tuation in fiscal and monetary policies, global competition,
the increasing strains on natural resources, and the effects
of all of these on how customers and clients are thinking and
feeling.

The organization's internal culture can be thought of under
two main headings: *habits* and *habitats*. By habits, I mean
the patterns of everyday work. These include the formal
structures of management and accountability: the horizontal
relationships between divisions; and the vertical relationships, if any, between layers of management. The habits also
include all the tacit, informal codes of social behavior that
give each organization its own distinctive feel. Another way
of describing organizational cultures and subcultures is 'the
way we do things around here.' By habitats I mean the physical environments in which people work: the structures of the
buildings, the design of workspaces and of the equipment and
furnishings. The physical habitat can have a profound bearing
on the cultural mood of the organization.

THE ROLES AND PRINCIPLES OF CREATIVE LEADERSHIP

Being a creative leader involves strategic roles in three areas of focus: *personal*, *group* and *cultural*. Within each of these there are three core principles of practice. These are not linear phases or steps. They are organic processes that should feed into each other in a continuous cycle of mutual enrichment.

Personal

Everyone in an organization is capable of contributing creative ideas to its development. The first role of the creative leader is: *To facilitate the creative abilities of every member of the organization.*

Principle 1: Everyone has creative potential
Many organizations associate creativity with specific functions, often with marketing, design and advertising. While these can be highly creative fields, creativity and innovation are possible in everything an organization does. For innovation to flourish, it has to be seen as an integral purpose of the whole organization rather than as a separate function. Everyone in an organization has different experiences of how it works and potentially valuable insights on how it might be improved. I worked for a time as advisor to an international cultural organization, which also has a major art museum. I was having lunch in the cafeteria one day with the head of security. He was obviously irritated and I asked him what the matter was. He asked if I had heard about the study that had been commissioned by the management on how to improve the 'visitor experience' to the museum. I did know about the study and that a New

> "For innovation to flourish, it has to be seen as an integral purpose of the whole organization rather than as a separate function."

York firm of consultants had been brought in to conduct it. I asked him what the problem was. He said, "Why doesn't the senior management ask us?"

He was leading a large team of security staff who spent much of their time in the galleries and corridors, in the car parks and public spaces, interacting with the visitors and answering their questions. They helped visitors to find the restaurants and restrooms, directed them to the exhibits and often to particular works of art. He said, "My staff probably know more about the nature of the visitor experience than any other group in this organization, yet the management is spending a small fortune on a firm of outside consultants who've never been here before; and we're not even being consulted. Apparently, the leadership thinks the sole role of security is to slap people's hands if they try to touch the exhibits. It's insulting."

Consciously engaging the whole staff in the creative life of an organization can have huge benefits: unconsciously disengaging them can have expensive consequences. Those who are not engaged in their work are operating in 'neutral'. According to recent studies, this is true of about one in five 'high-potential employees'. In 2001, Gallup published a study that estimated that 'actively disengaged employees' were costing the US economy alone between $292 and $355 billion a year.[3] Later studies show that engaged employees, in contrast, are more productive, profitable and create stronger customer relationships. Workplace engagement is also a powerful factor in facilitating creative thinking on how to improve business processes and customer service. According to Gallup, 59 percent of 'engaged employees' *strongly agreed* that their job brought out their most creative ideas, while only 3 percent of 'actively disengaged employees' said the same.

Being a creative leader means ensuring that everyone in the organization is playing to their creative strengths and feels that their contribution is valued as part of the overall performance of the organization. This is one of the primary arguments that I make in *The Element: How finding your passion changes everything.*

Human resources, like natural resources, are often buried deep. In every organization there are all sorts of untapped talents and abilities. People join companies from many different backgrounds and with many different profiles, but they are usually perceived only on the basis of their educational background and current job descriptions. I meet many people who do not enjoy the work they do. They endure it. It's not their life's mission: it is what they do to make a living. But I also meet people who love what they do and who couldn't imagine doing anything else. They are in their element. To say that somebody is in their element means firstly that they are doing something for which they have a natural aptitude. It can be for any sort of work: administration, design, teaching, cooking, working alone or with other people. The essence of diversity is precisely that people are very good at very different things: what deters one person may have an irresistible attraction for another. But being good at something is not enough. Plenty of people do things they are good at but do not really care for. Being in your element is not only about aptitude, it's about passion: it is about loving what you do. One of the signs of being in your element is that time changes and an hour can feel like five minutes. You look up and you wonder where the time went. If you are not in your element, five minutes can feel like an hour. The clock seems to have stopped. Being in your element is about tapping into your natural energy and your most authentic self. When that happens, as Confucius once said, you never work again.

Identifying individual talents is not simply a matter of conducting a formal audit. There are some general tests for creative thinking and a growing battery of instruments for assessing personal strengths and aptitudes.[4] The nuances of individual creative capacities, combined with the many factors that motivate or suppress them, mean that the results of most of these tests give only the roughest indication of potential. The best strategy is usually to put people in situations and give them challenges that reveal their abilities; some of which they may have been unaware of themselves.

One specialist advertising company I know in New York has established its own university, which offers a range of classes by external speakers and by members of the company's own staff. The company's designers run courses on design, the copywriters on creative writing, and people from the finance on accountancy and financial management. The program encourages a greater understanding between departments of each other's work and helps to create a strong sense of common culture. It also develops the skill base of the company and has stirred up the internal talent pool. Several people have moved to other departments because they found that they were good at and enjoyed something other than the job they were hired to do.

"Being in your element is not only about aptitude, it's about passion: it is about loving what you do."

Principle 2: Innovation is the child of imagination
Nourishing imagination is an essential part of growing a culture of innovation. A good deal of creative work, especially in the early stages of a project, is about openly playing with ideas, riffing, doodling, improvising and exploring new possibilities. The eventual quality of what is done depends on this process of interweaving, of making fresh connections, of breaking with convention and seeing from different perspectives. Consequently, a creative organization, as Peter Richards puts it, "is first and foremost a place that gives people freedom to take risks; second it is a place that allows people to discover and develop their own natural intelligence; third, it is a place where there are no 'stupid' questions and no 'right' answers; and fourth, it is a place that values irreverence, the lively, the dynamic, the surprising, the playful."[5]

Pixar is one of the most innovative and critically acclaimed film studios in the history of the movies. Since launching *Toy Story*, its first animated feature, in 1995, Pixar has produced a host of feature films, short films, and a variety of industry changing technological innovations. To date, the studio and its staff have won over 100 awards, including: over 20 Academy Awards, a handful of Golden Globes, and Grammys and has earned more than $5.5 billion worldwide. In 2001 the Academy of Motion Pictures Arts and Sciences introduced the Academy Award for Best Animated Feature. All seven Pixar features produced since then were nominated for the Academy Award and five of them received it. Pixar knows something about corporate creativity.

Pixar has a fascinating culture. It includes the Pixar University, a program of workshops, events lectures and seminars that takes place on the Pixar campus every day. It offers over a hundred courses including a complete filmmaking curriculum, classes on painting, drawing, sculpting and creative writing. The university offers the equivalent of an undergraduate education in fine arts and the art of filmmaking. Perhaps what is most distinctive about the program is that every member of the Pixar payroll, including the animators, accountants, security guards, catering staff, technicians, production assistants, marketers and security guards, is entitled and encouraged to spend up to four hours of every working week in the Pixar University.

Randy Nelson was Dean of the University for twelve years. Formerly a juggler and co-founder of the Flying Karamazov Brothers, he says that the university is part of everyone's work. The reason being that everyone on the Pixar payroll is a filmmaker. Consequently, everyone is given access to the same curriculum and people from every level within the company will sit alongside one another in class. At one class on 'Lighting and Motion Picture Capture', the students included a post-production software engineer, a set dresser, a marketer, even a company chef, Luigi Passalacqua. "I speak the language of food," he said. "Now I'm learning to speak the language of film."

The university has powerful benefits for Pixar. Since anybody can go to any course, there is a constant flow of new ideas running through the whole organization. People are constantly meeting each other from different areas of the organization and are reminded that they are all part of a single effort. The skills that are developed in the university are essential everywhere within the organi-

"Being creative is not only a matter of inspiration. It requires skill, craft in the control of materials and a reciprocating process of critical evaluation."

zation. A drawing class doesn't just teach people to draw. It teaches them to be more observant, no matter what their usual role. Nelson says, "There's no company on earth that wouldn't benefit from having people become more observant."

The Pixar University crest features the Latin motto, *Alienus Non Diutius*, "Alone No Longer." Nelson says, "It's the heart of our model; giving people opportunities to fail together and to recover from mistakes together." Above all, the Pixar University is a highly practical way of energizing the imaginations of everyone in the company, of uncovering often-unknown personal talents, and of cross-pollinating the culture of the whole organization.[6]

Principle 3: We can all learn to be more creative
There are techniques, procedures and practical skills that can be taught to most people that will facilitate some sorts of creative activity. I referred in Chapter 1 to the use of brainstorming. This is one of a number of approaches that are designed specifically to facilitate the first mode of creative activity: the generation of ideas. But simply being asked to have ideas is not enough. I was once sent with 40 or so other academics on a training program called 'Managing a University Department'. In the first session I sat with seven

other heads of department including professors of sociology, engineering, physics and social sciences. Just before coffee we were asked to have a brainstorming session on the future of education. We were given large sheets of paper and thick marker pens and five minutes. (If you ever lose consciousness and wake up wondering where you are, check whether you have a thick marker pen in your hand and a large sheet of paper in front of you. If so, there is a good chance you're on a management course.) What followed wasn't quite the monsoon we had been led to expect. We ventured a few self-conscious thoughts and then fell into general conversation until the croissants turned up. This wasn't so much a storm, more light drizzle – a faint condensation on the walls.

Being creative is not only a matter of inspiration. It requires skill, craft in the control of materials and a reciprocating process of critical evaluation. These are abilities that can be taught. Consequently, professional development in the general skills of creative thinking (including how to work in creative teams) is an important feature of creative organizations.

Professional development is at the heart of creative cultures but often, as I noted in Chapter 3, organizations are reluctant to invest in it.[7] Many take a short-term view of training needs. This kind of short-term thinking can ultimately be counter-productive because it eats away at organizational loyalties and the sense of common purpose on which creative cultures depend. The better approach is to invest in the talents and loyalties of the staff.

For McKinsey the moral is straightforward: "You can win the war for talent but first you must elevate talent management to a burning corporate priority. Then to attract and retain the people you need, you must create and perpetually refine an employee value proposition, senior management's answer to why a smart, energetic, ambitious individual would want to come and work with you rather than with the team next door. That done, you must turn your attention to how you're going to recruit great talent and finally develop, develop, develop!"[8]

One solution is "to form smaller more autonomous units, create the maximum number of P&L jobs each business will bear and use special project teams to provide new challenges and ways of working together."[9] Another, as Pixar and others have shown, is for organizations to establish in-house universities and award their own qualifications. In 1981, Motorola was the first company in the United States to develop a corporate university (CU). Today there are hundreds of such initiatives throughout the world. One study[10] drew from case studies of twelve such initiatives.

A corporate university is "an internal structure designed to improve individual and business performance by ensuring that the learning and knowledge of a corporation is directly connected to its business strategy." A corporate university's students are drawn from its employees. It has the capacity to offer formal accreditation for some of the learning it provides. The principal purpose is to offer learning opportunities that advance the organization's goals: by developing a sense of corporate citizenship; enabling staff to understand the context and priorities of the organization's work; and developing the specific skills and aptitudes that give the organization its competitive edge. The benefits are also highly personal.

I once spoke at the national conference of an international hotel chain, which included the awarding of degrees to the graduates of the company's new corporate university. One of them told me that this was her first experience of educational success. She had done very well in the company even though she had failed at school. This was the first time she had been on an education program that had uncovered her real strengths and raised her self-esteem and confidence as a learner. Providing these opportunities is a core role of a creative leader and one of the rewards of a creative culture.

Group

More often than not creativity in organizations is driven by teams, where there is a flow of ideas between people who have different areas of expertise. The second role of a great leader is: *To form and facilitate dynamic creative teams.* Great creative teams model the mind: they are diverse, dynamic and distinct. This leadership role includes *forming* creative teams, deciding which people to bring together for which project; *focusing* teams, setting constraints, boundaries and expectations within which the team will work; and *resourcing* the team so that it is able to tackle the brief without avoidable frustrations of time and materials.

Principle 4: Creativity thrives on diversity
Creative teams are diverse. Just as intelligence in a single mind is interactive, so too, organizational creativity is often interdisciplinary. From research organizations to commercial companies, the best creative teams bring together people from very different backgrounds: people who think differently, who may be of different ages and genders, or with different cultural backgrounds and professional experiences.

IDEO is one of the world's leading design and innovation consultancies. Based in Palo Alto California, it has offices in Chicago, Boston, New York, San Francisco, London, Munich and Shanghai. Since its inception, IDEO has worked with dozens of organizations to develop hundreds of products in industries as diverse as toys, office equipment, furnishings, computers, medical applications and automotives. It has been regularly ranked among the *Business Week* top 25 innovative companies, and has offered consulting advice to the other 24. IDEO's expertise is not in any of the industries it advises: it is in the process of innovation itself.

> *"Diversity is a powerful resource for creative teams and in the workforce as a whole."*

At the heart of its work is a process it describes as 'design thinking'. A signature feature of this approach is that for each project, a team of specialists is brought together from different disciplines, including: engineering, product and industrial, ergonomics, behavioral sciences, marketing and market research. Together they explore the task from many different angles and develop a range of different possible solutions. Each of them is then prototyped, critiqued and tested until the final version emerges. The diversity of an interdisciplinary team is vital. As Tim Brown, the CEO of IDEO, explains, "a competent designer could always improve upon last year's widget, but an interdisciplinary team of skilled design thinkers is in a position to tackle more complex problems."

Diversity is a powerful resource for creative teams and in the workforce as a whole. Not all companies have woken up to this. There is still a tendency for leaders and managers at all levels to hire people who look and seem like themselves. While from a cultural point of view this may seem understandable it creates long-term problems for the flexibility and creativity of the organization as a whole. I have worked with a number of organizations on the need to develop a diversity strategy. One is an international investment bank with offices in Europe, America and Asia. The bank was proud of its diversity strategy though it evidently had some way to go. I remember being briefed by one of the all-male, white, middle-aged senior management team. I asked him how the diversity strategy was coming along. He thought the company was doing pretty well. "In fact," he said, "I'm interviewing a diverse candidate tomorrow." I asked him what he meant by a diverse candidate. He said, "You know, a woman."

Diversity, naturally, takes many forms. One dimension is innate characteristics, including gender, age and sexual orientation. A second is cultural background, including ethnicity and nationality. A third is personal background, including work experience, education and expertise. In a rapidly changing world, there are unanswerable ethical reasons for promoting a culture of diversity in the workplace. There are also strong strategic reasons, especially in relation to innovation. A more diverse workforce enables an organization to be more in tune with the needs of the changing cultural environment in which it is operating. It also provides a deep resource of different perspectives that is essential to sustain a culture of innovation.

Principle 5: Creativity loves collaboration

Creative teams are dynamic. Bringing people together from different disciplines is no guarantee of creative work. Diversity can be an obstacle to innovation unless teams have working processes in which differences become strengths rather than weaknesses. Collaboration is at the heart of Pixar's creative processes. Collaboration, as Randy Nelson observes, is not the same as cooperation. Cooperation only requires that the efforts of different people be synchronized in some way. They may be doing completely separate tasks at different times yet still be cooperating, as long as one supports the completion of another one. This is the typical *modus operandi* of industrial assembly lines and the linear processing of many administrative tasks.

"The creative impulses of most people can be suffocated by negative criticism, cynical putdowns or dismissive remarks."

Collaboration, on the other hand, involves people working together in a shared process in which their interaction affects the nature of the work and its outcomes. Collaboration is a process of improvisation that, according to Randy Nelson, has to be based on two key principles. First, all participants, "accept every offer that is made." The aim is not to negate other people's contributions but to build on them, a process known as 'plussing'. Second, "always make your work partners look good." The aim is not to judge what they produce but to help make something of it and raise everybody's game.[11]

The creative impulses of most people can be suffocated by negative criticism, cynical putdowns or dismissive remarks. Effective collaborators 'amplify' each other's contributions. Tim Brown from IDEO makes the same point. The process of design thinking is collaborative, "but in a way that amplifies rather than subdues the creative processes of individuals; focused but at the same time flexible and responsive to unexpected opportunities: focused not just on optimizing the social, the technical and business components of a project but on bringing them a need and a design response."[12] The IDEO slogan is "None of us is smarter than all of us."

The purpose of collaboration is to benefit from the stimulation of each other's expertise. *Vis Viva* is a teaching and research group of artists and engineers in the United States. A leading member of the group points out a common misconception about interdisciplinary groups: "The notion that we are trying to bring aesthetics to engineers or conversely bring a rigorous empiricism to artists is not the point at all. The point is both of these groups do both of these things in different ways. Our group attempts to foster creativity by creating space for interaction between disciplines and viewpoints."[13]

Creative teams are diverse and dynamic. They are also distinct. They come together for particular tasks and when the job is done they break up and reconvene in other groups. I once worked on a number of creativity events with John Cleese from Monty Python. The five members of Monty Python were very different people but they had a wonderful collaborative process where their differences became highly productive. Added together they were much more than the sum of the parts of the team and they achieved many things collectively that are unlikely to have been conceived had they not met each other. A great leader knows who to put in a team, what work to give each person on the team, and when it is time to move onto something else.

Principle 6: Creativity takes time
Creative insights can take time to develop, and creative organizations understand that time is an essential resource for innovation. Some offer staff discretionary time to work on their own ideas. Perhaps the best-known example is Google, where engineers can use 20 percent of their time for discretionary projects. During this time they can pursue any interest they like. If they do come up with an idea that would interest the company, they can pitch it to senior management team. Since 2005, 5 percent of all products that have been launched by Google were developed in the 20 percent discretionary time. The 20 percent allocation is a flexible provision. It is valuable in itself but also because it sends an important signal to the workforce that the company values creativity enough to give people the freedom to do what they are most passionate about.

> *"The processes of creativity can also be stifled by a sense that ideas are unlikely to be taken seriously if they come from the wrong places."*

Culture

The quality of the creative work of individuals and of groups is deeply enmeshed in the general culture of the organization as a whole. The third role of a creative leader is: *To promote a general culture of innovation.*

Principle 7: Creative cultures are supple
There is no single strategy for developing a culture of innovation. The internal challenge is to evolve structures and processes that are supple and responsive. Some companies set up specific innovation programs or labs. The benefit of these special units is that they can focus on innovation without affecting the rest of the organization. The disadvantage is that they may become detached from the general organizational culture and rejected by it when they try to reintegrate. Like

tissue rejection when organs from one body are transplanted into another, antibodies from the host culture can attack the alien ideas until they are neutralized or destroyed. Anyone who has been on an off-site training course might know this feeling when they go back to work on Monday and try to 'cascade' what they have learnt.

The processes of creativity can also be stifled by a sense that ideas are unlikely to travel *up* the organization or will not be taken seriously if they come from the wrong places. Innovation can be stifled by pressure from above to deliver results over the wrong timescale: by demands for the wrong sort of accountability. Loosening hierarchies means that those who run the organizations should be accessible to those who work within them. The need for continuous innovation involves reviewing some of the most established practices in leadership.

The 2010 IBM study, *Capitalizing on complexity*, found that CEOs who are capitalizing on complexity have focused their attention on three areas:

- **Embodying creative leadership:** Creative leaders consider previously unheard-of ways to engage more actively with customers and partners and employees.

- **Reinventing customer relationships:** With the Internet, new channels and globalizing customers, organizations have to rethink approaches to better understand, interact with and serve their customers and citizens.

- **Building operating dexterity:** Successful CEOs refashion their organizations, taking them faster, more flexible and capable of using complexity to their advantage.

The report concluded that, "creative leaders expect to make deeper business model changes to realize their strategies. To succeed, they take more calculated risks, find new ideas, and keep innovating in how they lead and communicate."

When John Chambers took over at CISCO Systems in 1995, the company had annual revenues of $1.2 billion. In fiscal year 2009, they were estimated at $36 billion. Reflecting on the growth of the company, and the challenges it now faces, he has had to rethink his own role as CEO.

When he became CEO, Chambers thought of his leadership role with Cisco in three main ways: first, developing a vision and strategy of the company; second, building the team to implement that strategy; and third, communicating the strategy within and beyond the company. After he had been in the role for four or five years, he began to think differently about his role as a leader. He began to focus especially on the company's culture. Great companies, he says, have great cultures. "A huge part of a leadership role is to drive the culture of the company and to reinforce it." He has also changed his style of leadership away from command and control to collaboration and teamwork. "It sounds easy to do, but it is hard, because you are trained that way in MBA school, in law school. Around 80 to 90 percent of the job is how we work together toward common goals, which requires a different skill set."

As at Pixar, IDEO and Google, the processes that drive the culture of innovation at Cisco are collaboration and delegation. Engineers, says Chambers, "are part business leaders, part artists, and you've got to know which hat they have on." He now sees the need for a fundamental change in ways of working "that may be really important to the future of business in this country and the world." At Cisco, the emphasis is increasingly on collaborative teams, on cross sector groups drawn from sales, engineering, finance, legal, and other departments. "We're training leaders to think across silos. We now do that with 70 different teams in the company. So we'll have a sales leader go run engineering. A lawyer go and run business development; a business development leader go run our consumer operations. We're going to train a generalist group of leaders who know how to learn and operate in collaboration teamwork. I think that's the future of leadership."[14]

Sir John Harvey Jones, the former leader of ICI, the international chemicals company, made the same point in this way: "Every single person in business," he said "needs to acquire the ability to change, the self-confidence *"In all cases, in-* to learn new things and the capacity for *novation involves* helicopter vision. The idea that we can win *calculating risks."* with brilliant scientists and technologists alone is absolute nonsense. It's breadth of vision, the ability to understand all the influences at work, to flex between them and not be frightened of totally different experiences and viewpoints that hold the key. We need every single pressure from business at the moment to make clear that the specialist who cannot take the holistic view of the whole scene is no use at all."

Principle 8: Creative cultures are inquiring
Innovation involves trial and error, being wrong at times and sometimes having to back up and start again. There is a tendency throughout the corporate world towards short-termism. Ironically, these pressures arise in response to the very processes of change that require a longer-term view. As organizations compete in increasingly aggressive markets, budgets for experimental research, blue-sky thinking and long-range development are being cut back in the interests of immediate returns and instant results. The effect can be to stifle the very sources of creativity on which long-term success ultimately depends.

Being creative isn't all about chaos and risk. Creativity in any domain is a balance of freedom and control. In all cases, innovation involves calculating risks and the organization's tolerance for them. I talked about risk taking and creative leadership with one of the most successful unit trust managers in Europe. Like all financial institutions his was being borne along on a turbulent current of change. Meeting these new challenges has called for new styles of leadership, to make the most of the resources within the company. He describes how his own style of management has changed to meet these new circumstances:

"I have discovered, upon achieving a 'top' position in management, that there is nowhere to hide. One has to make a comprehensive attempt to get things right. This for me at first involved trying to decide everything – I had to know the answers myself, I thought. This led to a series of mistakes and then inertia; indeed I fell flat on my face in the metaphorical mud. I then found that I had to admit my mistakes rather publicly and ask for help from my colleagues to get myself back on two feet. This seems to have been the beginning of some sort of improved understanding of the manager's role.

"I began to delegate, realizing that actually others were more competent than me. I began to listen, rather than compete with others to produce the cleverest answer. I began to do what I knew I could do, which was to offer support and encouragement to my colleagues rather than seek to score points. I found myself gradually beginning to question and in many instances unlearn the very lessons I had spent most of my life learning, as I realized that being dogmatic is the fast road to disaster in a changing environment. Yet at the same time I found that I needed a sense of direction; otherwise it seemed that I would be abrogating responsibility rather than delegating it.

"I endeavored to balance directness and openness as closely as possible with a willingness to listen and consider positively the viewpoint of other parties. It seems in practice that it is precisely at the point of convergence of these two 'vectors' that the natural way forward always lies. It is hard to find and I'm sure that I never find it precisely as I'm certain that I'm never fully open nor do I fully listen and consider. But it seems to work a whole lot better than my previous approach.

"We are now trying to achieve the same balance in the firm as a whole. Admitting what we are not good at has led for example to outsourcing of certain functions. Willingness to listen has led to more harmonious senior management discussions, enhanced trust, and speedy decision-taking as colleagues have ceased second guessing each other, particularly in areas where the second guesser has little knowledge. It is also leading to more delegation and to more empowerment of younger members of staff, who often have clearer minds.

"This thinking has in turn engendered a greater sense of partnership – both within the firm, reflected in the Board's willingness to create stock ownership plans for all staff worldwide who have been with the firm for more than a year – and also with our clients, suppliers and shareholders through better communication. Interestingly, it is also coinciding with a greater consciousness that we can contribute to our local community. None of this seems to be at the expense of competitiveness. I believe that our competitiveness is enhanced and I think we are learning once again as an organization and new opportunities are arising continuously.

"The traditional design of office buildings and spaces is rooted in the nineteenth century."

"It has required us to increase training significantly, particularly at senior management levels, including the use of management psychologists, and has led us to introduce 360-degree appraisals for senior managers. In graduate recruitment we are relying much more upon internships. Most of all, it is fun, certainly for me and I hope for my colleagues. Interestingly being a multinational company with employees from a whole range of cultural backgrounds has been both a spur to re-examine our approaches and a rich source of different perspectives."[15]

Principle 9: Creative cultures need creative spaces
Finally, the physical environment is a powerful embodiment of organizational culture. The size and shape of workspaces, the configuration of furnishings and equipment, the quality of lighting, fabrics and colors all create ambiences that may encourage or discourage creativity. Until the 1980s, there was very little research into the effects of workspaces on the work done. Since then a growing number of studies have been published in what is now known as 'environmental psychology' and the obscurely named field of 'cognitive ergonomics'. The traditional design of office buildings and spaces is rooted in the nineteenth-century model of industrial work. When the emphasis is on efficient processing of tasks, the principal considerations in the workspace become productivity, maximum occupancy and uniformity. These are hardly the right environments for stimulating imagination, creativity and innovation.

More flexible patterns of working time and the pervasive effects of information technologies mean that there is a blurring of boundaries between the home and office, work, play and personal time. It is often important to allow staff to personalize their workspace in ways that they find most conducive to creative work. Where collaboration matters, there is a need for shared spaces for meetings and workshops.

BORN AGAIN

I said that organizations are like organisms. In some ways, the life cycles of organizations follow those of human lives. They begin in the mind of someone, as the first inkling of an idea. The idea is nurtured and cultivated and if it is viable it begins to grow. The most creative periods in the lives of organizations are often in the early stages of growth when there is a rush of excitement about possibilities to be explored and everyone lends a hand to do whatever is needed for survival. In its youth, an organization may burn great energy on new ventures and take heady risks in the pursuit of success. As a successful organization matures it tends to settle into fixed institutional structures and routines and to become more conservative. It enters middle age. Over time, it may suffer from a hardening of the categories and lose its original vitality and suppleness. If the process of sclerosis continues, it may grow old and die. And many organizations do. But an organization always has the possibility of being born again, or of being revitalized at any point in its development. This happens first and foremost by investing in the creative powers of the people who are the organization. The simple truth is that organizations that make the most of their people find that their people make the most of them. That is the power of innovation and the constant promise of creative leadership.

"Organizations that make the most of their people find that their people make the most of them. That is the power of innovation and creative leadership."

LEARNING TO BE CREATIVE

"Education is not a linear process of preparation for the future: it is about cultivating the talents and sensibilities through which we can live our best lives in the present and create the future for ourselves."

I HAVE ARGUED THROUGHOUT this book that one of the primary reasons so many people believe they are not creative stems from education and especially the systems of mass education that have evolved since the Industrial Revolution. There is a lot that individuals and organizations can do immediately, to revive their creative capacities. But there is an urgent need too to transform education.

There are many creative teachers who do wonderful work in their own classrooms, studios and laboratories. There are whole institutions that pursue innovative programs within their own districts, and whole districts that are battling to do the same in their regions. For the most part, though, these innovations are happening not because of the dominant cultures of education but in spite of them. The challenge is to take innovation to scale: to transform education into a process that genuinely addresses the real challenges of living and working in the 21st century. What is involved in this process of transformation?

TRANSFORMING EDUCATION

Let me begin with a note about terminology. Nowadays, 'school' refers to particular sorts of formal institutions that provide organized instruction, especially to young people. I am going to use the term here in a broader sense to mean any purposeful learning community, whether for children or adults, public or private, compulsory or voluntary. I include formal institutions and voluntary gatherings, from pre-kindergarten to universities, community colleges and home-based learning. Education is often associated with children and young people. By 'education', I mean all of it from pre-kindergarten to adult education. When I use the word 'student' I mean anyone who is engaged purposefully in learning, whatever their age and whatever the setting.

I have two reasons for this approach. First, my arguments are essentially about the qualities of teaching and learning wherever they occur. Second, institutions take many forms. Structures can be changed if there is a will to change them and the purposes are clear. Too often purposes are distorted by institutional habits. As Winston Churchill put it, "We shape our institutions and then they shape us." The challenge is to recreate our institutions by reframing our sense of purpose.

A culture of creativity

In 1997, I was asked by the British Government to form a national commission to develop a strategy for creative education in elementary and high schools. There was already a national strategy for literacy, a part of which recommended that one hour each day should be spent in elementary schools teaching all students the nationally approved literacy materials. There was a similar strategy for mathematics. I sensed from my conversations with some members of the Government that they hoped we might recommend something similar: a creativity hour perhaps; maybe on a Friday afternoon. That would have been a tidy strategy and easily accommodated within the existing system. However, our recommendations went a lot further. Promoting creativity systematically in schools is about transforming the culture of education as a whole.

The best way to achieve that aim is to do what policymakers keep asking and get back to basics. The 'basics' are often thought to be reading and writing and the so-called STEM disciplines: science, technology, engineering and mathematics. All of these are important. But before talking about curriculum, there are more basic questions about the purpose of education in the 21st century. What is it for, and what is at the real core of the process? There is a useful analogy with the theater.

Back to basics

Peter Brook is one of the most innovative and accomplished theater directors of our times. Brook's interest is in making theater as direct and vivid an experience as possible. He believes that too often, modern theater is neither. Its purpose has become corrupted by clutter. For Brook, the essence of theater is the relationship between an actor and audience. Nothing should be added to this relationship, he argues, unless it supports or improves it. "I can take any space and call it a bare stage. A man walks across this empty space whilst someone else is watching and this is all that is needed for an act of theater to be engaged." Yet when we talk of theater, says Brook, this is not quite what we mean. "Red curtains, spotlights, blank verse, laughter, darkness, these are all confusedly superimposed in the messy image covered by one all-purpose word. We talk of the cinema killing the theater and in that phrase we refer to the theater as it was when the cinema was born, a theater of box office, foyer, tip up seats, footlights, scene changes, intervals, music, as though the theater was by definition these and little more."[1] Over time the core business of theater has been blurred by every sort of encumbrance, like the incremental coats of varnish on an old master.

The analogy with education is direct. At the heart of education is the relationship between teachers and students. If students are not learning, education is not happening. In many education systems, the clarity of that relationship has become obscured by political agendas, terms and conditions of employment, building codes, testing regimes, professional territories, national and state standards, and so on. In the middle of these other interests, the needs of actual students are easily forgotten and often are. This is one reason why so many students are pulling out of the system. They feel, rightly as it happens, that the whole clattering system isn't really about them at all.

In education, as elsewhere, clarity of purpose is vital; especially when so many people are involved in so many roles. All complex systems depend on a multitude of roles in order to work: some of these are front-line roles and some are essential supporting roles. Organizations have to be clear about the core business upon which all of these roles should be focused, and to acknowledge that all roles have potentially creative contributions to improving it.

I recently visited a leading hotel chain, at their invitation, to discuss their approach to staff engagement. The whole company understands that its core business is the comfort and satisfaction of the guests and that every member of staff has a role, directly or indirectly, in ensuring that guests are satisfied and will come again. This understanding is shared not only by the staff who interact directly with the guests but also by the staff who do not; including the laundry staff, the dish washers and the maintenance crews. The success of the system as a whole depends on all of them. The dish washers know that one lipstick mark on a water glass can be enough to mar the whole experience for a guest and that their work really contributes to the quality of service at the hotel as a whole. It is this sense of common purpose and engagement that has driven the company's brand and expansion.

Though it is too often forgotten, the core business of schools is to improve the quality of students' learning. The principles of creative leadership apply in education at every level. School principals have a par-

"If students are not learning, education is not happening. Clarity of purpose is vital."

ticular responsibility to nurture a culture that achieves this, by facilitating the creative engagement of every member of the community, whatever their role. The culture includes everything that goes on in the school and everyone who contributes to it in one way and another, for better or for worse.

PRINCIPLES OF TRANSFORMATION

I suggested in Chapter 3 that education has three core purposes:

- **Personal:** to develop students' individual talents and sensibilities.

- **Cultural:** to deepen their understanding of the world around them.

- **Economic:** to enable them to earn a living and be economically productive.

The arguments that I have put forward about the nature of creativity and culture suggest specific principles through which schools can realize these purposes in practice.

Talent is diverse

The narrow focus on academic ability and particular disciplines in schools inevitably marginalizes students whose real
interests and abilities lie in other domains. Cultivating the full
range of students' talents calls for a broader curriculum and
a flexible range of teaching styles. This is not to suggest that
students should study only the subjects they like or have a
natural interest in. One of the roles of education is to broaden
and stretch the interests of students, into areas for which they
may not have a natural affinity: it is equally important that
they feel their own natural abilities are properly engaged and
valued.

When my wife Terry was in high school in England, she had
to spend most Wednesday afternoons in the winter outdoors
on a frozen hockey field. This was not her favorite part of the
week. She was surrounded by people who were taller, faster,
stronger and more committed to hockey than she was. For
most of the time she felt as if she was lying helplessly in the path
of an out-of-control freight train. She says she would not have
minded quite so much, had the girls who relished knocking her
down on the hockey field joined her in the ballet studio once a
week, where her abilities shone and she felt most at home.

The implication of diversity is that breadth in schools should
be balanced by depth. Alongside any common curriculum,
there have to be opportunities for students to go more deeply
into areas that interest them particularly. There should also
be equal encouragement for many different sorts of career
options. Not everyone needs or wants to go to college, for
example, and not everyone should go immediately after
high school. Some want to go to design school or to music
school or to a dance academy. Others want to get out in the
world and pursue their practical work immediately. Human
communities depend on a diversity of talents, not a singular
conception of ability.

Learning is personal

As Socrates famously expressed it, "Education is the kindling of a flame, not the filling of a vessel." All students have different interests, and learning styles. What and how they are taught has to engage their energies, imaginations and their different ways of learning. No one can be made to learn against his or her will. Learning is a personal choice. Of course, under conditions of compulsion and penalty even the most reluctant learners will grudgingly commit ideas to memory to avoid unpleasant consequences. But the spirit of democratic education requires that students learn willingly.

"It is possible to personalize learning for every student. One of the ways this can be done is through the creative use of new technologies."

When students drop out of high school and college there are many programs to encourage them to re-engage with education. The majority of these programs are based on individual attention and on personalized learning. If public education were personalized to begin with, far fewer students would pull away from it. Some people argue that personalizing education for every student is an impossible pipe dream: it would be too expensive and teachers simply could not give every student the necessary time and attention. There are two answers to this argument.

The first is that there is absolutely no alternative. Education *is* personal or it is nothing. Personalized learning is an investment not a cost. I cannot imagine there are many students who leap out of bed in the morning wondering what they can do to raise the reading standards of their local region. The only way to raise overall standards is to engage the energies and imaginations of every student in the system. We know already the massive cost of not doing so.

The second argument is that it *is* possible to personalize learning for every student. One of the ways this can be done is through the creative use of new technologies. Information technologies are among the driving forces of the economic and cultural revolutions and one of the reasons why the industrial model of education is becoming obsolete. Some of the most powerful tools for promoting creativity, communication and collaboration ever devised now offer unprecedented opportunities for education to be personalized: to cater for the interests, abilities and learning styles of every student. Some countries and states are already using web-based technologies to connect students and teachers in personalized learning programs of many sorts. They include Sweden, New Zealand, Singapore, the United Kingdom and parts of the United States.[2]

One example of radical innovation in schools is a pilot program in New York City known as the School of One.[3] The mission of the school is "to provide personalized, effective and dynamic classroom instruction so that teachers have more time to focus on quality instruction." The school has developed a suite of computer programs, which include *student profiles* based on detailed assessments together with input from parents and teachers, and a *lesson bank* of materials from many providers in various formats that are suited to different learning styles. At the heart of the system is a computer program known as the *learning algorithm,* which generates unique daily schedules and resources for each student and for each teacher. These schedules are posted on screens throughout the school and include group work, collaborative projects and individual study time. The teachers are freed from most of the routine tasks of administration that beset teaching jobs and can focus on "providing quality support and instruction to the students." According to their own judgment and discretion, the teachers can override the schedules for themselves or particular students. The scheme is in its pilot phase but the School of One promises other innovations using IT;

contributing, as the school intriguingly puts it, to "the mass customization of student learning."

In Chapter 3, I mentioned the distinction between digital natives and digital immigrants. The typical history of immigrant communities is that the children teach the adults about the new culture. The adults often recreate the culture of the old country in the new one, and aim to preserve the old ways for the sake of nostalgia and security. The young ones are thrust into a new culture and embrace it more vigorously. They bring it home and aim to teach the older generation the new values and ways of doing things. It is often this way with digital culture. Our children are living and breathing it while many adults hesitate to embrace its strangeness, customs and modalities. In education, our children have a lot to teach us about the possibilities of the tools and ways of thinking that they have grasped intuitively and that some of their teachers still hesitate to engage.

The evolution of online learning is also having profound consequences for conventional university education. More and more institutions are posting their courses online; and every day new resources from every quarter become available to would-be students. As the market value of university degrees falls and the cost of getting them increases, many more people are likely to explore the alternative routes to study and qualifications that the Internet is making available.

A proven example of the attraction of alternative forms of higher education is the Open University, a distance learning university that was founded by the British Government in 1969.[4] It awards undergraduate and postgraduate degrees, as well as non-degree qualifications such as diplomas and certificates and continuing education units. It has an open entry policy, which means that students' previous academic achievements are not taken into account for entry to most undergraduate courses. The majority of students are based in the United Kingdom, but its courses can be studied anywhere in the world. The university has thirteen regional centers around the UK and offices throughout Europe. The University has more than 180,000 students enrolled, including over 25,000 students studying overseas. It is the largest academic institution in Europe by student number and one of largest in the world. Since it was founded, more than three million students have studied its courses. It was rated the top university in England and Wales for student satisfaction in 2005 and 2006, and second in 2007. The success of the Open University and other online providers illustrates the widespread hunger for personalized routes into higher education and the growing appetite for innovative ways to provide them.

Life is not an academic exercise

'Service-learning' is a method of teaching, learning and reflecting that combines academic classroom curriculum with service throughout the community. It integrates community service with instruction and reflection, to teach civic responsibility and engagement and strengthen communities for the common good. The National Youth Leadership Council (NYLC) is one of the leaders in service education worldwide and defines service-learning as "a philosophy, pedagogy, and model for community development that is used as an instructional strategy to meet learning goals and/or content standards." Dr. James Kielsmeier founded NYLC in 1983, "to create a more just, sustainable, and peaceful world with young people, their schools, and their communities through service-learning."[5] The work of NYLC now reaches into every state in the US and 35 countries. NYLC programs have included partnerships with schools, colleges, major corporations, government, faith-based organizations and other nonprofits.

A fascinating and very different example of community engagement comes from an extraordinary initiative known as

Room 13. This is a social enterprise organization that includes an expanding network of artists' studios throughout the world and an international community of artists, educators and other professionals. Room 13 is a democratically run studio that works along normal business lines. The unique feature of Studio 13 is that its management team is aged between eight and eleven.

Studio 13 began in 1994 when a group of elementary school students established their own art studio in Room 13 in Caol Primary School near Fort William, Scotland. The guiding philosophy evolved through artist-in-residence posts held by the project founder, Rob Fairley. Fairley worked closely with a number of elementary schools and was asked by students at Caol Primary School to become artist-in-residence there. With his encouragement, they ran the studio as a business, raising funds to buy art materials and to engage other artists to work with them.

The core of Room 13 is a belief in the importance of each individual's integrity, and the importance of expressing that individuality. "Its stimulus," says Fairley "was exasperation at the lack of interest in teaching visual literacy and in teaching the basic technical skills necessary to express ideas through visual imagery."[6] By approaching children as artists and intellectual equals, Room 13 combines artistic development with the skills to run a successful business.

Slowly and organically, Room 13 has grown from a one-day-a-week voluntary project between Fairley and the children of Caol Primary into an international network of such studios, including sites in Austria, Botswana, Canada, China, Holland, India, Mexico, Nepal, South Africa, Turkey and the United States. Room 13 studios offer professionally run courses and creative workshops, painting holidays, expeditions, training and all manner of creative development for adults of all ages.

Each Room 13 studio is run completely by the students. An elected management team is responsible for the day-to-day running of the studio, for keeping track of the finances for each studio and for making sure all invoices are paid. No adult is allowed to sign the checks. Room 13 is not age or ability specific and there is no coercion. Students come because they wish to and stay for as long as they want providing they negotiate the time with their teachers and all class work is up to date. Room 13, devised and run by elementary school children now has an international reputation for creating high quality artwork and for pushing the boundaries in many forms of creative education.

Success creates success

When students find something they enjoy and can excel in, they do better in education generally. One of the most fascinating examples of this principle is the dazzling success of the system of music education in Venezuela known as El Sistema. El Sistema is a national music program that has produced a number of outstanding musicians and has dramatically changed the lives of hundreds of thousands of Venezuela's poorest children. The country now has 237 orchestras, 200 youth orchestras, and 376 choruses. Among the graduates of El Sistema are internationally renowned musicians such as Edicson Ruiz, Gustavo Dudamel and the extraordinary Simón Bolívar Youth Orchestra. Many children begin attending their local El Sistema center, called a 'nucleo' as early as age two or three and most continue well into their teens. They attend up to six days a week, three to four hours a day, plus retreats and intensive workshops. Participation is free for all students. El Sistema's primary focus is "to create a daily haven of safety, joy and fun that builds every child's self-esteem and sense of value." Discipline is relaxed but enforced. Hard work and true achievement are crucial to the success of El Sistema. However, a feeling of fun is never forgotten. El Sistema takes considerable time to work with the parents of students. Where possible, home visits to children aged two or three can be useful, to ensure that the family understands the level of commitment required of them. As the students begin to learn their instruments, teachers instruct parents on how best to support their child's practice schedule at home, giving feedback and encouragement. Emphasis is placed on creating a community where everyone supports one another. Teachers and students alike are committed to personal and community success, "creating a place where children feel safe and challenged. El Sistema graduates leave with a sense of capability, endurance and resilience, owning a confidence about taking on enormous challenges in their lives. A deep sense of value, of being loved and appreciated, and a trust for group process and cooperation, enables them to feel that excellence is in their own hands."[7]

> "Creativity is possible in every discipline and should be promoted throughout the whole of education."

Creativity is for everyone

Creativity is not confined to any particular discipline or activity. Often it is assumed to be associated mainly with the arts, crafts and design but it is not. The national commission, which I chaired, included scientists, economists, business leaders, educators, dancers, musicians, actors and performers. The report, called *All our futures* dealt with the whole curriculum. Yet some members of the government steadfastly referred to it as "the arts report." Creativity is not only about the arts. Work in the arts can be highly creative but so can work in anything that involves intelligence. There are many fundamental arguments for the arts in education. But associating them exclusively with creativity is a mistake. It implies that the arts are mainly opportunities for a break from more rigorous academic work: a chance to get creative for a time, a view that misunderstands both the nature of creativity and the arts. It also implies that other disciplines, including math and science, are not creative, which is simply untrue. Creativity is possible in every discipline and should be promoted throughout the whole of education.

Dennis Littky and Elliot Washor founded Big Picture Learning in 1995, "to encourage, incite and effect change in the U.S. educational system." With 30 years experience between them as teachers and principals in public high schools, they started Big Picture with the motto 'Education is everyone's business' and a commitment to show that education can and should be radically changed. They wanted to create schools in which students would take responsibility for their own education; would spend considerable time doing real work in the community with volunteer mentors and where they would not be evaluated solely on the basis of standardized tests. Students would be assessed, "on their performance, on exhibitions and demonstrations of achievement, on motivation, and on the habits of mind, hand, heart, and behavior that they display, reflecting the real world evaluations and assessments that all of us face in our everyday lives."[8]

The first school opened in South Providence, Rhode Island in 1996 with a freshman class of 50 students, mostly 'at-risk' African American and Latino students who did not fit in conventional schools. That class graduated in 2000 with a 96 percent graduation rate: 98 percent of the graduates were admitted to postsecondary institutions. Each subsequent graduating class has matched or bettered its predecessor. Many of these students are the first in their families to earn a high school diploma, and 80 percent of them are the first in their families to enroll in college.

In 2001, the Bill and Melinda Gates Foundation gave Big Picture Learning a grant to replicate the school design in other areas of the country. In 2003, after the continued success of Big Picture schools, the Gates Foundation gave a second grant to fund the launch of even more schools. Also, in 2003, the Foundation gave Big Picture a grant to become lead convener of the newly formed Alternative High School Initiative (AHSI). By 2008, over 60 Big Picture schools were operating in fourteen states and there were schools in Australia, Israel and the Netherlands that use the Big Picture Learning model. All of these schools, "from Tennessee to Tasmania, from New York City to the Netherlands, embody the fundamental philosophy of Big Picture Learning, educating one student at a time in a community."[9]

Big Picture schools believe "that all students should have the opportunity to learn in a place where people know each other well and treat each other with respect. Schools must be small enough so every student has genuine relationships with adults and other students and no one falls through the cracks. From assessment tools to the design of the school building itself, a truly personalized school approaches each student and situation with a mind to what is best for the individual and for the community." The culture of Big Picture schools is an integral part of their success. "Students are encouraged to be leaders and school leaders are encouraged to be visionaries. Our schools strive to create a respectful, diverse, creative, exciting, and reflective culture."[10]

Littky and Washor say that their mission is to change the way Americans think about the public education system: "Instead of one that judges students and sets limits for achievement, we are building a school system that inspires and awakens the possibilities of an engaged and vital life within our youth ... All of our work is intended to influence the national debate about public education. We want to help convince opinion leaders (policymakers, business leaders, media representatives, and educators) as well as parents and the public, that there are better ways to educate our children."

Creative schools are creative with the schedule

The schedule or timetable is the management tool for organizing the use of time and resources. In theory, the purpose of the schedule is to facilitate learning. In practice it can have the opposite effect. The rigidities of most school schedules can drive the whole culture of the school. Instead of the timetable flexing to meet the needs of teaching and learning, students and teachers alike are shunted through the day on the fixed rails of the timetable. Lessons take place in set units of time, irrespective of the activity, in patterns that repeat week after week. Different processes need different patterns of time. Practicing a language may be best in short but frequent periods of immersion: working on group projects in science or the arts usually benefits from longer blocks of time. The schedule should be sensitive to these differences. Another reason to rethink the schedule is that students' energy levels vary with the rhythms of the day.

There is some evidence that the circadian rhythms of teenagers may be different from those of adults. Neuroscientist Russell Foster, head of Circadian Neuroscience at Brasenose College, Oxford, has been conducting memory tests with teenaged students at Monkseaton High School in North Tyneside in the UK. His research suggests that teenagers' brains work two hours behind adult time. Young people's body clocks may shift as they begin their teens. Teenagers get up later not because they were lazy, but because they are biologically programmed to do so. Dr Paul Kelley, the principal of Monkseaton and author of *Making Minds*, says that continuous early starts create 'teenage zombies' and that allowing teenagers to begin lessons at 11 a.m. has a profound impact on learning.

Dr Kelley argues that depriving teenagers of sleep may affect their mental and physical health as well as their education. Though we don't need science to tell us this, rousing teenagers from their beds early results in abrupt mood swings, and increased irritability. It may also contribute to depression, weight gain and reduced immunity to disease. Dr Kelley said: "This affects all teenagers from about year eleven and stays with them until their university years and beyond. The research shows that we are making teenagers the way they are and that we need to do something about it." In the medium term, he aims to change the rhythm and timing of the whole school day. One immediate outcome of the research is a process known as spaced learning, in which teachers give short lessons, sometimes of less than ten minutes, before changing to a physical activity and then repeating the lesson. In one trial, the pupils scored up to 90 percent in a science paper after one session involving three 20-minute bursts, interspersed with ten-minute breaks for physical activity. The pupils had not covered any part of the science syllabus before the lessons.[11]

Some schools involve the students in radically rethinking the schedule and of the whole culture of education. The Sudbury Valley School was founded in 1968 in Framingham, Massachusetts in the United States. It is a private school, attended by children from the ages of four to nineteen and is organized on two basic principles: educational freedom and democratic governance. In this respect it sits in a long tradition of democratic schools that includes Summerhill School founded in 1921 in Suffolk, England by A.S. Neill. In Sudbury Valley as at Summerhill, students have complete responsibility for their own education. The school is run as a full democracy in which students and staff are equals.

Students of all ages decide for themselves what they will do and when, how, and where they will do it. This freedom "is at the heart of the school; it belongs to the students as their right, not to be violated." The fundamental premises of the school are that "all people are curious by nature; that the most efficient, long-lasting, and profound learning takes place when started and pursued by the learner; that all people are creative if they are allowed to develop their unique talents; that age-mixing among students promotes growth in all members of the group; and that freedom is essential to the development of personal responsibility." In practice, students initiate all their own activities and create their own environments.

Adults and students of all ages mix freely. "People can be found everywhere talking, reading and playing. Some may be in the digital arts studio, editing a video they have made. There are almost always people making music of one kind or another, usually in several places. You might see someone studying French, biology, or algebra. People may be at computers, doing administrative work in the office, playing chess, rehearsing a show, or participating in role-playing games. In the art room, people will be drawing; they might also be sewing, or painting, or working with clay, either on the wheel or by hand." The premise is that physical plant, the staff, and the equipment are there for the students to use as the need arises: "The school provides a setting in which students are independent, are trusted, and are treated as responsible people; and a community in which students are exposed to the complexities of life in the framework of a participatory democracy."[12]

Sudbury and Summerhill are not isolated experiments. There are now dozens of schools based on similar principles in more than 30 countries. Although they are mostly private schools, they are part of a growing movement worldwide to engage students directly in the design of their own education and to embody in practice the principles of democracy on which systems of public education were originally founded.

All schools are unique

Students experience their education in particular schools and not in the corridors of the state legislatures. Transforming education in general is always about transforming individual schools; and that process can begin in your school immediately. The challenge is not to take a single model to scale. It is to propagate the principles of creativity *throughout* education, so that each school develops their own approaches to the challenges they face as a unique community. Often the simplest ideas can have a huge effect.

For several years, I acted as mentor to a statewide program of creativity and innovation in Oklahoma. The state has a nationally recognized program of early years' education. One school in the Jenks schools district of Tulsa entered into an unusual partnership with an institution across the street. The Grace Living Center is a retirement home. The supervisor of the center approached the school district to ask whether they could participate in the district's reading program. As a result the district established an early years' classroom in the foyer of the retirement home and this is now where a group of young children goes to school each day. At the center of the partnership is the Book Buddies program, in which members of the home spend time, one-on-one, listening to the children read and reading to them.

The results have been remarkable. Over 70 percent of the children leave the program reading at Grade 3 level or higher, outperforming many other children in the district. The reason of course is that they have had personalized teaching. Second, they are learning much more than reading skills through their relationships with the members of home. They are learning about the rich traditions of life in Oklahoma. Third, medication levels at the home have fallen dramatically. The senior citizens have a new reason to live and a new energy for their days. They have a purpose. But every now and then the children have to be told that one of book buddies will not be coming back again, because they have passed. So at this young age the children are learning too about the natural cycles of life and death.

In most education systems, people are segregated by age. This project shows what can happen when the generations are brought back together and re-establish some their traditional relationships. As with all genuine innovations, the outcomes, as Elliot Eisner once said, are a surprise not a prediction.[13]

Small, creative changes in any school can have major benefits. Large changes may have correspondingly dramatic results.

We're all in this together

Schools can no longer be academic ghettoes. One of the principles for transforming education is partnership. Everyone has a stake in the future of education and in many parts of the world there are formal alliances between schools and the business, philanthropic and cultural sectors. In the United States, the Partnership for Twenty First Century Learning is a national organization that "advocates for 21st century readiness for every student."[14] The partnership and its members provide tools and resources to help the US education system keep up, "by fusing the three Rs and four Cs (critical thinking and problem solving, communication, collaboration, and creativity and innovation)." The partnership advocates for local, state and federal policies that support this approach for every school. The founding members included AOL Time Warner Foundation, Apple Computers, Cisco Systems, Dell Computer Corporation, Microsoft and the National Education Association.

Also in the US, the Council of Chief State School Officers (CCSSO) has formed a partnership with a consortium of states and foundations, entitled The Partnership for Next Generation Learning. The partnership is establishing a network of 'innovation laboratories' in education. Arguing that the design of education is no longer aligned with the needs of the country, CCSSO has called for a new education system, "one that is designed around the fundamental premise that we will provide each and every child with personalized learning experiences leading to success. There are many examples, in this country and abroad, in both formal education and other sectors, of what transformative learning looks like. Unfortunately, these examples remain exceptions rather than the norm. We are still falling short of wholly systemic transformation because existing federal, state, and local systems are not conducive to fostering innovation and making transformative shifts to new policy."[15] The aim of the strategy is to change the national conversation about how to improve educational outcomes: "Although many are working to improve various elements of the current system, the Partnership for Next Generation Learning is ready to engage those who are prepared to shift energy, time, and investment away from fixing what we have toward creating the public education system that we need ... and making this transformation a reality for all students."[16]

In the United Kingdom, The RSA (Royal Society of Arts, Manufactures and Commerce) has been a leading campaigner for educational transformation. In this capacity it coordinated the drafting of an 'Education Charter' with multiple partner organisations, committing to a more holistic education than one bound by one focused on narrow, instrumental concerns. This led to the development of the organization Whole Education, in which the RSA is one of a growing group of over 20 institutional partners. The national movement for Whole Education "knits together academic, practical and vocational learning calibrated to the potential of each individual." The basis of Whole Education is the conviction that education should "invest in the intellectual development of the young person as well as the development of social and emotional competencies. These competencies are a major part of the foundations that allow every young person to learn effectively and contribute positively to their own development and attainment and to the development of a good society." Whole Education partner initiatives work with over 5000 schools and colleges and numerous youth organizations and charities engaging directly with young people. The overall aim is "to ensure that all young people have access to a Whole Education, an education that equips them with the skills, knowledge, attitudes and resources necessary to cope and thrive in life beyond school make a positive contribution to their societies."[17]

MAKING IT HAPPEN

To transform education, it is essential to have a theory of change. In this case, it has to be built on school-based innovation combined with political advocacy. In my experience it's essential to work both ends of the system. National, state and local policies for education clearly have profound effects on the climate in schools. This is especially true of systems of public accountability like No Child Left Behind (NCLB). It is always important to engage policymakers whoever and wherever they may be and to change the policy climate in the best way possible. But schools cannot wait for policy changes before they do anything themselves and students cannot postpone their lives in the meantime. In any case, schools often have more freedom to innovate than they commonly think.

Creativity is not about a lack of constraints; often it is about working within them and overcoming them. The dynamics of culture are such that change travels in all directions. With the power of the Internet and of social networking, ideas and innovations can move quickly and inspire others to action. Sensitive policy makers will feel the change and may even say it was their idea.

THE CULTURE OF EDUCATION

I said in Chapter 9 that we can think of organizational cultures in terms of *habits* and *habitats*. In schools, the habits include several related elements: the *curriculum*, the *schedule*, *pedagogy* and *assessment*. The habitat includes the physical fabric of the school, its décor and the surrounding environment. All of these have profound effects on learning and all can be transformed with a systematic approach to cultivating imagination, creativity and innovation. National reform movements almost invariably focus on curriculum and assessment. They set national or state standards, sometimes specify content and put in place national systems of testing. The element that is most often overlooked is the only one that really makes a difference to student achievement and that is the quality of teaching.

Being a teacher is a creative profession. One of the reasons that schools fail and systems stumble is that teachers as well as students become disengaged. There are teachers who are not interested in learning or have no gift for teaching and should be doing something else that does fulfill them. This does not make them bad people but they should not inflict themselves on students who need and deserve better. But there are many good teachers whose creative instincts are curbed by standardized education and whose effectiveness is diminished as a result. A creative culture in schools depends on re-energizing the creative abilities of teachers.

"There are three related tasks in teaching for creativity: encouraging, identifying and fostering."

CREATIVE TEACHING

The task of education is not to teach subjects: it is to teach students. No school is better than its teachers. When you think of your own time at school it is the people you remember: your contemporaries, and especially the teachers: the ones who turned you on and the ones who turned you off; who built you up or knocked you down. In the right context, a casual remark by a teacher, or even a raised eyebrow or tone of voice can set you on a lifelong journey of discovery or put you off taking even the first step.

In Chapter 5, I distinguished between the two traditions of individualism: the *rational* and the *natural*. To some extent these have been associated with different styles of teaching. So-called traditional methods are usually associated with formal instruction to the whole class and with rote learning. These methods are often thought to be essential to promote conventional academic standards. The apparent decline in the use of these methods is often linked to the apparent decline in these standards. Progressive methods are associated with inquiry-based learning, with students working individually or in groups to explore their own interests and express their own ideas. I am not arguing against formal instruction, or for traditional approaches to be replaced exclusively by 'progressive' teaching methods. Both have an important place in creative education. Sometimes it is appropriate for the teacher to give formal instruction in skills and techniques, or to convey specific ideas and information; at others times it is more appropriate for the students to explore ideas for themselves, individually or in groups. Some of these methods do put a strong emphasis on creativity: some do not. Some of this work is excellent: some is not. A common failing is the tendency to misunderstand the nature of creative activity not only in education but more generally. Too often what passes for creativity has been an undisciplined and undemanding process. In general though, the emphasis in schools is on academic learning, which has tended to value only one mode of knowing and, in so doing, has displaced others. This has been to the detriment of all of them.

Creativity depends on interactions between feeling and thinking, and across different disciplinary boundaries and fields of ideas. Mastery in teaching is like mastery in any other profession. Expert practitioners in any field: doctors, lawyers, chefs, artists, scientists, have a whole repertory of techniques available; and wide knowledge and practical experiences to draw from. Knowing which to draw from to meet the needs of the present situation is a process of connoisseurship that expert teachers also share.

There is a difference between teaching *through* creativity and teaching *for* creativity. Good teachers know that their role is to engage and inspire their students. This is a creative process in itself. The philosopher of aesthetics, Louis Arnaud Reid, made a linguistic distinction between the use of a verb to describe the task and its achievement. Teaching is a good example. You may ask what someone is doing and be told that she is "teaching in room B." That may be true in the sense of the *task* of teaching, but unless there is some learning going on, she is not *achieving* it. Too many teachers are hired for knowledge of their discipline rather than their interest in students. Good teaching requires personal knowledge as well as the ability to engage others.

Teaching *for* creativity is about facilitating other people's creative work. The skill required may be generally creative or specific to a particular domain; like learning an instrument or techniques in dance or gymnastics. Teaching for creativity involves asking open-ended questions where there may be multiple solutions; working in groups on collaborative projects, using imagination to explore possibilities; making connections between different ways of seeing; and exploring the ambiguities and tensions that may lie between them. Teaching for creativity involves teaching creatively. There are three related tasks in teaching for creativity: *encouraging*, *identifying* and *fostering*.

Encouraging

Many people do not think of themselves as creative and lack the confidence to take even the first steps. The first task in teaching for creativity in any field is to encourage people to believe in their creative potential and to nurture the confidence to try. Other attitudes important for creative learning include: high motivation and independence of judgment; a willingness to take risks and be enterprising, to be persistent and to be resilient in the face of false starts, wrong turns and dead ends.

Identifying

A second role is to help students to discover their own creative strengths. Everyone can learn the general skills of creative thinking. In addition, we all have personal creative capacities. A creative musician is not necessarily a creative scientist; a creative writer is not necessarily a creative mathematician. Creative achievement is often driven by a person's love of a particular instrument, for the feel of the material, for the excitement of a style of work that catches the imagination. Identifying people's creative abilities includes helping them to find their creative strengths: to be in their element.

Developing

The third role is to develop the skills of independent creative work. Teaching for creativity aims to encourage self-confidence, independence of mind, and the capacity to think for oneself. In teaching for creativity, teachers aim to:

- promote experiment and inquiry and a willingness to make mistakes,

- encourage generative thought, free from immediate criticism,

- encourage the expression of personal ideas and feelings,

- convey an understanding of phases in creative work and the need for time,

- develop an awareness of the roles of intuition and aesthetic processes,

- encourage students to play with ideas and conjecture about possibilities, and

- facilitate critical evaluation of ideas.

The aim is to enable students to be more effective in handling future problems and objectives; to deepen and broaden awareness of the self as well as the world; and to encourage openness to new ideas.

CURRICULUM

The curriculum is the content – the knowledge, information, ideas, skills and values – that students are expected to learn. There is a difference between the formal curriculum, which all students have to follow, and the informal curriculum, which is optional, including for example afterschool programs. My interest here is in the whole curriculum, by which I mean all the learning opportunities that a school provides *including* the formal and informal curriculum.

The first purpose of the curriculum is to organize knowledge so that it can be taught. There are many things that are not taught in schools. Witchcraft and necromancy are not taught in most schools. One of the functions of education is to put a stamp of approval on certain sorts of knowledge and experience and by implication to suggest that others are not so worthwhile. As the French sociologist Pierre Bourdieu puts it, education distinguishes between the spheres of "orthodox and heretical culture."[18]

A curriculum has a second function; this is *managerial*. Schools need curricula so that they can organize themselves, know how many teachers to hire, what resources are needed, how to arrange the day, whom to put where, at what time and for how long. A curriculum is a management tool that is translated into the schedule.

As explored throughout the book, a distinction is commonly made between academic and non-academic subjects. Usually, for example, science, history or mathematics are seen as academic subjects; and art, music or drama as non-academic.

There are several problems in this approach. The first is the very idea of subjects, which suggests that different areas of the curriculum are defined by their subject matter: that science is different from art because it deals with different content. I much prefer the idea of disciplines. Mathematics is not defined only by propositional knowledge. It is a combination of concepts, methods and processes *and* of propositional knowledge. The student is not only learning about mathematics but also how to do mathematics. The same is true of music, art, geography, physics, theater, dance and the rest.

The idea of disciplines also opens up the dynamics of interdisciplinary work. It is because of these dynamics that disciplines keep shifting and evolving. This is what the linguist James Britton[19] had in mind when he said, "we classify at our peril. Experiments have shown that even the lightest touch of the classifier's hand is likely to induce us to see members of a class as more alike than they actually are and items from different classes as less alike than they actually are. And when our business is to do more than merely look, these errors may develop during the course of our dealings into something quite substantial."

Disciplines are constantly merging, reforming, cross-fertilizing each other and producing new offspring. When I first arrived at my last university, I went to a meeting of the professorial board, a committee of all professors in the university across all disciplines. There was a proposal from the professor of chemistry that the university should establish a new professorship in chemical biology. The board nodded sagely and was about to move on, when the professor of biological sciences opposed the proposal. He argued that what the university really needed was a chair in biological chemistry. As Britton implies, our categories of knowledge should be provisional at best.

The second assumption is that some subjects are academic and some are not. This is not true. All issues and questions can be considered from an academic point of view and from other viewpoints too. They can be investigated in the deductive mode or in other modes. These processes can be applied to any phenomena: plants, weather, poetry, music or social systems. Knowledge can be generated in many ways other than in words and numbers. Not everything we know can be put into words and numbers, nor are words and numbers all that we know. It is for all these reasons that schools have to offer curricula that are broad and balanced.

One of the consequences of standardization is that the curriculum has become increasingly narrow. In many school systems the emphasis is on languages and the so-called STEM disciplines – science, technology, mathematics and engineering – at the expense of the arts, humanities and physical education. It is essential that there is an equal balance between these areas of the curriculum because each reflects major areas of cultural knowledge and experience, to which we all should have equal access. Each addresses different modes of intelligence and creative development. The strengths of any individual may be in one or more of them. A narrow, unbalanced curriculum will lead to a narrow, unbalanced education.

On the basis of the arguments I have proposed throughout this book, a balanced curriculum should give equal status and resources to literacy and numeracy, the sciences, the humanities, the arts and to physical education. High standards in literacy and numeracy are essential in themselves and they are also the gateways to learning in many disciplines. Languages and mathematics offer much more than basic literacy and numeracy. The study of languages should include literature, and the skills of speaking and listening. Once the fundamentals have been grasped, mathematics can also lead into rich fields of abstraction and the conceptual languages of science and technology.

Science education has an essential role in the education of all students. Learning in science includes engaging with the store of existing scientific knowledge; using the methods of scientific inquiry to investigate hypotheses; and exploring the interactions of science with other fields, including technology. Science education encourages an understanding of evidence and the skills of 'objective' analysis; gives access to existing scientific understanding of the processes of the natural world and the laws that govern them; and provides opportunities for practical and theoretical inquiry, by which existing knowledge can be verified or challenged. Science education also promotes higher standards of scientific literacy: an appreciation of the scientific concepts and achievements that have shaped the modern world and of their significance and limitations.

The humanities are concerned with understanding human culture. These include history, the study of languages, religious education and aspects of geography and social studies. Humanities education broadens and deepens students' understanding of the world around us: its diversity, complexity and traditions. It aims to enlarge our knowledge of what we share with other human beings including those removed in time and culture; and to develop a critical awareness of our own times and cultures. Humanities education includes the study of these disciplines and also using the methodology and processes for students' own enquiries in human culture.

The humanities overlap in several ways with the sciences and the arts. In common with the arts is a primary concern with understanding the human dimension of experience; though they differ in the modes of knowledge they generate and in the forms of study they use.

The arts are concerned with understanding and expressing the qualities of human experiences. Through music, dance, visual arts, drama and the rest, we give form to the currents of feeling and perception that constitute our lived experience of ourselves and of other people. Learning in and about the arts, is essential to intellectual development. The arts illustrate the diversity of intelligence and provide practical ways of promoting it. The arts also provide the most natural processes for giving form to personal feelings and emotions and how they connect with our ways of thinking about the world; they are among the most vivid expressions of human culture. To understand the experience of other cultures, we need to engage with their music, visual art, dance, verbal and performing arts.

Physical education contributes directly to the physical health and well being of students. We are all embodied beings and there are intimate relations between mental, emotional and physical processes. Physical education can also enhance creative processes by quickening concentration and mental agility.[20] Physical education and sport are inextricably bound up in many different cultural traditions and practices and evoke powerful feelings and values, both in relation to the games themselves and through the sense of collective activity and belonging they can generate. They provide important opportunities to develop individual and team skills and to share success and failure in controlled environments. In these and other ways, physical education has essential and equal roles with other curriculum areas in a balanced approach to creative and cultural education.

ASSESSMENT

Assessment is the process of making judgments about students' progress and attainment. The problem for creative education is not the need for assessment, but the nature of it. Assessment should support students' learning and achievements. In practice, it tends to dominate the priorities and general ethos of education.

There are four related problems:

- a growing emphasis on summative assessment, in the form of testing;

- a related emphasis on measurable outcomes, in the form of 'league tables';

- the difficulties of assessing creativity; and

- the pressures of national assessment on teachers and schools.

An assessment has two components: a description and a comparison. If you say that someone can run a mile in four minutes or can speak French, these are neutral descriptions of what someone can do. If you say that "she is the best athlete in the district" or that "he speaks French like a native," these are assessments. The difference is that assessments compare individual performances with others and rate them against particular criteria. One problem with systems of assessment that use letters and grades is that they are usually very light on description and very heavy on comparison. Students are sometimes given grades without really knowing what they mean, and teachers sometimes give grades without being completely sure why. I once talked with a high school student who had just completed a three-year program in dance. I asked her what she had got out of the course and she said, "I got a B."

A second problem in grade-based assessment is that a single letter or number does not convey the complexities of the process that it is meant to summarize. And some outcomes cannot be adequately expressed in this way. As Eliott Eisner once put it, "not everything important is measurable and not everything measurable is important."[21] One way to enhance the value of assessment is to separate out these elements of description and comparison. Portfolios of various sorts allow for detailed descriptions of the work that students have actually done, with examples and reflective comments by themselves and others. Providing clear and detailed criteria is also a way of improving the transparency of assessments. Peer group assessment is a process by which students contribute to the judgments of each other's work and to the criteria by which it is assessed. These approaches can be especially valuable in both formative and summative assessments of creative work.

Assessment has several roles. The first is *diagnostic*. Students may be given tests and assignments of various sorts to help teachers to understand their aptitudes and levels of development in various areas. The second is *formative*, the purpose of which is to gather evidence on students' progress to inform teaching methods and priorities for further work. The third role is *summative*, which is about making judgments on overall performance at the conclusion of a program of work. Methods of assessment can take many forms: from informal judgments in the classroom, to formal assignments and public examinations. They can draw on many forms of evidence: from student participation in class, to portfolios of work, to written essays and assignments in other media.

Summative and formative assessment both have essential roles in encouraging a wide range of teaching and learning; in improving the quality of achievement; and in ensuring a healthy balance between factual knowledge and more open-ended styles of learning, all of which are necessary to creative education. National assessment systems tend to emphasize summative assessment. They are used to judge how well the school itself is doing when compared to other schools. The outcomes of these assessments are linked to the public status of schools, to their funding and sometimes to their survival. Generally, national assessments emphasize 'measurable outcomes' and focus on testing students' recall of factual knowledge and skills that can be measured comparatively. They generally take little account of experimentation, original thinking and innovation. The focus of teaching narrows, and so does students' learning and achievement. Some areas of the curriculum, especially arts and humanities; some forms of teaching and learning, including questioning, exploring and debating; and some aspects of particular subjects, are neglected.

Assessing creative development is more complex and nuanced than testing factual knowledge. Creative work has to be original and of value. But there are different types and degrees of originality. Judging value depends on a clear sense of relevant criteria. Teachers are often unclear about the criteria to apply to students' creative work and may lack confidence in their own judgment. As I argued in Chapter 5, the creative process usually passes through various phases. It may involve false starts, trial and error and a series of successive approximations along the way to the finished work. The educational value of creative work lies as much in the process of conceptual development, as in the creation of the final product. Assessment has to take this into account and teachers often need advice on how this should be done. Insensitive assessment can damage students' creativity and may encourage them to take a safe option, avoiding experimentation and never learning how to find and correct their mistakes. There are also issues of comparability. How should people's creative work be compared between schools or regions?

The difficulties of assessing creative development can be overcome and there is much research, experience and expertise to draw from. The problem is that tackling these issues is not yet a priority in many education systems. The net effect is to increase the emphasis on some forms of learning and to lower the status of others.

LOOKING TO THE FUTURE

I said in Chapter 8 that it is possible to analyze a culture in terms of its various elements, but that the lived experience of a culture is in how these elements flow into each other. It is the same with organizations of every sort, including schools. The culture of a school is much more than the curriculum, teaching styles and forms of assessment. Culture is about values, ambience, tone and relationships. In these respects, all schools are different and they should be. Diversity is essential to move the system beyond industrial models of standardization and conformity. Consequently, in many parts of the world, people are coming together to develop their own alternatives to standardized schooling. Many of them are in the public sector; some are independent schools and some are hybrids, like the charter schools in the USA.[22] A small but growing number of people are opting for more radical alternatives including home schooling and 'un-schooling'.[23] The new pioneers of alternative education come from many different backgrounds and often are driven by dissatisfaction with their own experiences in school and a determination to do better for their own and other people's children. One example is the work of New York's Blue School, which also illustrates how the dynamics of creativity in the arts and in business can interweave with the culture of education.

Blue Man Group is a world-renowned creative organization based in Lower Manhattan, New York City. The group was founded in 1988 by Phil Stanton, Chris Wink, and Matt Goldman. Blue Man Group produces unique performances that combine music, elaborate improvised instruments, comedy and multimedia theatrics. The group has also recorded music and scores for film and television and appears regular on television. The Blue Men wear black utilitarian clothes, blue make up on their hands, faces and bald heads and never speak. They meet everything around them with a childlike innocence and curiosity. Since it was founded the group has grown into an international creative phenomenon, with theaters in New York, Las Vegas, Orlando, Boston, Chicago, Berlin and Tokyo. And now they have started their own elementary school.

None of the group's founders had any of this in mind when they first set out on their journey together.

As Chris Wink says,[24] "When Blue Man first started we weren't a business, we weren't a company, we weren't a show. We were just a community of friends looking for something interesting to do. All we had was a character and a few principles that we shared. We had no idea what we were going to do: we just knew that we were going to explore these ideas using this character." None of the group remembers which of them first thought of becoming bald and blue. And as Matt Goldman says, it was not a very bankable idea. A trio of bald, blue, silent performers did not have obvious investment potential. They loved the character though partly because it was as neutral as they could imagine in terms of culture, age and gender.

Being bald and blue was hardly a long-term, linear plan; the evolution of the group was simply carried forward on the excitement of its own creative collaboration. Together they generated lives and careers that none of them could have foreseen. As Chris Wink puts it: "Some people are lucky and want to be rocket scientists or cellists. These are existing media. For others we wanted to be post-modern multimedia vaudevillians, who create instruments and explore popular culture in a sort of shamanic primal atmosphere. Where's that job exist? Because if we could have found it we would have signed up for it."

The group's work was guided by some clear principles. One of them was that everyone could be creative. "We needed that idea," said Chris Wink, "because we had gone through our educational experiences thinking maybe we weren't creative. And then we got together and said maybe that's not true. What if that isn't true?" For Phil Stanton, this was a vital principle from the outset, "and it influenced everything throughout our career." The group define creativity in a broad sense. Although they are a performance-based group, they aim to be creative in everything they do. As Matt Goldman put it: "Being creative wasn't confined to if you could mould clay or paint on canvas or write music. In the business setting you could be creative and in anything in any discipline."

Matt Goldman and Chris Wink have been friends since they were in elementary school together. Phil Stanton met them later when he moved to New York City in his early twenties. They had an instant rapport. One of the things that drew the group together initially, he says, "even before there was a Blue Man was that we were in our own ways disappointed with our educational experience. It seems like when we're all kids everybody paints and has fun. But somehow we throw away that kind of inspiration and get rid of a bunch of other things too."

When they had their own children, they and their wives faced the dilemma of where and how to educate them. After long reflection, they decided they should start their own school: The Blue School. As Matt Goldman explains it: "We wanted to create the kind of school that either we wished we had gone to or that we fantasized would be the school for our children: a school that emphasizes creativity as much as anything else, that teaches kids a special way to treat one another through social and emotional learning. A place where you don't lose your childlike exuberance, where you have such a zest for learning, a love of life all the way through, and not have it educated out of you."

As it has evolved, the educational model of the Blue School now consists of two main elements: the core curriculum, which represents the basic disciplines of the program: language arts, science, fine arts, lively arts, social studies, technology and media literacy, math, physical arts and fitness. The second element of the program is the school's values: creativity and expression, family and community connections, playfulness, exuberance and fun, self-awareness and well-being, global and environmental exploration, multiple perspectives and differentiated learning styles. Each of the Blue School's values relates in some way to the idea of connection, "whether it be the connection to a community, to one's emotions, to one's artistic voice, to one's body, to the world, to one's interests, or to one's sense of joy and wonder." The model reflects the work of and principles of The Blue Man Group itself and emerged from the school's commitment to achieve a new kind of balance between "rigor and enchantment" and a belief that both are essential in education.

According to Chris Wink, "on a metaphorical level, the traditional model of education is that children are freight cars and the school is a grain silo. It fills each of the kids up and then moves them down the track. We're creating a launch pad where kids are the rockets and we're just trying to find the fuse." The Blue School's approach, he says, "involves having the entire brain alive and exhilarated and tingling with life force. And that needs to be part of our educational model. That seems like a crazy revolutionary idea but it really actually seems to us to make sense, to make actual academic sense."

The work and ambience of the school also reflects the Blue Man Group's original commitment to trusting in our natural creative powers. As Chris Wink puts it, "People tend to think that the part of ourselves that feels different should be hidden or covered up. The Blue Man message is that you should not hide that part of you because it is the key to your individuality. Letting it out lets all this creativity out. You should have the courage to expose that part of yourself." There is a point in the Blue Man show when brightly colored paint pours from tubes around the performers' chests onto drums that they are pounding in a shared, primal beat. "When we drum on paint during our show," says Wink, "the vibrant colors are a way of expressing what happens when you let your outsider come out."

Whether in the public or the independent sector, in schools or at home, being creative in providing education and promoting creativity are not dispensable luxuries. They are essential to enable us all to make lives that are worth living and to sustain a world that is worth living in. The cultural and economic circumstances in which we and our children have to make our way are utterly different from those of the past. We cannot meet the challenges of the 21st century with the educational ideologies of the nineteenth. We need a new Renaissance that values different modes of intelligence and that cultivates creative relationships between disciplines and between education, commerce and the wider community. Transforming education is not easy but the price of failure is more than we can afford, while the benefits of success are more than we can imagine.

AFTERWORD

"Education and training are the keys to the future. A key can be turned in two directions. Turn it one way and you lock resources away; turn it the other way and you release resources and give people back to themselves."

A LL OF THE IDEAS about imagination, creativity and innovation that I have developed in this book are pointing to the need for a different conception of human ability, in education, in business and in our communities. I see these issues in terms of ecology. The concept of ecology has had a deep influence on how many people now think about the natural resources of the earth. More and more people recognize that since the Industrial Revolution we have squandered and damaged much of what the earth has to offer because we have not seen the value of it. We have jeopardized the balance of nature by misunderstanding how its many different elements nourish and sustain each other. Although the dangers persist, they are at least more widely understood.

I believe that there is a similar calamity in our use of human resources. In the interests of the industrial economies we have subjected generations of people to narrow forms of education that have marginalized some of their most important talents and qualities. In pursuit of higher levels of efficiency and productivity in our organizations we have overlooked the essentially human factors on which creativity and innovation naturally depend. We have wasted much of what people have to offer because we have not seen the value of it. Along the way we have jeopardized the balance of communities by not recognizing how our different talents and passions sustain and enrich each other. The dangers persist, and they are not yet widely understood.

These are not trivial matters. Our own times are being swept along on an avalanche of changes. To keep pace with these changes, we will need all our wits about us. It is often said that education and training are the keys to the future. They are, but a key can be turned in two directions. Turn it one way and you lock resources away, even from those they belong to. Turn it the other way and you release resources and give people back to themselves. To realize our true creative potential – in our organizations, in our schools and in our communities – we need to think differently about ourselves and to act differently towards each other. We must learn to be creative.

ENDNOTES

PREFACE

1 Sir Ken Robinson, "Do schools kill creativity?" TED Conference, February 2006. http://www.ted.com/talks/ken_robinson_says_schools_kill_creativity.html

2 "Sir Ken Robinson: Bring on the learning revolution." TED Conference February 2010. http://www.ted.com/talks/lang/eng/sir_ken_robinson_bring_on_the_revolution.html

3 Robinson, Ken (2009).

CHAPTER 1: OUT OF OUR MINDS

1 The pace of change has been picking up for the past 300 years. The 18th century saw political revolutions in Europe and in America. In the 18th and 19th centuries much of the world was convulsed by the rise of science and by the Industrial Revolution. The 20th century was the bloodiest on record. It saw two World Wars, numerous regional conflicts and tumultuous revolutions in Russia and China. Overall the 20th century was the most murderous in human history: it's estimated that more than 100 million people died in the 20th century at the hands of other human beings. It also saw extraordinary advances in science and

technology and massive cultural changes, especially in the old industrial economies.

2 Abraham Lincoln, Second Annual Message to Congress, December 1, 1862.

3 ILO Global Employment Trends for Youth 2010, ILO Geneva. Copyright © International Labor Organization, 2010.

4 Friedman, Thomas L. (2007).

5 The study was based on personal interviews with 1541 CEOs, general managers and senior public sector leaders representing different sizes of organizations in 60 countries and 33 industries. In addition, the study surveyed the views of 3619 students from more than 100 major universities around the world including students on undergraduate and graduate programs, including MBA and doctoral students.

6 Diamond, Jared (2006).

7 "No country has moved up the human development ladder without steady investment in education," Mrs. Irina Bokova, the Director-General of UNESCO, is quoted as saying, at the launch of the Education for All, Global Monitoring Report, Reaching the Marginalized, in January 2010. "The failure to stay competitive in the international playing field is a direct result of our failure to stay competitive in the education field," says Jeff Beard, the director general of the International Baccalaureate in Geneva, Switzerland.

CHAPTER 2: FACING THE REVOLUTION

1 Ian Pearson, British Telecom, interviewed in *The Sunday Times*, 4 June 2000.

2 For a fascinating discussion of the origins of the Center, moderated by Prof. Steven Pinker, see: "The Cognitive Revolution at Fifty: a conversation with Jerome Bruner, Noam Chmosky et al." http://www.veoh.com/browse/videos/category/educational_

and_howto/watch/v19047796rRck4D7Z Last (retrieved on 26 August 2010).

3 Ostman, Charles (1998). Reproduced with the kind permission of Charles Ostman.

4 *The Times*, London, October 2000.

5 Kurzweil, R. (1999). Reproduced with permission. Copyright 1999 *Scientific American*, a division of Nature America, Inc. All rights reserved.

6 Information from The Population Reference Bureau, 1875, Connecticut Avenue, NW, Suite 520, Washington, DC 20009-5728. http://www.prb.org

7 During the past two decades most of the world's fastest-growing countries were in the Middle East and Africa. Kuwait's population grew from 1.9 to 2.3 million between 1998 and 2008 and at the current rate the population will have doubled in less than 20 years. The population of the African continent is growing at 2.4 percent, yielding a doubling time of only 27 years (though the infant mortality remains the highest of any continent at 76 per 1000 live births). "Between 2005 and 2050, the populations of Afghanistan, Burundi, the Democratic Republic of the Congo, Guinea-Bissau, Liberia, Niger, Timor-Leste and Uganda are projected to increase at least threefold." Information from: World Population Prospects: 2006 summary, United Nations (ST/ESA/SER.A/261/ES)

8 "Between 2005 and 2050, half of the increase in the world's population will be accounted for by a rise in the population age 60 or over; whereas the number of children (aged under 15) will decline slightly." Information from: World Population Prospects: 2006.

9 World Population Prospects: 2006.

10 For a detailed and authoritative analysis of the economic and cultural significance of this sector, see, for example, Richard Florida, *The Rise of the Creative Class*, Basic Books, 2002.

11 Information sourced from: the Department for Information, Media and Sport, UK. www.culture.gov.uk/what_we_do/ research_and_statistics/4848.aspx (retrieved August 26, 2010).

12 Macrae, Hamish "The World in 2010," unpublished seminar paper.

13 Information from: Workwise UK website. http://www.workwiseuk.org/events/tucworkfromhomeday.html (retrieved August 12, 2010).

14 Full story can be found on the Newswatch page of the BBC website: "1930s: Technological changes in the newsroom" http://news.bbc.co.uk/1/shared/spl/hi/newswatch/history/noflash/html/1930s.stm (retrieved May 2010).

CHAPTER 3: THE TROUBLE WITH EDUCATION

1 Formal education for all was introduced in Britain in 1870. The government provided for all children to have a basic grounding in literacy and numeracy to the age of twelve. In the closing years of World War II, the government set about planning the post-war reconstruction of the country. Its plans for education were set out in the Education Act of 1944. One of the main aims was to provide post-elementary education for all young people.

2 Gutek, G.L. (1972), pp. 203–4.

3 Gutek, G.L. (1972), pp. 203–4.

4 New civic universities were opened in Birmingham (1900), Liverpool and Wales (1903), Leeds (1904), Sheffield (1905), Bristol (1909).

5 Robinson, K. (1992).

6 McMurrer, J. (2007).

7 See: "China pushes to ease grim Chinese unemployment", Reuters, 7 January 2009. http://www.reuters.com/article/idUS-TRE5062AD20090107 (retrieved July 2010).

8 Chambers, E. et al. (1998), pp. 44–57.

9 Details from The Institute of Management, 2 Savoy Court, Strand, London WC2R 0EZ.

10 Sourced from: Guthridge, M., Lawson, E. and Komm, A. (2008). http://www.mckinseyquarterly.com/Making_talent_a_ strategic_priority_2092 (retrieved July 2010).

11 Only 23 percent of the 6000 executives surveyed strongly agree that their company attracts highly talented people and just ten percent that they retain almost all the high-performers. Only sixteen percent think their company knows who their high-performers are and only three percent said their company develops high-performers effectively and moves low performers on quickly.

12 Sourced from: Guthridge, M., Lawson, E. and Komm, A. (2008). http://www.mckinseyquarterly.com/Making_talent_a_ strategic_priority_2092 (retrieved July 2010).

13 See: Farrell, Diana and Grant, Andrew, J. (2008). https://www. mckinseyquarterly.com/Organization/Talent/Chinas_looming_ talent_shortage_1685 (retrieved July 2010).

14 Alliance for Excellent Education, 'High School Dropouts in America' Fact Sheet, updated February 2009. http://www. all4ed.org/files/GraduationRates_FactSheet.pdf (retrieved July 2010).

15 Department for Education and Employment, (2000).

16 ILO (2010). Copyright © International Labor Organization, 2010.

17 "Ganga": from the English word gang; a term used by police departments in the United States to describe all people of color under 18.

18 See: Hilty, Lindsey (2009). http://www.journal-news.com/news/ hamilton-news/what-does-it-cost-to-educate-a-child--330984. html (retrieved July 2010).

19 "American Creativity at Risk: Report of a National Symposium," November 1996. Details from the Geraldine R Dodge Foundation, 163 Madison Avenue, Morristown, NJ 07962, USA.

20 Prensky, M. (2001).

21 I spoke recently at a national conference of the Consumer Electronics Association. Over lunch, the CEO told me that he had been with the Association for 30 years. When he started, there were just four electronic consumer products: telephone, television, radio and record player. Now there are thousands of electronic consumer gadgets, most of them using digital technology.

22 Hayden, Terry (2010). http://www.tes.co.uk/article.aspx?storycode=6048021 (retrieved June 2010).

23 *Guardian*, London, 27 June 2000. These figures and accounts are taking from a survey by the National Union of Teachers to members at all the city's secondary schools. Response to the survey was comparatively small – 116 useable replies – but the union is convinced they are typical. Seventy percent of teachers who had been assaulted had more than five years' teaching experience.

24 Alan Smithers, Director, Centre for Education and Employment Research, Liverpool University, in *The Times*, London, May 10, 2000.

25 O'Connor, R. and Sheey, N. (2000).

26 O'Connor, R. and Sheey, N. (2000).

CHAPTER 4: The Academic Illusion

1 Hemming, James (1980) in *The Betrayal of Youth*.

2 These tests are from the official Mensa website: http://www.mensa.org.uk/. The answers are:
  - *Question 1:* 'O.' The letters are the first and last letters of Mercury, Venus, Earth, Mars, Jupiter, Saturn, Uranus, Neptune and Pluto.
  - *Question 2:* '140.' The alphabetical positions of all the letters are added to give the amount.

- *Question 3:* South 'v.' The series is: south, east, north, south, west, east spirals clockwise from the top left-hand corner.

3 Galton built upon Darwin's ideas and considered that natural selection was potentially disrupted by human civilization. Because society sought to protect the underprivileged and weak, it was contrary to the natural selection process that generally forfeits the weakest.

4 Richardson, Ken (1999).

5 Richardson, Ken (1999).

6 Hernstein, R. and Murray, C. (1996).

7 Langer, S. (1951).

8 Kuhn, T.S. (1970).

9 Rada, J.F. (1994), unpublished. Reproduced with the kind permission of Dr J.F. Rada.

10 Tiner, J.H. (1975).

11 A great deal has happened in the theory and practice of science and philosophy to question these sequences. Chaos theory and complexity theory for example both try to grapple with the apparently chaotic relationships between events.

12 In England the term public school, schola publica, appeared in the twelfth century. The term distinguished them from private or home-based schools. It meant that they were open for those who could afford to send their children to them: literally public in that sense. These days, public schools are a particularly prestigious and self-appointed group of independent grammar schools.

13 St Paul's school founded in 1518 was funded by the Mercers Company and was independent of the church. During the reign of the Tudors there was a huge increase in the foundation of grammar schools. Many schools that had been closed during Henry's dissolution of the monasteries were reopened. Schools were established by successful individuals and by the city livery companies including the Merchant Tailors. King Edward VI also promoted and lent his name to the foundation of grammar

schools in many cities throughout the land. The growth of grammar schools continued under the Stewarts. There were 155 founded between 1501 and 1601; and 186 between 1601 and 1651.

14 The first three, grammar, rhetoric and dialectic, were known as the trivium and formed the basis of the grammar school curriculum. The remaining four, the quadrivium, were the foundation of the university curriculum.

15 Quoted in Davis, Robin (1967).

16 It was also seen as vital to address the manifest and, to many social reformers, offensive problems of social deprivation among the laboring classes.

17 By 1908 there were 663 grammar schools and by 1963 there were 1,295. This massive expansion was directly related to the development of the industrial economy and the need for a better-educated worked force.

18 From the outset, the grammar schools had been seen as a means of social advancement and as superior to the secondary moderns. One of their main purposes was to provide a route to the universities.

19 As Peter Scott (Scott, 1997) puts it, the university system has become a mass system in structure but remains elite in its private instincts. In universities, business schools are valued for their contribution to the balance sheet but have relatively low academic status. Philosophy and mathematics departments may generate little income but their intellectual capital is very much higher. In some ways these are typical problems for new disciplines. New fields of study are commonly disparaged by established ones.

20 Where the private system had been based on ability to pay the state system was founded on the idea of ability and intelligence quotient. Selection for different types of school was by a national test taken at the age of eleven, the eleven-plus, which was based on theories of IQ. Less than a quarter of children were accepted for a grammar school education. The rest, having failed the

eleven-plus, went to secondary modern schools. Understandably many thought of themselves as educational failures – and many still do, decades later. When children failed the eleven-plus they weren't told it was for economic reasons. They assumed they just weren't as clever as those who passed. It was a myth that only 20 percent of children were capable of passing the test. This was not true. Only 20 percent of children were required to pass it. The numbers of grammar school places were planned on that basis. It was harder to pass the eleven-plus in some parts of the country than others because of local variations in the numbers of grammar schools (Davis, 1967). It was harder in some years to pass the eleven-plus. If there was a particularly good year and 30 percent or more performed well, the authorities raised the pass level. (This is a system known as 'norm-referencing'. It means that the assessment of individual students is based not on absolute but on relative achievement. If all candidates were to be given 'A' there would be complaints about falling standards. A pupil's placing does not depend solely on personal performance. He or she may improve performance by 100 percent over a year, but if everyone else improves similarly, personal grades will be no higher than before.)

It was generally harder for girls to pass. Girls tend to mature earlier than boys and often perform better at such tests and not so many girls were expected to go into professional and managerial jobs. The prospects of passing the eleven-plus were greatly increased by coaching. Success relied as much on knowing the techniques involved as on natural aptitude. Many who failed the eleven-plus might have passed with training and many of those who did pass had had it.

21 Simon, B. (1978).

CHAPTER 5: KNOWING YOUR MIND

1 Laing, R.D. (1975).

2 This is the term used by the German philosopher Alfred Schutz. See Schutz, A. (1972).

3 Russell, B. (1970).

4 The American psychologist Thorndyke showed that learning poetry or Latin vocabulary did not improve the memory in general but merely the skill of learning poetry or Latin vocabulary.

5 Gardner, Howard (1993).

6 Sagan, C. (1978).

7 Ellis, P. (1989).

8 See: The Soundbeam website press release: "New sounds from Sunderland" http://www.soundbeam.co.uk/news/news-sunderland.html

9 With acknowledgement to "Derek Paravincini's extrordinary gift" 60 Minutes. A profile by Lesley Stahl. See: http://www.cbsnews.com/stories/2010/03/12/60minutes/main6292474.shtml
See also: Ockelford (2007).

10 Savants' abilities, though exceptional, seem highly localized. How does this square with my argument about the interactive nature of intelligence? The point I think is that there is still a dynamic process between different capacities in the mind of the savants. But in these cases it is between very high and often very low abilities in different areas of intelligence.

11 See Lichtman, Jeff, (2009). Reproduced with the kind permission of Jeff W. Lichtman, MD, PhD.

12 Hall, Alan (1999). See, for example, Deutsch, Diana (ed.), 1999.

13 Half the problem is the way they are taught of course. The best way to learn French is to go to France and have to speak it all day with French people. The worst way is to speak it for a few minutes a week with an English person who doesn't speak it properly. This is exactly how I tried to do it. Learning a language in 30-minute periods at school is something like trying to learn to swim on dry land. It would be like balancing children on desks

for 30 minutes a week miming the breast stroke and promising them that if they get the hang of it in three years' time they will be put into water. We know how they would get on.

14 Greenfield, S. (1997).

15 The participants who complete the program successfully receive a Certificate in Practical Performance Skills (Dance), which is accredited by Trinity College, London. Each individual builds their own portfolio and gains module credits as they progress through the program. They can also work towards a Young People's Arts Award at Bronze level. The Academy, with its partners, is committed to finding routes back into education and employment for its participants. The Academy sets out to help young people acquire the kinds of transferable skills that will help them engage with the world of work. However, those who wish to continue their dance training and their links with Dance United can join the weekly youth dance group or the emergent graduate performing dance company. All graduates are offered regular contact and tutorials with Academy staff with the aim of supporting them in whichever path they choose to follow. A few have already taken key steps on the ladder to successful professional careers as dancers by entering into further education and professional dance training.

16 The quotations in this section are from The Academy, a film by Dan Williams and Andrew Coggins. Further details from http://www.dance-united.com.

CHAPTER 6: Being Creative

1 This can be a highly dynamic process whose eventual outcomes can be quite different from those anticipated at the outset. Sometimes the objective changes as new ideas and possibilities come into view: sometimes, as with inventions and discoveries, new purposes are found when an initial product or idea has emerged.

ENDNOTES

2 For example, the groundbreaking studies of Benjamin Whorf, Edmund Sapir, Jean Piaget, Jerome Bruner and Noam Chomsky among many others.

3 Our sense of reality is not only a function of social convention of course. There is a difference between saying that social factors influence knowledge and that social factors determine knowledge. The fact that we distinguish in our culture between cats and dogs may be due to certain social conditions. The fact that we can distinguish between them "has something to do with cats and dogs." Any person's mental model will contain some images that approximate closely to reality, along with others that are distorted or inaccurate. But for the person to function, the model must bear some overall resemblance to reality: "Every reproduction of the external world, constructed and used as a guide to action must in some degree correspond to that reality. Otherwise the society could not have maintained itself; its members, if acting in accordance with totally untrue propositions, would not have succeeded in making even the simplest tools and in securing therewith food and shelter from the outside world." – Lawton (1975).

4 This argument is developed by George Herbert Mead. See Miller, D.L. (1973).

5 In developing this example, I am grateful for the advice and expertise of Barrie Wiggham, formerly of the Hong Kong Government and Hong Kong's Representative in Washington.

6 From a filmed interview with Richard Feynman, reprinted with permission of Melanie Jackson Agency, LLC. Available in the Masters of Science series from the Vega Trust. www.vega.org.uk. The Vega Trust was established to promote and deepen public understanding of the processes and excitement of science. One of its leading figures is the distinguished chemist and Nobel laureate, Professor Sir Harry Kroto.

7 Langer, S. (1951).

8 Polanyi, M. (1969).

9 Polanyi, M. (1969).

10 Kelly, George (1963).

11 Polanyi, M. (1969).

12 A notorious example is Carl André, the sculptor who displayed a pile of bricks in London's Tate Gallery and drew the outrage of every popular journalist.

13 Koestler, A. (1975).

14 Visit Edward De Bono's website at www.edwarddebno.com

15 William J. J. Gordon and George M Prince were the co-founders of Synecticsworld (www.synecticsworld.com). Synectics theory is based on three fundamental assumptions:

• Creative output increases when creative people become aware of the psychological processes that control their behavior.

• The emotional component of creative behavior is more important than the intellectual component; the irrational is more important than the intellectual component.

• The emotional and irrational components must be understood and used as precision tools in order to increase creative output.

16 I'm grateful to John Haycraft, the distinguished English auctioneer and valuer for helpful background information and advice.

17 Kelly, George (1963).

CHAPTER 7: FEELING BETTER

1 Actually it isn't. I invented Dombey to save the blushes of the student and of the real town.

2 The exile of feeling is obvious in everyday language. Arguments are often dismissed for being only 'value judgments' or 'merely subjective'. It is hard to imagine any argument being dismissed as 'merely objective'.

3 Quoted by Peter Abbs in "Education and the Expressive Disciplines," Tract, No. 25, The Gryphon Press (1979). A special issue devoted to the contemporary visual arts.

4 Siroka, R.W. *et al.* (1971).

5 Marx and Maslow would argue that the economic prosper-
ity of the times provided the material comfort for this sort of
introspection. Herbert Read would have seen it as a response
to the dehumanization of society brought on by industrialism.
Certainly people finding themselves removed from the products
of their own labor, exposed to ever widening horizons through
the new media, and whose roots in community life are loosened
by massive social upheaval, are more likely than their parents or
grandparents to feel a loss of identity and personal significance.

6 Frankl, V. (1970).

7 Jung, C.G. (1933).

8 Goleman, Daniel (1996) A report in 1999 by the Mental Health
Foundation, The Big Picture, gives graphic evidence of this
among children at school.

9 Goleman, D. (1996).

10 In Hemming, J. (1980).

11 It is commonly said that the literal meaning of education is to
draw out, from the Latin word educo. The more common Latin
word for drawing out is educere, a third conjugation verb, which
gives us the English words 'educe' and 'eduction'. But education
derives from educare, a first conjugation verb meaning to bring
up or educate. So this doesn't really help.

12 Board of Education (1932).

13 In the early 1970s, Robert Witkin, a British sociologist, published a book looking at the creative processes of the arts. He
called it The Intelligence of Feeling. He develops in a different
way some of the themes that are elaborated in detail in Goleman,
D. (1996).

14 In certain cases, of course, emotional states are caused by physical disturbances as in some forms of depression or through the
metabolic changes associated with illness.

15–18 Goleman, D. (1996).

19 In the modern world science came to be seen as the largely
unquestioned source of authoritative knowledge. Scientific

methods enjoy the claim of being factually true, "... even if they are in no way demonstrable, even if they must be taken on faith, even if they tend to answer what are, after all unanswerable questions. Scientific methods have the great advantage in this self-conscious society of not appearing as myths at all but as truth, verified by the inscrutable methods of the scientist." – Carey, J.W. (1967).

20 Simon, Brian (1978).
21 Polanyi, M. (1969).
22 Descartes, R. (1968).
23 Pivcevic, E. (1970).
24 Popper, Karl (1969).
25 Forster, E.M. (1974).
26 Grotowski, J. (1975).
27 Reid, L.A. (1980).

CHAPTER 8: YOU ARE NOT ALONE

1 Ministries of culture throughout the world and national cultural policies often focus particularly on the arts.
2 Williams, Raymond (1966).
3 Understanding the complexities of cultural experience and identity is essential in many fields of study: in social history, sociology, culture, anthropology, and in cultural studies. The field of cultural studies is often concerned for example with examining relationships between patterns of development, changes in forms of government, their accumulative effects on the shape of communities and the organization and content of education. These long revolutions, as Raymond Williams has called them, in industry and democracy are also enmeshed in a broader revolution in social values, which is in turn being interpreted and "indeed fought out very complex ways in the world of art and ideas."

4 This idea was developed by the cultural theorist Walter Benjamin in a celebrated essay, "The Work of Art in the Age of Mechanical Reproduction," in Benjamin, W. (1980).

5 He continues: "The pleasure lies not in watching the play develop in a straight line but in the parodies, the lifelike contradictions, the surprises possible within the worldview of the play ... When the rules are broken audaciously we are delighted as when (a tennis player) throws his racket at the umpire. But the success of these effects rests on our pleasure in seeing conventions smashed." – Robinson, K. ed. 1980, p. 97.

6 The emergence of modernism in painting in Europe marked a break with the formal structures and constraints of the classical tradition. The great movements in Western Europe in painting are characterized by painters turning to new frameworks of creative expression. The Impressionists aimed to break free from the existing preoccupations with figurative painting. They wanted to explore the use of color and texture as a way of capturing the feelings they experienced in contemplating their subjects rather than in trying accurately to reproduce their physical appearances.

7 Levitas, M. (1974).

8 Polanyi, M. (1969).

9 Geertz, Clifford (1975).

10 Department for Education and Employment (1999). For a fascinating discussion of the growing links between the arts and sciences, see Ede, S. (2000).

11 The idea of modernism fired intellectual energies to the late 1960s. They were gradually replaced by new ways of thinking that have come to be grouped under a general heading of postmodernism.

12 The ideas that underpinned the growth of the scientific method were not invented in the fifteenth century. They date back to the ancient Greeks and beyond. They found a new resonance in the fifteenth century and later because of contemporary cultural conditions. The applications of these ideas interacted with the

development of new technologies, which they had also helped to make possible. In turn these created new opportunities for the development and application of scientific ideas.

CHAPTER 9: BEING A CREATIVE LEADER

1 Amabile, T.M., Conti, R., Coon, H. *et al.* (1996). http://jstor. org/stable/256995 (retrieved July 2010).

2 Both Total Quality Management and Six Sigma strategy are systems of quality control devised to reduce errors that occur during the manufacturing and supply chain process.

3 "What Your Disaffected Workers Cost," *Gallup Management Journal*, 15 March 2001.

4 For a comprehensive survey of the development of creativity testing see Sternberg, R.J. (1999).

5 Richards, P. quoted in Alliance of Artists Communities (1996), p. 5. http://www.artistcommunities.org/files/files/American_ Creativity_at_Risk.pdf

6 "How Pixar Adds a New School of Thought to Disney," William C. Taylor and Polly LaBarre, *New York Times*, January 29, 2006.

7 For some people, one of the most powerful forms of development can be taking on new roles that stretch their existing expertise into different areas of responsibility. Yet, according to one study only 10 percent of 200 executives surveyed said that their company uses new job assignments as a lever for professional development, whilst 42 percent have never made cross-functional moves, 40 percent have never worked in an unfamiliar business unit, 34 percent have never held positions with responsibility and 66 percent say they have never had a leadership role in starting a new business.

8 Chambers, E. *et al.* (1998).

9 Chambers, E. *et al.* (1998), pp. 44–57.

10 Department of Trade and Industry (2000).

11 "Pixar University's Randy Nelson on Learning and Working in the Collaborative Age" See: http://www.edutopia.org/randy-nelson-school-to-career-video (last retrieved August 2010).

12 Brown, Tim (2009).

13 Quoted in American Creativity in Crisis: report of a national symposium.

14 Newsweek, 04.06.10.

15 These comments are from a personal interview.

CHAPTER 10: LEARNING TO BE CREATIVE

1 Brook, P. (1995) *The Empty Space*, Touchstone, p. 9.

2 McKinsey Education (2009).

3 School for One website: http://schools.nyc.gov/community/innovation/SchoolofOne/default.htm

4 The Open University: http://www.open.ac.uk/

5 See: National Youth Leadership Council website. http://www.nylc.org/

6 See "Room 13 Ideology" on their web page: http://www.room13scotland.com/room13network.php?which=ideology. See also Adams, J. "Room 13 and the Contemporary Practice of Artist-Learners", *Studies in Art Education*, 47:1, pp. 23–33, 2005.

7 See: El Sistema web page http://elsistemausa.org/el-sistema/venezuela/. Reproduced with permission of El Sistema USA.

8–10 See the Big Picture Learning website at: http://www.bigpicture.org/big-picture-history/. Reproduced with permission.

11 Kelley, P. (2007). See also story from BBC News: "Head urges lie-in for teenagers", published 2009/03/09. http://news.bbc.co.uk/go/pr/fr/-/2/hi/uk_news/england/tyne/7932108.stm

12 Sudbury Valley School website: www.sudval.org

13 Eisner, E (1996).

14 Partnership for 21st Century Learning Skills website: www.p21.org

15,16 See: CCSSO (Council of Chief State Schools Officers) website: http://www.ccsso.org/What_We_Do/Next_ Generation_Learners.html. Reproduced with permission.

17 See www.wholeeducation.org. Reproduced with permission.

18 Bourdieu, P., in Young, M.F.D. (ed.) (1971).

19 Britton, J. (1972).

20 Kelley, P. (2007).

21 Eisner, E. (1996).

22 Charter schools receive public money but are not subject to some of the rules, regulations, and statutes that apply to other public schools. They do have to meet agreed terms of accountability, which are made explicit in each school's charter. Charter schools provide an alternative to other public schools, but legally they are part of the public education system and are not allowed to charge tuition.

23 Unschooling is a range of philosophies and practices centered on allowing children to learn through their natural life experiences, including child directed play and household responsibilities and work experience rather than through a formal school curriculum.

24 The Blue Man quotes are all from a short video that they recorded and made for my use. Reproduced with permission.

REFERENCES

Abbs, P. (1979) "Education and the Expressive Disciplines," *Tract*, 25, The Gryphon Press.

Adams, J. (2005) "Room 13 and the Contemporary Practice of Artist-Learners," *Studies in Art Education*, **47** (1), 23–33.

Alliance for Excellent Education (2009) "High School Dropouts in America," Fact Sheet, updated February.

Alliance of Artists Communities (1996) *American Creativity at Risk: Restoring creativity as a priority in public policy, cultural philanthropy and education*, Report on Symposium, November 8–10. Available from 225 South Main St, Providence, Rhode Island, RI 02903.

The Geraldine R Dodge Foundation (1996) *American Creativity at Risk: Report of a National Symposium*, November, The Geraldine R Dodge Foundation, 163 Madison Avenue, Morristown, NJ 07962, USA.

Amabile, T.M., Conti, R., Coon, H. *et al.* (1996), "Assessing the work environment for creativity," *Academy of Management Review* **39** (5): 1154–1184.

Bajer, J. (1999) "The Paradox of the Talents," in *People Management Magazine*, December.

Barber, M., and Mourshed, M. (2007) *How the World's Best Education Systems Come Out on Top*, McKinsey Education, London.

Benjamin, W. (1980) *Illuminations*, Fontana, London.

Board of Education (1932) *Report on Primary Schools,* HMSO, London, 1932.

Boden, M. (1994) *The Creative Mind,* Abacus, London, 1994.

Bourdieu, P. (1971) "Systems of Education and Systems of Thought," in Young, M.F.D. (ed.) *Knowledge and Control,* Collier MacMillan.

Britton, J. (1972) *Language and Learning,* Penguin Books, Harmondsworth.

Britton, J. *et al.* (1975) *The Development of Writing Abilities: 11–18,* Macmillan Education, London.

Brook, P. (1995) *The Empty Space,* Touchstone, New York.

Brown, T. (2009) *Change by Design,* Harper Business.

Carey, J.W. (1967) *The Antioch Review,* XXXVII, Yellow Springs, Ohio.

Chambers, E. *et al.* (1998) "The War for Talent," *McKinsey Quarterly,* No. 3, pp. 44–57.

Davis, R. (1967) *The Grammar School,* Penguin Books, Harmondsworth.

Department for Culture, Media and Sport (1998) *Creative Industries Mapping Exercise,* DCMS, London.

Department for Education and Employment (1999) *All Our Futures: Creativity, Culture and Education,* HMSO, London.

Department for Education and Employment (2000) *Skills for All: Proposals for a National Skills Agenda,* DfEE Publications, London.

Department of Trade and Industry (2000) *The Future of Corporate Learning,* HMSO, London.

Descartes, R. (1968) *A Discourse on Method,* transl. Sutcliffe, F.E., Penguin Books, Harmondsworth.

Deutsch, Diana (ed.) (1999) *The Psychology of Music,* 2nd Edition, Elsevier.

Diamond, J. (2006) *Collapse,* Penguin Books, London.

Ede, S. (2000) *Strange and Charmed,* Calouste Gulbenkian Foundation, London.

Editorial (2001) "What Your Disaffected Workers Cost," *Gallup Management Journal*, 15 March.

Education for All (2010) *Reaching the Marginalized*, January.

Eisner, E. (1996) *Cognition and Curriculum Reconsidered*, Paul Chapman.

Ellis, P. (1989) *Touching sound – Connections on a creative spiral*, Department of Arts Education, University of Warwick, Coventry, United Kingdom CV4 7AL, in *Education and Computing* Volume 5, Issues 1–2, 1989, Pages 127–132, Elsevier B.V., Oxford.

Farrell, D. and Grant, A. J. (2008) "China's looming talent shortage," *The McKinsey Quarterly*, 2008, No. 1.

Feynman, R. filmed interview in the 'Masters of Science series', The Vega Trust, CPES, University of Sussex, BN1 9QJ. www.vega.org.uk

Forster, E.M. (1974) *Two Cheers for Democracy*, Penguin Books, Harmondsworth.

Frankl, V. (1970) *Psychotherapy and Existentialism*, Souvenir Press, London.

Friedman, T.L. (2007) *The World is Flat 3.0: A Brief History of the Twenty First Century*, Picador, London.

Friedman, T.L. (2009) "The New Untouchables," *New York Times*, October 21.

Gardner, H. (1993) *Frames of Mind: The Theory of Multiple Intelligences*, Fontana, London.

Geertz, C. (1975) *The Interpretation of Cultures*, Chicago University Press, Chicago.

Goleman, G. (1996) *Emotional Intelligence*, Bloomsbury, London.

Gould, S.J. (1996) *The Mismeasure of Man*, W W Norton & Co., New York.

Greenfield, S. (1997) *The Human Brain: A Guided Tour*, Weidenfield & Nicholson, London.

Grotowski, J. (1975) *Towards a Poor Theatre*, Methuen, London.

Gutek, G.L. (1972) *A History of the Western Educational Experience* (2nd Edition), Waveland Press.

Guthridge, M., Lawson, E., Komm, A. (2008) "Making talent a strategic priority," *McKinsey Quarterly*, No. 1.

Hall, A. (1999) "Speaking in Tones," *Scientific American*, November 1.

Harvey-Jones, J. (2003) *Make it Happen: Reflections on leadership*, Profile Books.

Haydn, T. (2010) "Behaviour Now – the classroom – how good is discipline today?" Analysis, *TES Connect*, June 18.

Hemming, J. (1980) *The Betrayal of Youth*, Marion Boyars, London.

Hernstein, R. and Murray, C. (1996) *The Bell Curve: Intelligence and Class Structure in American Life*, Simon & Schuster, New York.

Hilty, Lindsey (2009) "What does it cost to educate a child" *JournalNews*, October 5, Ohio, USA.

Husserl, E. (1970) *Logical Investigations*, Routledge and Kegan Paul, London.

International Labour Office (2010) *ILO Global Employment Trends for Youth 2010*, Geneva.

Jay, R. (2000) *The Ultimate Book of Business Creativity*, Capstone Publishing, Oxford.

Joint Council for Education Through Art (1957), *A Consideration of Humanity, Technology and Education in Our Time*, Report of the Conference at the Royal Festival Hall, London, 22–27 April 1957.

Jung, C.G. (1933) *Modern Man in Search of a Soul*, Routledge and Kegan Paul, London.

Kelley, P. (2007) *Making Minds: What's wrong with education and what should we do about it?* Routledge, London.

Kelly, G.A. (1963) *A Theory of Personality: The Psychology of Personal Constructs*, W W Norton & Co., New York.

Koestler, A. (1975) *The Act of Creation*, Picador, London.

Kuhn, T.S. (1970) *The Structure of Scientific Revolutions*, Chicago University Press, Chicago.

Kurzweil, R. (1999) "The Coming Merging of Mind and Machine," *Scientific American*, **10** (3).

Kurzweil, R. (2006) *The Singularity is Near: When Humans Transcend Biology*, Penguin, New York.

Langer, S. (1951) *Philosophy in a New Key*, New American Library, New York.

Laing, R.D. (1975) *The Divided Self*, Penguin Books, Harmondsworth.

Lawton, D. (1975) *Class, Culture and Curriculum*, Routledge and Kegan Paul, London.

Levitas, M., (1974) *Marxist Perspectives in the Sociology of Education*, Routledge and Kegan Paul, London.

Lichtman, Jeff (2009) "Neuroscience: making connections," *NatureNews*, January 2009, *Nature* 457, 524–527, doi:10.1038/457524a.

MacKenzie, D. A. (1981) *Statistics in Britain, 1865–1930: The social construction of scientific knowledge*, Edinburgh University Press.

McKinsey Education (2009) *Shaping the Future: How Good Education Systems Can Become Great in the Decade Ahead*, Report of The International Education Roundtable, July 7, 2009, Singapore.

McMurrer, J. (2007) *Choices, changes, and challenges: curriculum and instruction in the NCLB Era*. A report published by the Center on Education Policy, Washington, DC.

Mental Health Foundation (1999) *The Big Picture*, The Mental Health Foundation, London.

Miller, A.I. (1996) *Insights of Genius: Imagery and Creativity in Art and Science*, Springer-Verlag, New York.

Miller, D.L. (1973) *George Herbert Mead: Mind, Self, Language and the World*, Texas University Press.

O'Connor, R., Sheehy, N. (2000) *Understanding Suicidal Behaviour*, Wiley-Blackwell, London.

Ockelford, A. (2007) *In The Key of Genius*, Hutchinson.

Ostman, C. (1998) "Techno Marvels in the Making," *Magical Blend* magazine, No. 47, October.

Peters, T. and Waterman, R.H. (1982) *In Search of Excellence*, Harper & Row, New York.

Pivcevic, E. (1970) *Husserl and Phenomenology*, Hutchinson University Library.

Polanyi, M. (1969) *Personal Knowledge*, Routledge and Kegan Paul, London.

Popper, K. (1969) *Conjectures and Refutations: The Growth of Scientific Knowledge*, Routledge and Kegan Paul, London.

Prensky, M. (2001) "Digital Natives, Digital Immigrants," *On the Horizon*, Vol. 9, No. 5, NCB University Press, October.

Rada, J.F. (1994) "The Metamorphosis of the Word: Libraries With a Future," Fifth Mortenson Memorial Lecture, University of Illinois, Urbana Champaign, 7 October. Unpublished.

Reid, L.A. (1980) *Yesterday's Today: A Journey into Philosophy*, unpublished autobiography.

Richardson, K. (1999) *The Making of Intelligence*, Phoenix, London.

Robinson, K. (ed.) (1980) *Exploring Theatre and Education*, Heinemann.

Robinson, K. (1992) *Arts Education in Europe: A Survey*, Council of Europe, Strasbourg.

Robinson, K. (2009) *The Element: How finding your passion changes everything*, Viking Penguin, New York.

Rogers, C. (1969) *Freedom to Learn*, Merrill, New York.

Russell, B. (1970) *The Problems of Philosophy*, Oxford University Press, Oxford.

Sagan, C. (1978) *The Dragons of Eden*, Coronet, London.

Schutz, A. (1972) *The Phenomenology of the Social World*, Heinemann, London.

Scott, P. (1997) *The Meanings of Mass Higher Education*, Open University Press, Bristol.

Simon, B. (1978) *Intelligence, Psychology, Education*, Lawrence Wishart, London.

Siroka, R.W. *et al.* (eds) (1971) *Sensitivity Training and Group Encounter*, Grosset & Dunlop.

Sternberg, R.J. (1999) *The Handbook of Creativity*, Cambridge University Press, Cambridge.

Taylor, W.C. and LaBarre, P. (2006) "How Pixar Adds a New School of Thought to Disney," *New York Times*, January 29.

Tiner, J.H. (1975). *Isaac Newton: Inventor, Scientist and Teacher*. Mott Media, Milford, Michigan.

Toffler, A. (1970) *Future Shock*, Random House, New York.

United Nations (2006) *World Population Prospects: 2006 summary*, United Nations (ST/ESA/SER.A/261/ES).

Williams, R. (1966) *The Long Revolution*, Penguin Books, Harmondsworth.

Witkin, R. (1974) *The Intelligence of Feeling*, Heinemann, London.

Yeats, W.B. (1978) *Collected Poems*, Macmillan, London.

INDEX

ACKNOWLEDGMENTS

I WAS ONCE ASKED how long it took me to write *Out of Our Minds*. One answer is twelve months; the real answer is that I have been concerned with the issues in this book for most of my life. For as long as I can remember, I've been concerned that so many people have such a diminished view of their own possibilities, in part because of the deficits and foibles of our national education systems. I've been driven too by first-hand knowledge that there are many better alternatives to these systems. No-one has ideas in a vacuum and I have been deeply influenced in my own thinking by a lifetime of work in and around education with many brilliant people, some of whom knew it and many of whom did not. I can't list them all but many are referenced in the book and I thank them all.

For their particular roles in making this edition possible, I do want to thank Holly Bennion at Capstone Publishing, for suggesting a new edition in the first place and for calmly pursuing me to make it happen; my agent Peter Miller, for his expert advice and constant support for all I do; and Tom Fryer at Sparks Publishing Services for turning an unadorned typescript into a beautiful book in record time. I especially want to thank my wonderful editor Sarah Sutton, for her judgement and skill in commenting on my drafts, for her sensitive prodding where I needed to be clearer, and for her calm and unwavering enthusiasm for the whole project. For several intense months we exchanged a constant flow of emails and phone calls in which she showed a selfless disregard for the wildly different time zones in which we were actually working. But for her nocturnal tendencies, this edition might not have seen the light of day.